Some Came Early
Some Came Late

994
PHE

Hertfordshire

7/12

Please renew/return this item by the last date shown.

So that your telephone call is charged at local rate, please call the numbers as set out below:

	From Area codes 01923 or 020:	From the rest of Herts:
Renewals:	01923 471373	01438 737373
Enquiries:	01923 471333	01438 737333
Textphone:	01923 471599	01438 737599

L32   www.hertsdirect.org/librarycatalogue

Nancy Phelan

Some Came Early,
Some Came Late

Macmillan

© Nancy Phelan 1970

First published 1970 by
The Macmillan Company of Australia Pty Ltd
107 Moray Street, South Melbourne, Victoria 3205
and 155 Miller Street, North Sydney, NSW 2060

Associated companies in London & Basingstoke England,
New York, Toronto, Dublin, Johannesburg, Madras

Australian National Library card number and
ISBN 0 333 11896 0

Typeset in Monotype Imprint and printed by
Associated Printers (DNP) Ltd Hong Kong

Contents

Illustrations

Plates 26 – 45 are between pages 148 and 149

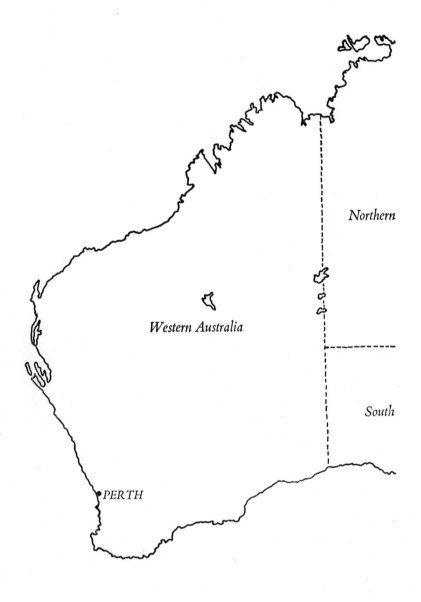

Northern

Western Australia

South

PERTH

Miles

0   500

For Axel and Roslyn Poignant

Acknowledgements

Many people gave me help and hospitality while I was writing this book and I am most grateful to them all.

In South Australia, I should like to thank Mr and Mrs B. Calman; Rhonda Radbone; Mr 'Robbie' Robinson, of Adelaide; Mr Alan Aubrey of Charleston; Mr and Mrs Frank Tscharke, Mr and Mrs Rupert Tscharke, Mr and Mrs M. Gramp, Pastor Reuther, all of the Barossa Valley, as well as all the other people there who gave me information; Mr and Mrs Jack Rosewarne, of Kadina, and the National Trust of Kadina.

On Phillip Island, Victoria: Mr and Mrs Robert Cross, for lending me 'Strawberry Farm'; Mr and Mrs Frank Janssen, Mr and Mrs K. Lang of Rhyll Village; Mr and Mrs O. Underdown, of Newhaven; Miss Margaret Campbell of Churchill Island.

In New South Wales: Mr and Mrs John Downes, of 'Brownlow Hill', Camden; Miss Llewella Davies of Camden; Miss Clarice Faithful-Anderson of 'Camelot', Cobbity; Mr Franklyn Pain, of Artarmon; Mr Arno Varima, of Sydney; the Estonian community at Thirlmere, particularly Mr and Mrs Arno Enno and the Estonian Ladies' Committee; Mr Lipping, Secretary of the Estonian Senior Citizens' Home; Mr and Mrs V. Kaasik, of Pheasants Nest; Mr and Mrs Max Kuusik of Thirlmere.

In Queensland: Mr and Mrs Duncan Fraser, of 'Fleurs', Clermont; Mr and Mrs D. Comerford and Mr Errol Comerford of 'Exmoor Downs' and 'Turrawulla'; Mrs Frank Kelly of Ravenshoe; Mrs E. Wallis-Smith of Atherton; Mr Stan Boyd of Cooktown.

The poem in Chapter Seven is by the Estonian poet Bernard Kangro. The lines quoted in Chapter Eight are taken from *John Brown's Body* by Stephen Vincent Benet, published by Oxford University Press.

I am also extremely grateful to my husband, R.S.Phelan and my friend Norma Ferris, for all their help in the emergencies that occurred during the final production of the book.

NANCY PHELAN

1

Arrival

Travellers to Australia are often amused by the way so many of the inhabitants reverence anything 'very old' whether it is worthless or not. Far from an ancestor's household gods being destroyed they are preserved unless lack of space or a move compels their abandonment. As time goes on this urge to cherish the past becomes more evident. Conservation societies spring up. The most hideous 'antique' brings a high price.

But what becomes of the folk-ways, customs and attitudes that our forbears brought with them? Are these equally cherished? Or are they shaken off as the migrant joins the Australian community? By going among the different communities of migrants, around the southern and eastern coasts, you might come by intimate and elusive knowledge never included in statistics. It might be possible to assess the tenacity of traditional behaviour and attitudes.

Adelaide was clearly the starting point. Here, if anywhere, old traditions are preserved. There are blue domes of a Russian cathedral, the minaret of a mosque built by Afghans who used to take camel trains across the desert. The city is calmer, mellower, than earlier more swashbuckling capitals. When I think of

Adelaide, it is of tranquil stone houses in leafy settings, openness, an almost Georgian grace.

To study the survival of customs and ways I planned to stay with the descendants of German settlers in the Barossa Valley, beyond the Adelaide hills. I wanted to live on some small family orchard, and a Mrs Tscharke of Stockwell near Nuriootpa would take me in. She was not only a Barossa German but a member of the Tanunda Historical Society who did voluntary work for the museum, had written a short history of the Valley, and drove the Angaston ambulance; probably an elderly widow with glasses, I thought, rather schoolmistressy and severe.

'If you can't stand it,' my Adelaide friends assured me, 'just ring and we'll come out and rescue you.'

To meet the formidable Mrs Tscharke I thought I had better wear stockings and a dress with sleeves. Unhappily, as we drove to the Dairy Vale Cheese factory, the pretty villages were in a torpor of heat; the countryside shimmered, and I nearly melted. Mr Aubrey of the cheese factory near Charleston was to carry me forward to meet Fay Gramp whose husband's family made Orlando Wines. Adelaide friends had arranged these introductions.

Mr Aubrey came out of his cool room to meet us, smiling and wiping his forehead. Kindness seeped from him like honey from a Greek pastry. He was trained with Danish cheesemakers and his house is full of silver trophies won at shows. Although it was a working day, nothing seemed to be a trouble to him. 'Do you like cheese? Ah, then, just a minute!'

He disappeared and came back with a cheese in his arms, carrying it like a baby. He plunged it in a tester and offered a cylindrical piece. It was a fine cheese. 'For you to take to the Valley,' he said, handing it over. It weighed nearly half a stone. 'Now before we start off for Barossa we'll just go across to my house and have a cup of tea. Or perhaps you like yoghurt? Ah, then you *must* taste mine. I don't mind saying I pride myself on my yoghurt.'

In the big dim kitchen Mrs Aubrey made tea while her husband served his yoghurt out of a great pail. He gave me a pudding-basin full, and although I could not eat it all, it was the best yoghurt I have tasted apart from Turkish. It was rather like being in rural Turkey – the yoghurt, the cool shadowy room, the dry heat outside, drowsy animals stretched on the step, the slow friendly voices, the long pauses and feeling of endless time.

We set out when it was cooler, the light was mellow. Our road wound between orchards and hills skirting the old German town of Lobethal. At last we came to a crossroads with a little bluestone hotel. Here at the crossroads Alan Aubrey took a deep breath of pleasure, and said, 'This is Lyndoch. Now we're in the Valley.'

There were grapes growing all round; the road ran between vineyards. I saw Orlando and Rovalley signs; we passed through Rowlands Flat, then the road twisted and climbed a slope into Tanunda. An arch spanning the road said:

GRAMPS WELCOME YOU TO THE BAROSSA VALLEY

2

Barossa Deutsch

In Fay Gramp's cool sitting room we drank iced hock while she gave Alan directions for finding the Tscharke vineyard. I was not sure what was happening, there was such an air of leisure and having arrived. We wandered in the garden where roses were giving out scent in the warm evening air. On the green lawn there was a barbecue shaped like a bottle which the family used for entertainments to raise money for charities. Rustlings came from an aviary where wood ducks, black ducks, teal, South African doves, finches, golden and silver pheasants, fluttered and flashed. In the garage beside an ancient family buggy stood Mervyn Gramp's pots of avocado pears and barrels of cucumbers pickled to his own special formula. The fern house was built on to the wall of one of Tanunda's oldest pug houses. The strange collection of objects and creatures increased the feeling of unreality brought on by travel, heat, fatigue and, probably, hock.

The Valley was named by Colonel Light, Surveyor-General for the South Australian Colony, who came here in 1837, seeking a way to the Murray River. It reminded him of *Bar Rosa* (Hill of Roses) in Spain, where he fought during the Peninsular War. The name was misspelt on early maps and became Barossa.

The valley is wide and shallow, thickly embroidered in green. Dark green squares lie flat like hooked rugs, or curve over gentle rises like candlewick counterpanes on featherbeds. The roads run very straight and direct; church spires and steeples among clusters of trees mark the villages. The hills do not shut out the sky, they lean back very low, very mild, with the flat-topped Kaiserstuhl in the distance. Cloud shadows move gently across them and in late afternoon light they are full of blue haze. Sunsets and evenings are long and serene, sometimes flaring and splendid with orange and purple, sometimes delicate pastel, with a childlike sky.

By the time we reached Nuriootpa we had forgotten all Fay's directions and had reached the village of Truro before we discovered our mistake. As we turned back and found the house among the vines, it was growing dark and I wished I was going home with the others instead of composing myself to meet a severe hostess. But as we entered the drive a woman came out and stood waiting.

She had soft black eyes, a cloud of black hair and a moonlit pallor. With a shy smile she introduced herself as Dulcie Tscharke. Here was no trace of traditional Teuton. Dulcie, whose maiden name was Materne, has French blood; her husband Frank has Russian; but they are true Valley people with a married daughter and a grown-up son.

Dulcie's great-grandfather migrated in 1858 and settled at Greenock, eight miles from Stockwell. Some of his original vines were taken out only a few years ago, and her brother still has one of the biggest private vineyards in that district. The Tscharkes migrated from White Russia in 1861 and planted the vineyard where I am staying. It has been divided into three, and belongs to Frank, his brother Rupert and their father. Once the family made their own wine; now they sell their grapes to the big wineries.

Dulcie and Frank describe themselves as *most ordinary people . . . German farmers . . . Barossa peasants*. They both have a keen sense of humour.

Though I had always heard that Barossa people were hospitable,

I had not expected to feel at home quite so quickly. The Tscharkes had just taken me into their family and though it is their busiest season, Dulcie has set aside all other plans to look after me.

On the first morning, humouring my request to help with the picking, I was given rubber gloves and clippers. At the vineyard, which the Tscharkes call 'The Garden', people were already at work in overalls and shady hats – Frank's brother Rupert, his wife Joan, various neighbours and helpers, men and women, all with German names. Each picker had two buckets which they were filling very fast and emptying into a waiting truck. This was early picking, green Semillon grapes for effervescent wines.

I was shown how to cut without slicing fingers and given a bucket. As we moved along the vines, bending and clipping and reaching through the twisted branches, Dulcie kept glancing round nervously as though expecting me to collapse. The sky was overcast but the air was sultry, and my rubber gloves were soon full of sweat. It ran down my bare arms in dirty streaks, my jeans and thongs became plastered with mud. There were lizards and spiders among the leaves, and inextricably tangled vines into which you had to grope. I had never given much thought to picking, had rather assumed the grapes would hang in graceful convenient bunches and that you just reached up and cut. The others were delighted at my disillusionment.

'You don't have to take so much trouble,' Frank said, watching my careful manoeuvres.

'I won't!' I said, slashing away with abandon, and soon my bucket was full.

'*Please!*' said Dulcie imploringly. 'Please don't feel you have to go on. Really, we don't expect you to.'

I emptied my bucket into the truck and took a second one. I was enjoying myself. I was hot, sticky, dirty, but the people were friendly, the country was beautiful. The green vines stretched out all around into the distance, like a sea. Here and there, the roofs of homesteads seemed half-buried in leaves. The shallow mountains made a low wooded wall against the grey sky. Red trucks ran like toys along the country roads, taking grapes to the wineries.

As each truck filled it went off with its green, sour-smelling cargo. The grapes go wherever they are needed – one day to the Kaiserstuhl Co-operative at Nuriootpa, another to Yalumba, to Seppelts or Buring. Though the vintage had just started here the wineries were already working full time, crushing grapes that had come in from other areas. Growers have no trouble selling to the winemakers; the demand exceeds the supply and prices are good. Private vineyards are prospering, though sometimes the small growers say with a frown that the big wineries are increasing their planting. If they can grow most of the grapes they need they will be able to dictate prices.

About half-past ten we stopped for a drink and *schnitte* – thick sandwiches of German sausage – then moved to another garden. To general surprise and amusement I stuck it out till the end of the morning. As we drove home to lunch Dulcie said dryly, 'Despite the photographs, the vintage is not all dirndls and headscarves. It's damned hard work, especially in the heat; and for the men, in winter, standing for hours in the bitter cold, pruning the vines. But it's a good life.'

The first white inhabitants of the Valley, in the late 1830s, were British farmers, but soon German immigrants began to arrive. Frederich Wilhelm III of Prussia had commanded the Lutheran Church to unite with the State Church. Those who resisted were persecuted, their form of worship forbidden, land and property confiscated, extortionate fines and penalties imposed. By 1835 many Silesian Lutherans had decided to leave the country. While they were still uncertain where to go, their leader, Pastor August Ludwig Christian Kavel, met George Fife Angas, a director of the South Australian Company. Angas realized the Germans would make ideal settlers for the young colony and offered to help with their passages to Australia.

The first party of Lutherans arrived in 1838 and settled a few miles from Adelaide, on the Torrens. They called the village Klemzig, after their home town in Germany. As more Germans came they moved out to found settlements at Glen Osmond,

Hahndorf and Lobethal, and when Angas offered land in the
Barossa some came to the valley and established the village of
Bethanien – Bethany – in 1842.

The district was known as Neuschlesein – New Silesia.
Gradually, as more Germans arrived, churches were built and
villages grew up around them. Life was very hard, but the settlers,
mostly illiterate peasants, were not afraid of work. They valued
peace and freedom of worship. They were brave, devout, thrifty
and industrious, but often ignorant, obstinate, narrow-minded
and rigidly conservative. They could contribute little to the mental
life and development of the Barossa Valley but they laid the
foundations for others to work upon. On these foundations, later
German settlers, families with more education, by their vision,
hard work and intelligence, established and maintained Barossa's
unique character.

At first there was no wine grown here, though a German
geologist, Johann Menge, had predicted the land would be good
for vineyards. It was not until 1847 that the first grapes were
planted at Pewsey Vale, near Lyndoch, by an Englishman named
Joseph Gilbert, and at Jacob's Creek by a German named Johann
Gramp. A few years later, Samuel Smith, a brewer from Dorset,
Samuel Hoffman, a German farmer, and Joseph Seppelt (who had
started by growing tobacco) turned to vines. Gramp's grapes
have now become Orlando Wines, Smith's are Yalumba, Hoffman's, North Para Wines, and Seppelt's are still called Seppelts.

The Tscharkes live about five miles beyond Nuriootpa, off the
Sturt Highway to the Murray. Our nearest village is Stockwell,
out of sight on the other side of the Highway, our nearest church
Ebenezer, just across the fields, very white with a high tower and
white witch's hat. It was established in 1852 by Wends from
Saxony. The Valley is full of churches; they say there are thirty-
seven within a radius of thirty miles. Whenever a theological
disagreement arose among worshippers, the dissenters would
move off and build another church. Light Pass, a very small
village, has two large churches, a stone's-throw apart.

For shopping we go into Nuriootpa or even Tanunda. Tanunda has a museum, many old cottages, four fine Lutheran churches, one containing the tomb of Pastor Kavel who led the first immigrants, and a sort of village green called Billygoat Square. The long main street is lined with trees and handsome stone houses; it has an air of peace and prosperity. By the Para River is Langmeil, the second settlement established after Bethany, where there are disused stone wineries and houses covered with vines. On the other side of the town is Chateau Tanunda, where Seppelts brandy is made, a large rather grim stone building with a tower, like a French provincial railway station on a grand scale.

The road from Tscharkes' to Tanunda goes through vineyards bordered with olive and almond trees. There is an old brickyard called Kreigs just beyond Nuriootpa and on the far side, Penfolds, Kaiserstuhl, Tintara and Basedows wineries. Near Kaiserstuhl is the Tarac factory where they make cream of tartar from grape pips. The stench tells me where I am, even in the dark.

Nuriootpa, which the locals call Nuri, is said to be Aboriginal for Meeting Place, but its earlier name was Angas Park, after George Fife Angas. It is the Valley's commercial centre but quite innocent of bustle. In the window of the bakery, where Dulcie goes to buy *Deutscherkuchen* (Germancake) the notices say:

ASK FOR BALFOUR'S CAKES
PLEASE DO NOT BRING DOGS INTO THIS SHOP
KITTENS, TO GIVE AWAY

On the outskirts, set back in lawns and fruit trees, is Coulthard House, graceful, two-storied, with shady verandah, now restored by a young American couple who have migrated to Australia.

Despite all the tourism, the crowds that flock to the Valley for Vintage Festivals, most of the Barossa people and towns seem unspoilt. Angas Park Hotel, in the main street of Nuri, still serves sherry in tumblers.

The 'pub' I like best is our local. The Stockwell Hotel is not smart; its walls are sulphur-yellow, poison-mauve and electric-blue, but its simple colonial lines are still visible and there are small rooms with low ceilings and wavy floors clustering around a closed courtyard.

In the old bar, men from the vineyards and farms drink and make cheerful noises as their ancestors have done there for a hundred and thirteen years. Out at the back is a stone building said to have been the lock-up, with a hole in the wall connecting it with the hotel, so prisoners were sometimes found dead-drunk in the morning. In this barn Dulcie and I found an antique mahogany sofa, in bad repair, but with a beautiful carved frame. The licensee let her have it for three dollars.

He was a friendly, kindly man; he and his family seemed to love the building, to care about its history. They showed us the list of licensees going back to 1857. The first was a Michael Quigly; after that, all German names.

'Have a drink on the house,' the publican said, waving us into the electric-blue parlour. 'I'll send it across.' We sat on plastic-and-chrome chairs at a vinyl-topped table and presently two tumblers arrived, one of neat *creme-de-menthe*, one of sweet sherry. We did not want to hurt the friendly licensee's feelings by saying these were too sweet for us, so when we were alone Dulcie poured my sherry into a vase of feathery-grass while I smuggled her *creme-de-menthe* outside. A few miles away was an older hotel, its licence going back to 1846, but when we visited it, there seemed to be far too many lace tablecloths and young men from Adelaide being knowledgeable about private bins.

Dulcie's best friend, Val Krushel, lives in a handsome white house just beyond Stockwell village. Her family bought it from George Fife Angas in 1862. It is called 'Carrara', after the hill where it stands, for a marble ridge runs through the property. There is a flagged courtyard shaded with grape vines and a mellow garden. White chairs and tables are set on the colonial verandah; inside are curiously-shaped rooms with fine antique furniture, elegant yet homely. When we go there for supper Val produces masses of cakes, including *Deutscherkuchen*. Everyone knows by now that I cannot resist it.

Stockwell itself, seen from the hill behind, is a green bird's-nest set in sand-coloured grass. Here and there, from the low dark bushes that form the nest, eucalyptus, cypress and pine stand out, and among leaves and pale glimpsed houses, an old flour mill, a white toy church with steeple and spire.

Beyond, the bleached grass stretches on towards vineyards and hills. Far off is the Kaiserstuhl. The sky leans over the valley, cloudless but for a white ethereal foam behind the church tower. Among its powdery scents the flour mill grinds and puffs as it has for over a hundred years. The streets are quiet; most of the residents are at work in their houses or vineyards and there are no tourists. Dogs doze in autumnal warmth.

It is not Australia yet it could be nowhere else. As copra underlies all other smells in some parts of the world, Australia's air is redolent of eucalyptus. Behind the sweetness of English flowers, aromatic pine and blossoming shrubs persists the ghostly breath of the gumtrees; a little harsh, faint but subtly persuasive; a scent that means Space, a silent reminder that we and our gardens are alien here.

Dulcie is very well named. She is gentle, warm, diffident and compassionate, yet for all her shy manner, strong when it comes to helping others or her work with the ambulance. She is off-duty while I am here, apart from emergencies. We drive around the Valley, visit old people to hear their reminiscences, spend hours talking at the kitchen table. Sometimes we go into Tanunda museum where the Historical Society has collected relics of the early settlers. These possessions are pathetically rough and poor; cheap German china, home-made cradles and clothes-chests, wooden shoes with hinged soles, sausage-fillers, wooden bowls for curing pigs, homeopathy kits, which most families owned and which were their only form of medical aid.

The clothes are the most poignant: poor, plain underwear, brown faded wedding-wreaths, rusty black wedding-dresses with high neck and long sleeves. Brides always wore black. They sit there, in photographs, looking blankly out from under their wreaths, which would later be framed and hung on the wall, like some kind of tribal trophy. Only the wreaths and the stiff bridegrooms in boots, with button-holes trailing streamers, show that it is not a funeral.

There are also silvered wreaths in frames. These were presented by the children of the marriage on their parents' silver wedding.

When I said I felt a touch of brutality behind it all, Dulcie told me that even in her childhood there were still harsh customs and almost sadistic cruelty. She remembers her brother's tonsils being torn out without anaesthetic (when he cried, he was hit over the head by the doctor), and but for her father's stubborn refusal to allow amputation, she would have lost an injured arm.

'And the funerals!' Despite the heat of summer the body was kept at home for three days, and family, friends, neighbours, including young children, must file past to pay their respects. The dark halls of certain houses, Dulcie says, are still places for her of fear and horror, filled with the stench of corruption and heavily-scented flowers. The coffin was placed on a bier called a *totenbahre*, and borne to the graveyard shoulder-high by men in frock-coats and top hats with streamers. The pastor walked before the coffin and behind it came the mourners, all male. The procession was led by a young boy of the departed's family, carrying a black wooden cross with streamers. These funerals continued into the mid-1960s.

The bereaved family went into full mourning for a whole year; as late as 1948 a married woman was severely censured for buying a black-and-white dress six months after her father's death. No social occasions were allowed for at least six months. Young widows were closely watched and heavily condemned if they showed signs of recovery before sixteen months had elapsed.

Birth was almost as sombre as death. Pregnant women must shroud themselves in concealing garments and not appear in public, especially at church, after the sixth month; in fact, not until the child had been christened and the mother given thanks and been purified by the church.

Even now, Valley people assured me, the hard old ways persist

in more remote villages. I know of a family who refused to let a
child be christened Diana because it was the name of a pagan
goddess; families who do not allow sport, partly because it is
ungodly and partly because it wastes time. They take their
children from school as early as possible and put them to work
on the farm. They despise and distrust education. There are
still employers who feel that semi-educated staff can be more
easily trained, and older people who have never fully benefited
from literacy. They can read and write and may have a peasant
shrewdness but they cannot handle paperwork. They bring all
such affairs to 'educated people' they know and trust, to lawyers,
agents, as illiterate peasants have always done in all parts of the
world. One day in a Tanunda office I saw an elderly German
farmer having his Medical Benefits form filled in, which he
laboriously signed, with a hand like a ham, without reading
what had been written. I was told this was the usual process. I
must admit I am with the peasantry when it comes to filling in
forms.

Frank's parents live down our road, beyond Rupert's vineyard.
Mrs Tscharke senior moves lightly, though she is bent with
rheumatism. Her beautiful complexion is barely touched by age
or hard work, her eyes like golden-brown pansies, with a shy
trusting youthful expression. She looks frail but Dulcie says she
spends all her time helping people, minding their children, cooking
their meals, giving things away left and right, always beaming
her beautiful smile. She and Dulcie love each other dearly.

Mr Tscharke, who has been ill, moves slowly but sits very
straight in his kitchen armchair. Despite his Russian blood he
looks a perfect Saxon, fair and fresh-faced, with very blue eyes.

In the kitchen is a big table, a steeple clock, an oil lamp with
engraved glass sphere, a glass-fronted secretary full of china
ornaments and family photographs. Round about are objects
Dulcie would like for Tanunda museum – a trivet made of
horseshoes, a long-handled flat shovel for taking *Deutscherkuchen*
out of the German oven, a wooden trough with a lid, the shape

and size of a cradle. For years Mrs Tscharke used it for mixing bread and Germancake.

'Take it, dear, take it for the museum,' she tells Dulcie. 'I'll use something else for the firewood.'

Behind the house is the original cottage built by the first Tscharke settlers. It has earth floors, thick walls, low doors and ceilings. There are only two rooms and water came from a pump, yet each door is carved and panelled. The windows are set in deep recesses and in the back of the high open fireplace is the iron door of the German oven. It makes a large square hump outside the kitchen wall. The old Tscharkes are amused and rather touched by my enthusiasm, but Dulcie understands. I am lucky to be with someone brought up in Valley traditions and ways who can see their historical value.

Barossa cuisine is certainly fattening. For breakfast we have cheese, bread, wurst and coffee. In the old days, most of these would have been made at home: Boiling *Kochkäse* – a boiled cheese, and *Stinkerkäse*, which speaks for itself. Boiled cheese is made by draining off the whey in a calico bag, usually hung under the shade of a tree, then mixing it with caraway seeds, salt and carbonate of soda. It is cooked in a double boiler, stirred till it has a honey consistency. It can be eaten, straightaway, on bread.

Stinkerkäse takes longer. When the whey has been drained from the sour milk and the caraway seeds added, the mixture is made into balls, wrapped in cabbage leaves and put in a stone jar. They are left for a couple of weeks till matured. By this time the cabbage leaves have almost rotted off and the stench is high. *Stinkerkäse* is eaten on bread.

'It smells perfectly ghastly!' Dulcie says. 'Worse than any strong cheese *you* have ever known.'

The big pitfalls are the breads, biscuits and cakes. Apart from *Deutscherkuchen* there are *Honigkuchen* – honey cake; *Pfefferkuchen*–spiced honey cake; *Pfannekuchen*–sugar buns; *Käsekuchen* – cheesecake; *Bienenstich* – bee-sting; gingerbread men, fancy biscuits and cakes for offering with beer at Christmas.

Germancake is till a standard item in Valley households, at Valley functions. There are various recipes – the *Barossa Cookbook* gives two – but it is always made with yeast and has a *streusel* top of mixed sugar, spices and fat. Dulcie keeps a constant supply for my benefit. She tells me it has – or had – a certain social significance. If you were a welcome visitor it would be offered with tea; if not, you should take the hint and not come again.

One day we called to see Mr Fromm of Tanunda Historical Society. It was late and we could not stay long, but he was deeply shocked at the thought of our leaving without tea and Germancake. 'Oh! Oh! but will you not have tea and *Deutscherkuchen?*' he cried, his kindly old face quite anguished. 'But you must, you must! Wait! Wait!'

He ran into his house and came out with several large slabs in his gnarled hands. 'Oh, you can't leave without! You must have a little . . . ' he pleaded, following us to the car, passing the cake in through the window. He was consoled only to see us eating it as we drove away.

Though most of the Valley people are winegrowers, in summer they usually drink beer at celebrations but in winter they like *Glühwein*. Mervyn Gramp, called Snow because of his flaxen hair, is Barossa's *Glühwein* expert and often produces vast quantities for fund-raising events. Last winter he made forty-eight gallons for 1,256 people at a *Melodienacht*. The local paper said, 'if patrons weren't warm before sampling this potent brew they certainly were afterwards.'

Music is woven through all Valley life and *Melodienachts* and Band Contests are part of Barossa tradition. The male choir of *Liedertafel*, which has existed for over a hundred years, meets for practice each Tuesday night in Tanunda, from March to November. During the year it often gives concerts for charity, sometimes travelling to other districts, and always sings at the Vintage Festival.

At the end of the year the *Liedertafel* has a *Kaffeeabend* or Coffee Evening as its Christmas breaking-up. It is a wonderful

mixture of drink and song. Hundreds of people come from all
districts, bringing their own refreshments. Dressing is very
informal and the grog is carried in anything, from sugar bags over
the shoulder to portable refrigerators. The audience sit round at
tables, as at a cabaret, swaying and beating time to the German
drinking-songs, and about half-past ten, eighty gallons of milk
coffee are made and served. The singing goes on all night.

Rupert Tscharke, who has a beautiful tenor voice, took me
one night to *Liedertafel* practice. When he came to collect me,
very fresh and well-groomed in a dark suit with collar and tie,
he showed no signs of having picked grapes all day in the heat.
Most of the other choir members had also been working in their
vineyards.

In the basement hall of the Tanunda Club, at a long table,
men were drinking beer. They stood, glass in hand, talking,
emanating good cheer. Some were rotund and rosy, others faded
and pale but nearly all had Teutonic heads and features. All
were introduced by German names.

They smiled at me rather shyly. I had thought I would slip
in unnoticed and sit at the back, but the chairman made a
welcoming speech and invited me to take a front seat. They
kept reminding me it was only a practice, very dull, rehearsing
the same phrases.

Mr Fritz Homburg, over eighty, who has been *Liedertafel*
conductor for years, tonight sat beside me, listening critically
while his son conducted the singers. From time to time he translated words, and as the evening went on other men leaned across
to offer musical scores.

The first items were rather hearty drinking songs for the
Vintage Festival – *Weinland* . . . oh-ho-ho . . . *Trink, Brüderlein,
trink* . . . The accompanist pounded the piano, the singers grew
red in the face; but as these songs gave way to simple melodious
German *lieder*, the mood changed. The men sang quietly, thought-
fully, seeming to treasure each note. These were songs they knew
well and sang for love, nostalgically, sadly, with spectacles on the
ends of noses, holding their scores at a distance or singing from

memory. Their rich voices came together and blended and harmonized with moving sweetness. They sang with closed eyes, from the heart, in the language of a land they had never known, yet which was in their blood; a lost, innocent Germany of forests and market squares, snow on gables and storks on chimney-tops.

Röslein, Röslein, Rö-ho-slein Roooooose . . . the day's work in the vineyards forgotten, peaceful content on each face.

The last song was so beautifully sung that a spell lay over us all. Some eyes were moist, some closed, some focussed far away. Mr Homburg, smiling peacefully, murmured, '*The forest is sleeping . . . The birds are all sleeping . . . And soon you will be sleeping too* . . . Ah, if only I could translate the real beauty of the words! *Abendlied!*'

This was more than a practice, a pleasant night out. These men singing in such perfect harmony were creating another unity. Only the song mattered, the joy of singing together.

On Sundays, when the air is still, you can hear church bells chiming all around. Dulcie says that on New Year's Eve, just before midnight, they toll the bell twelve times for the death of the Old Year; then they ring in the New. The whole Valley is full of sound.

Today it is cold and the wind is blowing the wrong way. We can hear only our own bells, from Ebenezer, across the fields. Ebenezer – *Hitherto hath the Lord helped me* – is part of Barossa history. In 1866, fifty members of the congregation, with six others from Light Pass, set out from here with covered wagons and carts to migrate to New South Wales, a journey known as the Trek. Their small holdings had become exhausted and land was cheap in the Albury district. The families, including children, travelled for nearly six weeks through all kinds of country and all kinds of hardships, never failing to hold morning and evening services or observe the Sabbath, till they reached Walla Walla, near Albury. Here they settled and founded what is now the biggest Lutheran congregation in New South Wales.

The little house near the church, from which they set out, is still there; but Gottlieb Nitschke's shop, on the Truro Road, where they held farewell prayers with their friends, is only a heap of stones.

The turkey has gone into the oven, the hock pudding into the refrigerator, and we are ready for church. Dulcie has given me a Lutheran Order of Service, told me the hymns are sung sitting down and you do not kneel for prayers, just sit with bowed head.

At Ebenezer there is no leisurely standing round talking; only a quick friendly nod and a clutch at the hat as we hurry in out of the wind. Smiles and handshakes take place in the church porch.

The bells rang out over our heads, very clear and innocent, silvery, like English bells; they stopped and the church was filled with the most angelic sweetness, at once rich and pure. It was an eighteenth century sound, fluting, warbling, no hint of the slurring or blaring of bigger organs; beautiful, mellow yet somehow *modest*.

Dulcie noticed my expression. She whispered, 'It's a very famous German organ. Oh, but this isn't our regular organist. If you could hear it played properly . . . Our organist makes it *speak*!'

It could not have spoken more clearly, even under Bach's fingers. It was the quality, the tone that communicated. The plain church, the altar with only a vase of flowers and two pairs of candles were the perfect setting for the other-world Saint Cecilia voice.

The young pastor appeared in black robes. At the neck were the two white vertical bands that symbolize the tablets of the Ten Commandments.

'In the name of the Father and of the Son and of the Holy Spirit.'

The services used to be in German, but hostility during the last war put an end to the German services. We sat with bowed heads. In front were Rupert and Joan with their two sons; behind were neighbours I had met in the gardens, helping with grape-picking. Across the aisle two little girls with flaxen hair whispered and dangled their legs. It was all very homely.

The service was simple but whole-hearted. Everyone sang. It was easy to read the notes of the chanting and I knew the tunes of the hymns, thougy the words were different. I enjoy singing hymns, even if I don's understand the words – as in Welsh chapels – but today all my attention was on that organ's dulcet fluting, innocent as a blackbird's whistle yet full of velvet compassion.

Pastor Pieter climbed into the pulpit and gave a sermon about roots and faith and spiritual growth. He was very sincere, very direct, and the congregation listened attentively, except the two little girls who whispered together rather loudly. No one seemed to mind.

We sang again. The plate came round and we put in our contributions. Then Dulcie beckoned and we walked out, quietly but with none of the guilty sneaking that often afflicts early leavers. The others stayed on for Communion.

As we drove away I could still hear the organ. The sun had come out and all the hills were blue.

Our turkey ready, the smell in the kitchen was as wonderful in its own way as the old German organ.

With the beautiful bird on the table we bowed our heads. Frank said:

> *Komm Herr Jesu*
> *Sei unser Gast*
> *Und segne uns*
> *Was Du bescheret hast.*
> (Come, Lord Jesus, be our Guest,
> And bless what Thou hast given us.)

'*Unser Gott der Vater, Gott der Sohn, und Gott der Heilige Geist*. Amen,' said Dulcie.

We were eating the hock pudding and filling up corners with *Käsekuchen* and *Bienenstich* when Rupert and his family came in. Dulcie had made the cheesecake but Frank and I had found the *Bienenstich* (Bee-sting) in the store at Truro, fresh from the bakery over the road. It is a delicious kind of yeasty sponge-sandwich, sweeter than *Deutscherkuchen*, with streusel top and custardy centre.

It was warm and cheerful around the table with these friendly people, laughing and eating too much. When we had finished the two brothers gave After-meal Thanks:

> *Habe dank Herr Jesu Christ,*
> *Dass du unser Geber und Gast gewesen bist,*
> *Vor einem schnellen und bösen Tod,*
> *Behüt uns lieber Herr und Gott.*   Amen.

'Oh yes, many families still say Grace in German,' Dulcie said. 'All over the Valley.'

3

In einem Kühlen Grunde

Ebenezer has a new mural which seems not quite right for the simple church. One hot afternoon Dulcie and I were sitting there quietly discussing it when a woman came in, wearing a battered hat and overalls. She had very blue eyes and an innocent childlike expression. She said gently, 'Someone in the church I hear.'

'Only me, Mrs Boehm,' Dulcie said. 'We won't steal anything.'

Mrs Boehm shook her head.

'Ah no. Good people never stealing,' she said, wandering away with her sweet vague smile. We found her standing absently out in the sunlight, as though listening to something we could not hear. She is very poor and lives in a small cottage in the church grounds, nominally to look after the building. She is a little simple, very gentle and serene though her life has been far from tranquil – drunken family, brutal beatings, endless work and poverty. Her English has the verb at the end of the sentence. A number of the old people, brought up on German, still speak this Barossa English.

There is no Barossa English about Pastor Reuther, though he was nine before he spoke our language. He is famous all over the Valley, not only as a pastor but a fearless defender of right and his people. He lives in Nuri, limping with arthritis, grown rather thin and frail since I first met him but still with a wide smile. For all his Lutheran sternness he is humorous and kind. One day, just to please me, he put on his black gown and stock and despite our protests stood on the porch in bitter cold so that I could take a photograph. Though he is now retired, he still drives vast distances in all sorts of weather to give services for old people who have no pastor.

He is always ready to answer questions. It was he who told me that the white bands of the Lutheran gown represented the Ten Commandments; that the narrow white stole, which some pastors wear and others reject, was originally worn by Luther. ('I like it myself; but some call it *that magpie business.*')

He comes from a family of pastors. His mother was the daughter of a famous Barossa pastor, G.J.Rechner, and was first married to Pastor Steltz. She was left a widow with a young family, in such straits that they had to live in the vestry of Immanuel Church, at Point Pass, about forty miles north of the Valley– 'Mum was a wonderful pray-er' – and the new young pastor, named Reuther, overheard her. He was so impressed that he decided immediately he must have her for his wife, to help in his work. They were married, and went to the mission station, Bethesda, on Lake Killalpaninna, forty miles east of Lake Eyre, to work among the Aborigines of the Dieri tribe.

Our Pastor Reuther spent his childhood on the Mission and spoke the Dieri dialect before he spoke German or English. He was nine years old when they left Bethesda and came south. The tribe, like the Mission, have now almost vanished. He showed me the dictionary his father compiled and the New Testament he translated into Dieri. A copy was sold last year in London for £570.

As a young man, Pastor Reuther trained at Point Pass College for three and a half years, then for three and a half years at Wartburg, in Iowa. When he returned from the United States, he was sent to the Lutheran congregation at Bethania, in Queensland, where he spent thirteen years. He married there and brought his wife back to the Valley. He was pastor at Light Pass for thirty-one years.

By 1939, more than a hundred years had passed since the first Lutheran migration. The Barossa people were now Australians, a wonderful example of integration. Nevertheless, there was strong hostility towards the Valley inhabitants during World War II. They were said to be 'arming' to fight for Hitler; non-German residents 'informed'; eminent Barossa citizens were interned. There was a stigma attached to German names and people dared not utter a word of the German language. Houses were searched, German literature done away with in the most senseless and brutal manner; even the churches were suspect. Dulcie's brother, a peaceful Lutheran pastor, had his library ransacked and his priceless irreplaceable old German church books destroyed.

But when Pastor Reuther found his house had been searched by the military in his absence he stormed down to Adelaide and extracted official apologies from the authorities. He never ceased fighting the smears, the accusations, the internment of those whose crime was to be born with a German name. He is not very big but he can be fierce.

'Why should I be afraid of officials? I work for God! God is my master! I answer to Him for myself and my people and I knew we had done no wrong.'

During World War I, German names had been wiped from the Barossa map – names that were part of its history – though some have survived. *Kaiserstuhl* became Mt Kitchener; *Guadenfrei* became Maranaga; *Schönborn* – Gomersal; *Neukirch* – Dimchurch; *Langmeil* – Bilyara; *Krondorf* – Kabminye. Even the children must ask for Kitchener buns instead of *Pfannekuchen* (sugar buns); but in 1914 German was still widely spoken in the Valley, there were German schools where the children honoured the Kaiser as well as the King. Old people remembered their homeland and had close relations living there. Anti-German hysteria at this time was more understandable; but some of those who suffered or were interned in the 1939 war are still very bitter. Others, like Dulcie, prefer to treat it as past. There were good harmless Italian settlers in Queensland who received the same sort of treatment from obtuse officials.

When Dulcie and I drive about the Valley, looking at churches and villages, she often finds changes. One day we went to look at Italian olive orchards and found all trace gone. Many old houses and cottages have been destroyed, leaving only pieces of pug or stone walls and scraps of thatched roofs, yet, in general, conservation is good. Tanunda Historical Society, which runs the museum, is very active.

The Society was meeting soon after I arrived. As on the night of the *Liedertafel* practice, everyone seemed to have German names, German heads or faces. We sat in rows facing the chairman and secretary and after the welcome, apologies and minutes came the general affairs. These included discussion on Tanunda's candidate for Miss Vintage Queen; Tanunda's decorated float for the Festival; the erection of a sign informing tourists that they were entering the Valley; new premises for the Museum; the purchase of an old German cart seen by a member in an outlying district; reminiscences by Mr Fromm about hours of work and pay; the donation of a jinker by someone in Adelaide and how to get it to the Valley (Drive it, with pretty girls on board in period dress).

A lady member stood up and proposed that tourist buses bringing sightseers to Tanunda be directed to drive around Billygoat Square. This made rather a stir. People turned to their neighbours, some maintaining there was nothing for tourists in Billygoat Square, others that its old cottages were unique.

Nevertheless, the lady insisted, the Square was of historical interest.

'Only because they tied their goats there in the old days,' cried a member.

That, the lady pointed out, was historical.

'But it's not very interesting for strangers,' another member objected. 'There are no goats there now. There's nothing for tourists to see.'

The secretary suggested that a few goats might be put there specially for tourists. A more serious member asked who would look after the goats. The secretary thought that perhaps they could be brought out just when the tourist buses were coming. The solemn member felt that would not be feasible. Besides, billygoats smelt. The secretary asked, 'Well, how about plastic goats?'

The lady member sat down with the matter unfinished.

Another member got up.

He knew the Society was delighted that the old Coulthard House at Nuriootpa had been taken over by a young American couple who were carefully restoring it; but there were rumours that they meant to open a museum which might threaten Tanunda Museum. He had therefore invited Mr Streuver to come along tonight to set people's minds at rest.

Young Mr Streuver, with very short hair and Edwardian moustache, rose and earnestly assured the meeting they need have no fears. Though it was true he planned a museum at Coulthard House it would not affect Tanunda's museum which he greatly admired. His museum would contain only bottles. He had a collection of 22,000.

There was an astounded silence. Misinterpreting Mr Streuver's accents I thought he meant paintings of battles; but he explained that bottle collecting was very popular in the States, it just hadn't got here yet. It would come: there was a great bottle potential here. These 22,000 bottles had all been collected by him in this country and he wanted a home for them, now he had brought his family to live in Australia.

Everyone looked relieved. A member stood up and expressed pleasure that Coulthard House was in such good hands. He was sure the Historical Society would wish the bottle museum the best of luck. In fact, he would like to suggest that perhaps Tanunda Museum might display cards directing visitors to the bottle collection.

This was agreed. Mr Streuver thanked the members and said that he would be happy to reciprocate by displaying cards for

Tanunda Museum in his bottle collection. There was a murmur of appreciation. Another member got up and suggested Mr Streuver be made an honorary member of the Historical Society.

The meeting concluded in a glow of warmth and goodwill; and we all gathered round for tea and Germancake, dealt out from a long table at the end of the hall.

Mr Streuver had invited us to visit him; but when we called in we found his wife, Sally, half-distracted – a crying child being rushed to the dentist, a very young baby in tears, the house in the throes of repairs, piles of work to be done and no bottles yet on display. Six months later when I came back to the Valley the scene had changed. Sally was now painting the hall, all was calm, the garden in order, a large bellows hung outside as a sign. Even Mr Streuver, whose name is Kelly, was far more relaxed and less earnest.

'Come in,' he said hospitably. 'Be our guest.'

Coulthard House was in full swing as a bottle museum, with visitors wandering about. The Streuvers had worked hard all the winter; the beautifully proportioned rooms now had white walls, Hong Kong matting and white paper Japanese lampshades. From the deep-set small-paned windows were views of fruit trees and green lawns where old German wagons were displayed. Some of the 22,000 bottles were arranged in flat glass cases back-lit to show off their shapes and subtle colours; mauve, blue, light green, beer-brown, clear glass and stonewear. Upstairs was a gallery of paintings, mainly Barossa scenes.

A piercing Siberian wind blew in at the open front door. The Streuvers do not live here. They have another old house in Tanunda. I asked how things were going.

'Well, slowly. So far at a dead loss. We have put all our capital into restoring this house and now it's bills up to here! Sally's taken a secretarial job to keep us going. I had a job for a while with the wine people – but the pay is so low. The pay in Australia is frightful. Besides someone has to be at the museum all the time. But don't think we regret it. We don't! We're glad we decided to come. This is just a difficult stage and when we come through it will be okay. We plan to open a restaurant at the back, something with proper atmosphere; but right now we just don't have the money.'

It was no good asking one of the wineries to back him. That would mean they could sell only that company's wines.

He and his wife, he said, came from Los Angeles. They decided to emigrate because they wanted a better life. In the States, he had been a Real Estate Appraiser – he guessed here we'd call him a valuer – and though he had family and friends over there it had suddenly dawned on him that there he was, waking up every day to the same old grind, the same old rat-race. Why not get out of it?

Australia was not so different from California in many ways; life here was closest to the one they knew back home but quieter and more peaceful. Life in the States was getting kind of mad; so they decided to sell up and move here.

'I read an article in an American magazine about coming here to live. It said *If you have $20,000, go! If you have only half that, don't*. We had less than half. So we came!'

At first they had lived at Newport, along the coast from Sydney. They were delighted to have a magnificent house right on the Pacific, quite cheap; but it was off season and when summer came the rent increased four times. Kelly found Sydney rents so high and wages so low they decided to move on. They bought a land-rover and trailer and travelled all over the country, deciding where they would settle. That was when they started collecting the bottles. They had left a collection behind in the States and had not expected to find any here; but as they drove around Queensland and the outback they discovered old bottles in demolished houses, ruins, junkyards. Finally there were 22,000; the trailer was full. They figured to find a house where they could display them.

'How did you come to choose the Barossa?'

'Well, we both like wine and this is a wine-growing area; yes, sure, I do have a German background. And then this house was available. It's an old house and perfect for a museum. And the Valley's a good place for tourists.'

At one stage they had thought of buying an antique shop in

the Blue Mountains of New South Wales, not far from where we have a cottage. I told him there was another American couple there, who had been working their way around the world to decide where to settle. They thought they might stay in the Mountains if they could make a living.

Kelly knew about them; but he had made his decision. He and his family were here to stay.

'But if all your people and friends are still in the States, and if you say wages are so much lower here and the cost of living so high, what is the advantage?'

'Well, maybe it's just the different tempo; more casual, more time to live. And of course there is far more opportunity. This country's only just starting. It's like the U.S. a hundred years ago.'

'Do you want to go back?'

'For a visit, maybe, to see our folks, but this is our home now. We're settlers.'

I remembered young Americans I had talked to in India and Nepal. Some were no-hopers. others were genuinely searching for a less materialistic way of life that they could respect and believe in. Kelly was not one of these.

'No. It's not that. I'm not a drop-out. It's partly that the pace of life being slower here you have time to live and also that there's greater opportunities, not just for us, but for our kids. We feel this is the place of the future.'

It is pleasant when you come back from a visit or drive and find the pickers finishing work in the vineyard, gathered around a flagon of claret. It is like harvest-time in other countries, the women in floppy hats, the braces on fat jovial German stomachs, the late glinting sunlight, the shadows falling, the laughter ringing out through the cool evening air.

One day, at Light Pass, we were leaning against the car outside Pastor Reuther's Strait Gate church when a blue Mercedes drove up smartly and Mr Bert Boehm hopped out to empty his mail-box.

He is seventy-one years old, slim, spry, with a fresh silky skin and bright blue eyes. He has a very big vineyard nearby and, though in official retirement, claims he is still the hardest working man in the place.

We had been soaking in sun, too indolent to move on, and Mr Boehm spared a moment to join us. He told me his ancestors migrated from Germany in the 1840s and came to Bethany, in the Valley. They stayed in the village for ten months but their land was at Light Pass, eight miles away. Every Monday they walked across to Light Pass to work on the house they were building and every Saturday night walked back to Bethany so they should not miss church.

'That was nothing in those days. Life was tough for everyone. You were lucky to have a house at all.'

In fact, one family at Bethany lived in the trunk of a tree for a time.

My oldest inhabitant was Mrs Steike, who is 96. She is the daughter of Johann Gottfried Schilling, one of George Fife Angas's shepherds. Her father was born on the ship coming out to Australia, in the late 1830s, and his brother, who was born in a clay dug-out, was the first white child in Angaston. You can see where the Schillings lived as you leave Angaston on the way to Lindsay Park, the old Angas estate.

Mrs Steike is a direct link with the earliest days of the Valley but her brain is perfectly clear and her memory excellent. She answers questions without hesitation and hears so well she only once had to ask me to repeat a word.

We found her staying with a friend, Mrs Kurtz, near Light Pass. Her own house of pug and log is so derelict it is falling down; but she had no complaints. Her voice is quick and birdlike, with a trace of foreign accent. Both she and Mrs Kurtz were brought up to speak German and still do when they are alone. Her features are rounded, her pink cheeks plump, and her eyes very large and blue. With smooth white hair in a net and blue cotton dress and white apron she might be a benevolent granny from a German fairytale; a little old lady who lived in a neat gabled house in the forest.

Mrs Kurtz, who comes from Eden Valley on the Keyneton side of Barossa, is younger with dark eyes, rosy cheeks and white hair. She is straight, strong and competent. Her house is stone with white iron lace, solid, substantial, full of massive furniture, gleaming wooden chests, shining brass beds inlaid with mirrors, and walls hung with two generations of family photographs behind well-polished glass. She does all the work herself.

In her garden, no space is wasted on lawns; just wide beds of roses, dahlias, Michaelmas daisies, ladies' slippers, fuschias, geraniums, gladioli, delphiniums, all growing together. These are not modern deodorized flowers; the roses, like dark red cabbages, are fragrant; there are sweet honey-scents and the aromatic tang of yew. A meticulous yew hedge, high as the house, closes in the garden, with arches cut through. Mrs Kurtz's son trims it twice a year and it takes him a week to do it.

Next door is the vineyard where two of her married daughters were helping the pickers; smiling sunburnt women in wide hats and flowered dresses. Across the road are Australian paddocks and gum trees; but here, with her hedge, her cottage flowers, her neatly-raked orchard, her almond trees and trays of kernels drying in the sun, this old German woman has re-created a home-land that she has never seen.

The two old ladies, with *schirtzes* over their good dresses, entertained us in a high shaded kitchen. The floor shone, the walls shone, the saucepans shone; so did the china, the glass of the framed text and religious pictures, the tiles around the stove. On the stove was Mrs Kurtz's large preserving pan full of beans; in the larder, rows and rows of bottles and jars – jams, jellies, pickles, preserved fruit and vegetables, all made by Mrs Kurtz, all from her garden and orchard which she tends herself.

'We don't starve,' she said dryly.

It was cool in the kitchen. A clock with antler-like carvings ticked on the mantelpiece; the cloth on the table was starched and embroidered and bordered with Mrs Kurtz's crochet. She sat

up straight, doing complex crochet as she talked, from time to
time glancing briefly at a design. She never reads directions, just
copies visually.

She was one of thirteen children. She grew up at Grüenberg,
walking miles every day to school. Her parents were strict as
well as poor and she was never allowed to go to parties. Work
and religion were their life. The big entertainment of the week
was confirmation class on Saturdays, which lasted from nine
in the morning until two o'clock, with a break for lunch. She
always looked forward to it, though it was an hour and a half
walk each way. The girls wore black dresses for their confirmation
and usually black veils when they went to Communion.

'And always on Good Friday,' said Mrs Kurtz.

'When the vintage time came,' Mrs Steike said in her faintly-
accented chirrup, 'we went to work in the gardens. We got two
and sixpence a day for picking and we worked from seven in the
morning till six at night. We brought our own food. We walked
miles to work and miles back home at night, unless we were lucky
to get a lift on a wagon. That was great fun. We got tired but we
always slept well. We never laid awake. We were strong. It was a
healthy life.'

You had to be strong; the weak went to the graveyard. There
were no hospitals, only a midwife and a few people who understood
homoeopathy. The doctors who first came to the Valley relied
mainly on chopping off and tearing out. The old ladies remembered
a woman having an arm amputated without anaesthetic.

'We all helped each other in those days.' They delivered the
babies and minded the children, nursed the sick and laid out the
dead. Though life is so different now, that community feeling
is still very strong in the Valley.

They began to talk about weddings. First of all, there were
Federschleissen parties where all the young people gathered, boys
and girls, to strip feathers for the bridal pillows and featherbed.

'We put tumblers upside down on the table and as you stripped
off the fluffy feathers you put them under your glass. When it
was full it tipped over. The first glass that tipped, we all stopped

work and had games and dancing and Germancake.'

There was also tin-kettling, which even Dulcie remembers. The night before the wedding the local boys would come to the bride's house and make a frightful noise, rattling sticks in tins till the parents brought out wine and Germancake; and often the bride and groom would be stopped coming back from the church by village boys holding a rope across the road. They were not allowed to pass till drinks were given.

The weddings went on for three days. On the first day the guests gathered from all over the Valley, in their German wagons and carts; the ceremony was on the second day, and on the third the party broke up and went home. Marriages did not take place on Saturdays; the middle of the week – Wednesday, Thursday, Friday – was the best time. People could then enjoy carousing and feasting without breaking the Sabbath.

Dulcie, who as a child, had been flowergirl at such weddings, pointed out that in the heat of summer they were often more fun for the guests than for the bride. Apart from the fact that she might, for strategic reasons, be marrying a much older man or even one she hardly knew, she usually worked till the last minute, cooking and scrubbing and polishing the house. Then she put on her veil and wedding-dress and went to the church. She kept on her veil and wedding-dress during the celebrations, which went on for hours, then there was another ceremony and the veil was replaced by a hat. She changed to her going-away dress and the guests sat down to a three-course meal – soup, meat, steamed pudding, no matter how hot the weather – all kinds of sausages, cakes and drinks. After this they took a drive, usually to the mausoleum at Seppeltsfield, to cool off.

Old Mrs Steike listened to the conversation, her ear cocked, smiling her pixy smile, from time to time putting in a word, and Mrs Kurtz would look up from her crochet to remind or correct.

'Yes, we worked hard,' she said. 'But we enjoyed ourselves more than they seem to do now, though they say they have everything.'

'Yes, we were happy,' Mrs Steike said, very convinced. 'We had a good time.'

From Menglers Hill on a warm afternoon you can see the whole Valley closed round with its hills, basking in drowsy light. The sun shines into your eyes, birds flutter and cheep nearby; the white church spires shine, deep green vineyards make patterns with lighter fields. It is rich and domestic yet too open, too serene for complacency.

If you go out of doors just after rain, with the sky still low and weighted, all the air smells of wet leaves. There is soaked earth, and the heavy silence that comes when rain stops and birds have not yet ventured to sing. Fresh scents drift from roses and orchards, the smell of grass is so powerful it brings an image of translucent beads on green spears. Then the clotted sky thins and cracks and a sudden shaft of late sun strikes the roads and pale roofs across the glistening vineyards.

When I arrived there was hardly a soul in the grape gardens; now quite suddenly they are full of bending figures and shady hats. The white grapes are being picked first, then will come the red. Buses have started to bring tourists to the wineries, where crushing is going on full swing. The picking, which ends with the Barossa Vintage Festival, lasts for six weeks and work must not stop, no matter how hot the weather. If the weather changes, the grapes could be spoilt. Already, since the rain, Frank has been worrying about a grape condition called *odium*.

A visit to a well-known winery is included in most Barossa Tours, and after the showing-round the members do a little massed tasting. These outings are not for wine snobs. The bigger wineries have fixed times for public inspection. Some of the smaller ones make appointments, or you just wander in if you know them. Hoffmans (North Para Wines) has been a family affair since 1847. Part of the house that Samuel Hoffman built for his eight sons and daughter is still used, loved and cared for. It has been added to in a rambling way, united by creepers and flowers and trees. It seems to lie down among the vineyards on the banks of the Para River, with the winery on the other bank. There is a grassy picnic ground with tables and benches under the trees. It is simple, homely and charming.

Mrs Hoffman, with a broken leg in plaster, was hobbling about in a large kitchen full of cooked chickens. The air smelt of chicken, they were piled on the table, on side benches. She is always organizing entertainments at the winery to raise funds for good causes and did not see why a broken leg should interfere with her plans. Her enthusiasm, exuberant kindness and open-handedness are reflected in her garden, where plants all grow together lavishly, generously. Across the river, at the winery, her son, the present vigneron, had some kind of official inspecting the books and men were rolling casks about, loading them on to a truck, but he found time to bring out a beautiful claret, which we drank perched on the office table.

It was different at Yaldara, a winery outside Lyndoch which Dulcie thought I should see. This is a show place with everything for tourists: a brand new chateau, well-kept gardens, a winery built like a village church, pink champagne and French antiques. The owner came from Germany in 1947, bought a derelict shell, constructed his chateau with old stones from demolished buildings and was soon in production. Coloured postcards and brochures go out; people flock in. The wines are good; the air smells of success. There is nothing worn or sagging, no ancient creepers to pull things down, no old buildings or happy vague gardens. Any creepers that grow are kept in order, lawns are clipped, trees trimmed. Buses line up in a parking lot; the bar in the sale-room is crowded. Bottles of sparkling burgundy and pink champagne are recklessly bought, and flushed tourists giggle and shout.

Over at Seppelts, where Mr Seppelt, with shirt hanging out, was chatting with his carters, we wandered freely around the vast winery, looking into seething tanks, talking to friendly workmen. I like Seppeltfield; it is Teutonic fantasy on the grand scale, a mixture of modern stainless steel and old stone arches, thick walls and iron lace, stone balustrades and high chimneys. Crenellated cement storage tanks, like castle keeps, loom out from aloes and cactus gone mad. There is a monstrous avenue of palms stretching for miles and a small neo-Greek temple on a green hill. The palms are oppressive in this gentle countryside but they were planted by Oscar Seppelt to give work to his unemployed staff during the depression.

The temple on the hill, built of reddish stone, is the family mausoleum. This is where wedding guests, flushed and stupefied with food and drink, came in their German carts and wagons to cool off.

Across the fields is Gnadenfrei church (Marananga) with a square tower and four little ears, and nearby a handsome old bluestone house with white trimmings. The fields and vineyards stretch out all around, rising and falling in mild waves, their neat lines of green like spaced out tea bushes.

The Barossa people are Australians, apart from their German names and German faces. Yet all through, there is an un-Australian lack of self-consciousness. It is hard to define, for the Valley is far from being a nest of earthy peasants in pug huts. It has all kinds of people, all kinds of lives, from the primitive to the most sophisticated, from the very poor to the very rich. New settlers have come from Europe; the most scientific methods of agriculture and wine-making are used; yet every now and then something opens a door on the past: old Mrs Kurtz's garden; the German songs at the *Liedertafel* . . . a simpler world that is still part of the present.

One night at the Gramps' house in Tanunda, Fay produced a strange zitherlike instrument called a *tricla*. It was brought out from Germany by great-grandmother Gramp over a hundred years ago. Half-lit, half in shadow, Fay sat at the table turning the handle, gently plucking the strings. Slow, sweet, poignant, a little tinny, a little mechanical, the music came grinding out. *In einem Kühlen Grunde*. A touch of the barrel organ, of the musical box, of the harp. The thin little sound was so vulnerable, but how melodious and moving the beautiful old German song! Like the night when the *Liedertafel* sang *Abendlied*, it spoke of an innocent Germany, a land of castles and forests, of goose-girls and good simple people living in peace.

The hot night, the pleasant room receded. In a cool grove the old millwheel turned and homesick immigrants listened.

4

Never get anywhere people don't meex

As I was about to leave the Valley Dulcie Tscharke was called upon to go to Adelaide with a patient in the Angaston District Ambulance. It was hurriedly arranged that I should go also, sitting beside the driver while she sat inside with the patient. If on the way the amublance was called to an accident, I was to disembark and sit with my bags by the roadside. The sight of Gawler, old and charming, on the way in, or Elizabeth, new and sterile, did nothing to reconcile me to leaving the Valley. But my friends at West Beach, vital and brimming with plans and arrangements for me, swept me forward.

Bette Calman I had known in Sydney as a fellow Yoga student; now she runs the Adelaide Yoga Centre. From her house I could come and go as I liked. At Bette's house, you never know if you will find swamis in saffron robes and loin cloths, dieticians, vegetarians, conservative business men passing through, osteopaths, Scandinavian masseuses, beauty experts.

Children come in for ice-creams; dogs leap and bark; the telephone rings. Women may be milling around the stove concocting witches' brews that turn out to be new health recipes. Trays of drying seaweed from the beach add ozone to the vegetable casseroles. Fresh fruit comes in crates with jars of nuts, cartons of yoghurt, pots and bottles of vitamins. Shrieks of laughter and endless chatter mingle with television and transistors from different rooms, while downstairs a holy man may chant OM or sit rapt in meditation.

Through it all Bruce Calman, Bette's husband, maintains a calm that would not disgrace the holy man, while pursuing his way as a top-flight business executive. Bette has reduced her need for sleep to a minimum and may be found wandering about at night writing letters, doing accounts, practising asanas or making pots of tea. Her hospitable nature makes life in this house at West Beach complete freedom. She greeted me with the news that everything had been arranged for me to go to the flat, rather dreary country of market gardens not far from Adelaide which is worked by Italian, Greek and Bulgarian migrants. After that I was to go to Kadina to stay with the descendants of Cornish miners.

Bruce Calman drove me to the Salisbury district and left me with Mr Robinson, known as 'Robbie', who has worked there for twenty-five years and now has his own garage at Parooka where he sells motor and farm machinery parts. He has a tolerant, fatherly air and it is easy to understand why migrants like and trust him.

We set out to visit an Italian family, but a call on Robbie's two-way radio asked him to go to Angle Vale to help a young Dutch orchardist with his tractor. Angle Vale was a sterile stretch of hot brown grass with stiff, dried-out artichokes. The parched air stung the nostrils, the heat haze made the low hills look mangy and barren. But the Dutchman had planted thousands of almond trees and they were growing well. Robbie said with respect that he was very intelligent and not discouraged by setbacks. He has a jewellery business in Salisbury and works in his orchard after hours and at weekends. By the time he retires the almond trees should support him and his family.

He was waiting for us, a sturdy young man in shorts and heavy boots. Robbie began tinkering and tapping. Dick, his Dutch friend, made the tractor rev and roar. I sat by the roadside waving off flies, squinting against heat and glare. Dick said he had been here eighteen years. Holland was just a place where his relations lived. He and his wife and family were Australians. Presently the tractor hiccupped and lurched away taking Dick back to his hard work. Almonds, he said, were a good commercial crop but also in spring there was nothing so beautiful as an almond orchard in blossom. There were no trees in sight apart from the orchard but Dick was happy here.

The Italian family we visited next were out in a bleak paddock picking onions. Mario, Domenica and their son Francesco were all good-looking with that social Italian merriness. They have thirty-five acres of market garden and were prospering. After sixteen years in Australia Domenica still spoke with an Italian accent.

'Mario comes first, from Cosenza, then send for me and the children. Australians very friendly to us. A lot of hard work but a good life.'

Francesco on his knees in the dirt paused among his onions. He is a student and has just finished second year chemistry, but was taking a year off from examinations. Domenica beamed with delight when I commented on his fluent English.

'Well, I went to school here. I've been here since I was five. I'm an Australian.'

'Do you speak Italian too?'

'We all talk Italian at home and Mum cooks Italian food. We grow our own olives and Mum pickles them.'

Once, Domenica said, they had had cows and made their own cheese but now there were Italian shops and so they had sold the cows. All the Italians made their own wine. They bought grapes from the vineyards and made the wine themselves.

'The New Australians buy up all the old mangles,' Francesco said. 'They're good for crushing grapes. You put the mangle on its side with some wire-netting to keep the grapes in, put the grapes through and collect the juice in a tub.'

'*Bagnio*,' said Domenica, much amused. 'Old bath.'

'One Italian was poisoned the other day,' Francesco told me, 'from using an old bath. The paint got into the wine and he got lead poisoning. It must have been some wine to take the paint off.'

Francesco would have an easier life than his parents. They had been peasants in Italy and here they were small landowners. He was not too proud to dig earth and help with their work, and he regarded his mother fondly.

'He's a good boy,' she said, rising from the box on which she had been sitting, to kneel down among the onions again.

There were tomato glasshouses beside the road along which we drove. These were owned mainly by Bulgarians. They were always welcoming you into their houses, Robbie said, to have coffee, a meal, a glass of wine. The wine was 'pretty raw' and some kept it only a few days before they drank it. Not that that sort of wine ever improved no matter how long you kept it, but they'd be hurt if you didn't accept some. So you drank it even if it killed you.

Most of the houses were fibro in pastel colours cheered by geraniums. Others were brick villas with lawns, scalloped blinds and television antennae. These belonged to prosperous long-established Italian families.

On the outskirts of Virginia we drew up at a small fibro house facing the railway line. It was poor, hot and bleak.

'Now this may be rather difficult,' Robbie said. 'This is a Greek who has got behind with his payments and I have to be firm. Perhaps you had better stay in the car.'

A dry wind had come up, swirling red dust about. The Greek was not too deep in financial waters for a television mast which gave the last touch of ugliness to the scene. At the side of the house two young men were struggling with a tractor. They looked glum and perplexed as the engine roared, stopped, roared again. A sense of failure and disappointment hung in the air as thick as the heat. The young men turned away, shrugging. They gathered their tools and moved towards the house. As they passed the car they said, 'Good day,' and their smiles were so gay my spirits went up like a rocket. Heat, hardship, poverty were nothing new to Greeks. Even the poor little house seemed to brighten. Instead of a regretful Robbie a young girl came out.

'Please come in. Please take coffee.'

Worn but hospitable, she led me through a hot little back verandah to a half-furnished kitchen. They were down to their last penny but they must give hospitality. A handsome young man pulled out a chair and offered a cigarette. His young wife making coffee seemed listless and weighed down but she had large, soft eyes and was pretty and gentle. She brought Turkish coffee and biscuits and sat beside me.

Robbie, who had wished to spare me the Greek's embarrassment at his sternness, was listening sympathetically as Con said that it was true enough he could not pay until he was paid by those who owed him money. The glasshouse owners pay only twice a year. He had to wait while debts piled up, but if his boss was honest he would be paid. Meanwhile he urgently needed a new tractor. Con's hands were held forward, clasped in prayer. The old tractor would not even start.

'Ring now, Mr Robinson, ring your office and ask. If *you* ask them they will agree!'

Robbie was presently at the telephone pleading Con's cause. Vicki led me round the bare little house. In the sitting-room was only the television set and photographs of the baby boy, a younger prettier Vicki, a younger carefree Con, dashing in an army beret.

'From Salonika we come. Ah, if you have been in Greece, you know Salonika? In Greece we are poor but have many family. Here we are poor and I am always alone. Con is working. I take the boy to school morning, bring him back afternoon. No one.'

She was so homesick, so gentle and shy in her apron and ankle socks, with her hair pushed back with a half comb. The view from the window was all red dust and railway lines, no more arid than Greece but how much emptier! Each week a man came with supplies for cooking and she could buy Greek food at an Italian shop in Virginia. It was not food she was hungry for.

In the kitchen Robbie was saying, 'I can't promise it will come off, but I will do my best.' As we drove away he said,

'He's a good boy but he's had bad luck. What he's asking is rather unusual but I'll have to see what I can do . . . '

On the other side of Virginia there were more glasshouses. Johnny da Costa and his wife, both Calabrese, grow mainly tomatoes. Mrs Johnny was shifting hoses, soaking the soil ready for planting. She sat down on an oil drum saying she was tired and would like a holiday, but how could you go with the kids and the tomatoes? Her mother-in-law, all in black with a black veil over her head, sat on the verandah, erect on a kitchen chair and for the duration of my visit she did not move nor speak nor show a sign of life.

Italians, Mrs Johnny said, lived all down the road, mostly newcomers. The women wouldn't bother to learn English.

'It's different with me. I came out here when I was twelve. But these others, they can't seem to settle. Things aren't so bad in Italy now but they were glad enough to come. Assisted passages!'

'The Good Neighbour Council in Salisbury told me the young men used to have trouble meeting girls . . . finding girls to dance with.'

'That's right. Our fellows got different ways. Australian girls didn't understand; they thought they were getting too fresh. It may be better now.'

'What about Italian girls? Could your men dance with them?'

'In Italy girls don't go out. Not many Italian fathers around here would let their girls go out with a fellow. But the boys meet more Australian girls now. I think they are getting used to each other. Then the Australian boys get jealous. You've got to see both sides.'

Migrants who have been absorbed into the community are often intolerant of newcomers. They have forgotten how it feels. Those who are bilingual are the ones who can bridge the gap. Giulio is Australian although he can never be anything but Italian. He has two thousand olive trees, the biggest and first olive orchard in South Australia. The substantial house is set among olive trees that form high hedges around the garden. In the big, cool kitcken Mrs Giulio set about making coffee. 'Giulio's olives, my coffee – the best.'

She spoke fluent, grammatical English with an Australian accent that seemed strange with her rich Italian voice.

'Ah, but I've been here thirty-six years, Mr Robinson. Don't forget that.'

She was short, pale, with thick waving hair springing back from her alert, good-humoured face. Giulio, who came rushing in from his olive groves, was going grey, a broad-chested, dramatic man. He raised eyebrows, hands, shoulders, thumped the table, shouted with laughter. One hand was cupped for the other clenched fist to hammer, palms were brought up, turned outward. He was orator, conspirator, clown, rebel, hero. The words poured out, the thick whispers, the quick turn of the head as he lowered his voice, swore, paused for effect.

Robbie sat back looking benevolent. Mrs Giulio watched her husband indulgently. Forty-seven years ago he came from northern Italy to Australia, twenty-four years ago he started growing olives. He knew nothing about them. He was a builder, and earlier had had a delicatessen shop.

'I build myself a house. A man comes – wants to buy my house; so I sell. Start a garden – celery. Then,' eyes narrowed, hands making weaving motions, 'then I think, maybe grow olivi. I take *wild* olivi. One thousand I plant, I grow. Bloody hard work!'

'Fifteen years I work in a factory,' said Mrs Giulio. 'While he grows olives. Can't make a living at it.'

'Everyone *now* wants my olivi. All Australia. Look! I show you the letters: *Giulio send more olivi*. Many pickers.'

'It wasn't always so easy. We had our bad times. We had to do this grafting so we hired a man.'

'Three years! No bloody good. He come. He cut. No olivi. I say to my wife, "We are ruined. Finish. Finish!"' A sob in the voice. A wail of despair. 'Then (*crescendo* up to *forte*) I cut. I cut myself! Olivi come up. Good as gold!'

'Did his grafting himself after that,' Mrs Giulio said. 'The man didn't know anything. We trusted him and he ruined our trees.'

'Arrh!' Giulio leant forward. 'But now comes scales. More troubles . . . Trees sick inside. I spray – I spray. No more scales. Now, Mr Robinson, Giulio makes new invention to pick olives. All the time pickers raise the hand up to the tree, down to the bucket. Now – I show you. No waste time up and down.'

I was drinking my fifth cup of coffee enthralled by the drama. Giulio moved on from bloody scales to bloody Dagos.

'Bloody Dagos, Mr Robinson. Don't want to work. Complain all the time. Make trouble. Want to buy my land cheap. All this road I own. What I buy with? My two hands. Make work, make money, two thousand trees now, many pickers. Now these bloody Dagos want me to give my land away . . . '

'Yugoslavs, Hungarians, Czechoslovakians,' said Mrs Giulio. 'Out for what they can get. In the old days, Mr Robinson, everyone helped each other, worked hard, minded their own business. Now it's all grab. Keep to themselves too, the new ones.'

'Bloody snobs!' Giulio roared. 'All the time say Australians are no good. Hey? Bloody Dagos stick together – not meex. No good! Never get anywhere people don't meex. Italia, my mother, but little ones grow up, leave the mother for the work, the life. Giulio now Australian. Bloody Dagos! This my country!'

5

Goodbye, Cousin Jack

Kadina, with Moonta six miles farther on, was once known as Australia's Little Cornwall. It lies ninety miles by road north-west of Adelaide, but the train takes the long way round to this part of Yorke Peninsula, struggling through curious shaved hills called the Hummocks. We had passed Port Wakefield, which was once the port for the Burra copper mines, and there had been glimpses of the distant blue St Vincent's Gulf. Right out in open country was a little old cemetery with enormous angels rearing up.

I was to stay with a Mrs Rosewarne, and with a Cornish name I pictured her plump, wearing a towcer (sacking apron). There would be saffron buns for tea and pasties, just as there were when I lived in the West Country where I had liked the Cornish people and become used to their ways.

The scenery was, I thought, flat and uninteresting after Clare, where I had been living. At Clare, the green hills and ploughed red earth, the harvest fields embroidered with haycocks, gave way to vineyards curving out towards Watervale where Quellthaler wines are made and to Seven Hills where the winery was founded by Polish priests. Clare had been all trees and pale stone, the main streets avenues of shade. Stone cottages in back lanes were

draped in vines and bees droned among sweet-scented, unfashion-
able flowers. At the far end of the town was an old mill, and
beyond a grove of trees, mellow buildings with oak casks against
rough white walls. This was Knappstein, the winery of a German
family.

When we stopped at Kadina, I saw my landlady on the platform,
shaped like a cottage loaf, with rosy cheeks and hair screwed
up on top. She ignored me. Instead, a woman in a floral pants-
suit, who looked amusing and lively, came forward and said she
was Gillian Rosewarne. She laughed when she looked at me, and
I laughed too. As we left the station she glanced at my Mrs
Rosewarne and said affectionately, 'There's a real Cousin Jenny
for you.'

I realized why she had been amused when we drove in a white
sports car to a stone house that certainly did not take in boarders.
She ran in calling, 'Jack! Jack! Our visitor's here and she's not a
bit like we expected.'

The town clerk had handed over my letter to the National Trust
and they had been nonplussed at my asking for a family of Cornish
descent to board with. One of the members said, when Gillian
offered to take me, 'Cheer up, she mightn't be so bad after all.'
That I had been ready for lumpy beds and West Country grammar
struck her as humorous.

It was fun at the Rosewarnes'. Gillian, who is really a busy
woman, is easy-going, always ready to laugh. The house was often
filled with young people, the atmosphere was casual and relaxed.
The day an American student came, she made Cornish pasties
for lunch – proper pasties, not the phoney kind with pre-cooked
meat, and gravy put in afterwards. They should be of fine-cut
raw steak, sliced onion, potato and turnip cooked very slowly so
meat and vegetables can give out their juices and the pastry is well
browned. The early settlers had to make do with what they
could get for meat – goat, rabbit, kangaroo. Though Cornish
pasties have a crimped join, which is a typical feature, they could
be related to Russian *piroshki*.

The one thing that drives Gillian to fury is the refusal of

some local residents to give heirlooms to the National Trust museum.

'Here we are, trying to preserve things for them, keep them for posterity, and they won't part up! Or the dealers get round them. The dealers come here, scrounging from the other States and all our antiques are being taken away. I feel like putting up notices: PEOPLE OF KADINA – UNITE. DON'T LET YOUR HEIRLOOMS BE TAKEN OUT OF THE STATE. GIVE THEM TO THE MUSEUM!'

The museum is in Matta House, built a century ago for the manager of the Matta Matta mines. Caroline Carleton, who wrote *The Song of Australia*, is said to have died there. Outside are displayed Cornish wheelbarrows – without legs, for going into the mines – and all kinds of early agricultural implements and vehicles. Inside are the furniture, kitchenware, pillowshams, bedspreads, watch-pockets and relics of the mining families. Like Tanunda Museum, it is all very personal, very poignant now that the owners have gone. Little Cornwall is only a memory. A few years more, and no one will remember the miners and their Cornish ways. Only the Cornish names, and perhaps the Cornish eyes, will survive.

Gillian is not Cornish herself but is deeply interested in the district's Cornish background, and in her husband's family history. The house is full of antiques. Jack's great-great-grandfather, Nicholas Rosewarne, emigrated from Hayle, in Cornwall, in 1857.

'He was only nineteen, two years younger than the Colony, all alone, homeless and penniless. It took eighty days in the ship to Port Adelaide and three weeks by bullock dray to the copper mines at the Burra. When he arrived he slept under the counter of an empty shop.'

Nicholas Rosewarne had come to Kadina in 1861 when the Wallaroo copper mines opened, with his young wife whom he met on the ship coming out. After seven years he left the mines and bought a grocery-hardware store. His son became a wheelwright and started a blacksmith's shop. From this Rosewarne's had grown to be one of the most important motor and machinery dealers in the State. The blacksmith's shop is still behind the modern showrooms. Gillian plans to restore it and fit it out with old equipment.

'I wish I had known great-great grandma Rosewarne. Her son Willie died young – he fell down the cellar – but she never stopped thinking of him. Even when she was quite old she used to sigh and say, "Poor Will. I wonder what fashion 'e do be lookin' now?" They say he had the *biggest* funeral and the *biggest* plot and the *tallest* monument in the cemetery!'

Cousin was a friendly form of greeting with the Cornish. Although as Gillian says, the only real Cousin Jacks and Cousin Jennys are now in the cemetery, you will still see unmistakeable Cornish figures and faces in the streets: stocky, short-legged, with straight features, rather broad, flat-topped heads, a long upper lip and strange dark eyes and eyebrows.

Many of the Cornishmen who came to Kadina and Moonta when copper was found were experienced miners. In Cornwall, mining goes back to the Bronze Age. The Phoenicians came to the West Country, where they are said to have left traces of their blood, for Cornish tin. When the Cornish came to the Yorke Peninsula they brought with them their passion for singing in choirs and playing in bands. Most of the miners were Methodists. In the Peninsula, they created little Cornish villages, living as much as possible as they had done at home and marrying among themselves. The Cornish are ancient Britons, like the people of Wales and Brittany, and regard anyone outside their country as *furriners*. Mere migration to the other side of the world would not seem to them an adequate reason for changing their ways.

The mine near Kadina was named Wallaroo, after the sheep station where copper was discovered. 'Wallaroo, or Wallawaroo, means wallaby urine,' Gillian said, rolling her eyes. Both Wallaroo and Moonta ('impenetrable scrub') mines were on the same property, very poorl and, which belonged to a Scottish sea-captain named Hughes who believed it might contain copper for he noticed his shepherds' fires sometimes burning with a greenish flame. He told the men to watch out for copper and how to recognize it.

In 1859, one of the shepherds, James Boor, found a green mineral thrown up by a kangaroo-rat in digging its burrow. It was copper. Captain Hughes took out a mineral lease and Wallaroo Mine opened. Two years later another shepherd, Patrick Ryan, found copper a few miles away at Moonta Moonterra, this time thrown out by a wombat. There was a wild race to lodge a claim; people rode all through the night to Adelaide; there were dramas, false statements, strange flukes, and a law suit, but Captain Hughes won the mining rights and Moonta mine opened. The lodes were so rich that no capital was needed to finance it. Eventually the two mines were run together and made over £20,000,000. Captain Hughes became Sir Walter Watson Hughes. Part of his fortune helped found the University of Adelaide.

The mines flourished until 1925; then they closed because of falling prices, labour troubles and overseas competition. The Cousin Jacks had to look elsewhere for work. Some went to Broken Hill or other mines, some turned to farming, others died. As people drifted away, the whitewashed villages began to disappear. Cottages decayed through neglect or were pulled down for their materials. There are a few left at the mines, picturesque from outside, with thick walls and chimneys, but often dark and cramped inside and sometimes with earth floors.

The mines settlement was a little way from Kadina (*Caddy-yeena*-Lizard Plain). A small monument marks the place where James Boor caught his foot in the kangaroo-rat's diggings. Low scrub covers the land where the miners' cottages stood in their little gardens, fenced to keep out goats. The cottages were built anywhere, paths wandered among them; there were no streets. Most were of lath and pug with shingle or iron roofs, though better houses were stone with a brick pattern around windows and doors. The cottages were whitewashed every year, as at home in Cornwall, with lime and water.

Beyond the cottages were the school and the churches and farther off, the buildings for mine offices, engines, machine shops, plants and works, poppet heads, high chimneys, the houses of personnel. Old photographs show a crowded busy sky-line;

now there is only a high stone engine building, a grey and saffron mountain of skimps which blows over everything, covering all with a fine earthy dust. It is slowly decreasing in size and perhaps one day will be gone, but meanwhile its surroundings are uninhabitable. The abandoned schoolhouse is thick with its dust. It brings a hopeless feeling, as when one thinks of those Japanese who live in the dunes and spend their lives shovelling away the encroaching sand.

The schoolhouse is large and has been handsome, but the roses have grown wild in the gardens and vandals have wrecked the inside. There is desolation and ruin in every room and always the silent dust sifting down.

Across an empty stretch is an old stone Methodist church with a graveyard and a belfry out in the grounds. The other mines' churches have gone. With evening shadows it becomes eerie. People once disappeared here, children strayed away from home and fell down abandoned holes in the ground. Now, though the unsafe ground is overgrown and harmless, there is a strange touch in the air. The feeling could be one of association for it comes in parts of Cornwall. In pagan times, the Cornish built bonfires to drive evil spirits away, on Midsummer Night, 24 June, and the miners brought this ancient custom with them.

There are still many people who remember the days of Little Cornwall, even a few old miners.

'I were one of Cap'n 'Ancock's men,' said Mr Trenwith, scowling into the sun. He is over eighty but still tall and upright. 'I remember the Cap'n.'

I had not expected to meet anyone who had known Captain Hancock. He was the famous Mines Superintendent who made many improvements in working the mines, a dignified, bearded Methodist. He was held in such awe by his men that they combed their hair before speaking to him on the telephone.

I said Mr Trenwith must have been very young if he worked for Hancock.

'I started at the mine when I was thirteen. I were a pickey-boy. I got five shillings a week. And when I were old enough I went down the mine and got an extra one-and-sixpence increase a week.'

Most of the old miners still living started above ground, at the pickey-table, taking out high-grade ore from loads wheeled up in barrows. Boys did not go underground till a certain age.

Though he has no Cornish accent, Mr Trenwith's voice is a rich un-Australian growl. I asked if he had been a singer.

'Ah, I sang. Everyone sang. And I were in the band. I played trombone.'

'And euphonium,' said his little dark-eyed Cornish wife, who does not come up to his shoulder.

'My mother used to talk funny,' Mr Trenwith said. 'They all talked funny in those days. Oh yes, she made saffron buns and pahsties. She had an oven like, in the wall. My dad took a pahsty for lunch every day. My dad were a miner. He came from Redruth.'

All the Trenwith family photographs are stuck in the glass doors of the kitchen dresser. When I sent him his picture, Mr Trenwith put it right at the top. 'Best place for the old sire,' he said.

Mr Laffin was another of Hancock's men. He left school at fifteen and worked as a pickey-boy till he was sixteen when he went down the mine. At one time, he said, he earned as much as £4 a week.

'Most unlikely,' an elderly lady told me rather tartly. 'The average miner's wage was about £1.18.0 a week, though it went up to £2.0.0. Unless he was a tributer or on tutwork, which I doubt. He was only a boy.'

On tutwork (contract), pay was based on the quantity of ore the men raised, no matter what grade; tributers were paid according to the value of its metal content. Sometimes, if they were lucky, tributers did make money, but most miners' earnings were small.

I was more interested in old Mr Laffin's personal life than his earnings. He leaned over his gate, talking slowly, with long pauses for reflection, while a meal cooled inside on the table. He was born here, he said, he grew up at the mines. His mother came out from Cornwall when she was twelve.

'She were an orphan; she worked in the Cornish mines when she were only eight years old. She never went to school, never could read or write. But she could cook proper – pahsties and saffron buns and potato cakes ....'

'My mother couldn't read or write ... ' 'My grandfather never got beyond mixing cement ... ' 'My father never went to school ... ' Everyone was so straightforward; no one pretended to be grander than they were. They are all proud of their Cornish background; they all know what part of Cornwall their family came from and the date and name of the ship that brought them here. So many South Australians, no matter what occupation or background, know these family facts. It seems strange to a native of New South Wales, but gives an impression of continuity, of not rejecting the past. This Colony was always a land of free settlers.

Though the Kadina people often said there was *Nothing Left*, we talked in kitchens with steeple-clocks and china dogs on the mantelpiece, brass candlesticks and wooden chests, all brought out from home. Though they spoke with Australian voices, they looked at me with Cornish eyes.

When they described the old days at the mines it was like Cornwall as I knew it. There were exceptions: possums stealing domestic utensils and food; water so scarce that families drank it from roofs or underground tanks contaminated by drainage, even collected from cart tracks. Though government water was later sold for a few pence a bucket, hundreds, particularly children, died of typhoid, diphtheria or other epidemics.

There was also trouble with goats. Most families kept a goat, which got out of hand, broke down fences and ate vegatable gardens, washing off the line, shoes, anything lying about.

But the chairs, the singing, the carols, the daily life was much as I remember in parts of rural Cornwall: the spotless cottages, lime-washed, with polished furniture, the parlour with a round table holding the family bible, family photographs hoisted up high and colour prints, slightly smoke-stained, of 'The Battle of Alma'. The harmoniums, the white marcella or honeycomb bedspreads and Staffordshire figures, the steeple-clocks and brass candlesticks were all familiar; the pig slaughtering ritual – washing the insides to make sausages, the smell of fried chitterlings, the laying down of bacon and sending away of pork loins to friends and relations. I knew, had even used, the *brandis*, an iron four-legged pot stand in the open fireplace, the huge cauldron for boiling clothes or water for Saturday night baths.

The Misses Mitchell live in a stone house next door to the Rosewarne's. Inside is fine old furniture lovingly cared for. The sisters entertained me in a room with mahogany armchairs and sofas and a steeple-clock on the mantelpiece. Miss Winifred has grey-green eyes, Miss Marion dark eyes under very black eyebrows. Both have soft gentle voices.

They told me with affectionate pride how their father, who was brought out from Cornwall at the age of ten and left an orphan, educated himself and became a well-known saddler in Moonta, a leading personality in the Methodist Church. Miss Winifred has been home to Cornwall to see his village and meet her relations. Miss Marion had nursed in Adelaide and Miss Winifred had been a teacher, but both had worked in Kadina for years and knew the life and the people. They smiled when I said some had suggested Little Cornwall might have survived if the mines had not closed and the miners dispersed. For all their Cornish stubbornness and distrust of new ways, life was changing even while the Cousin Jacks were here.

All the original miners spoke the West Country dialect, and though at school more orthodox English was taught, when children went home they lapsed back into archaic words, inverted pronouns, the confused and wonderful Cornish grammar; but as they grew up they wanted to speak like other Australians. They dropped the Cornish accent and as the older generation died it went with them.

More changes came with better education. Many of the first settlers distrusted the hospital, regarded it as the place to die in, were reluctant to send their families there. It was good that such attitudes had gone; but the sisters regretted the choirs, the beautiful singing. Bands of young men would wander about, singing, and every Sunday night after church men and women would parade up and down the street, eight abreast, from the mill corner to the town hall, singing and harmonizing until nine o'clock when they all went home. People gathered together to sing in their houses; and at Christmas there were the carols, such beautiful Cornish carols, some composed by Mr Thomas of Moonta.

Since the Mitchells are devout Methodists I did not like to bring up the subject of revivalist meetings and waited until I met Ken Reid, a native of Moonta whose humour is typically Cornish. Though he grew up in Moonta he lives now in Wallaroo, the old smelting town and port of Little Cornwall. His house is crammed with antiques, furniture, silver, glass, china, curios, stuffed birds, Aboriginal artifacts, geological specimens and paintings, from primitives to valuable works of contemporary artists. There are also some delightful Grandma Moses-like scenes painted by his father, perhaps the only existing records of very early life at the mines.

'The dealers would like to get in here,' Ken said, showing us his collection. 'They sniff round the hospitals, waiting for people to die, if they think there's a chance of a few antiques. There's going to be a wonderful scramble when I drop off. It'll be the event of the year. It will make a nice send-off, something to remember.'

Ken has diabetes. When it began to affect his sight he decided to go into Wallaroo Hospital. We found him in the geriatric ward. 'They didn't know where else to put me,' he said in his young surprised voice. 'I can't say that it's exactly riotous here.'

In a corner a form crouched, silent, under its covers; next door an elderly man wheezed and groaned, getting ready to die. Another lay flat on his back, playing a concertina. The dismal tune seemed familiar.

'*For he's a jolly good fellow,*' said Ken. 'Sounds different, doesn't it, played *lento* like that. It's for the funeral service they had in Wallaroo today. A local boy was killed in Vietnam. That fellow's been at it all day. At other times he plays dirges and hymns of a funereal nature. This is a change, I don't mind the tune. It's just a bit like Marmite, too much spoils the flavour.'

Ken sat up very straight in his flannels and blazer, his blue eyes wide and innocent.

'Oh, the revivalist meetings were great affairs. Do you know, there were eleven churches out at Moonta mine, not counting five in the town and others here and there. At the mines, they were so close together you could hear people repenting in several at once. Dozens of churches, mainly Methodist – Primitive, Wesleyan, Bible Christian. One would get up and call out *Praise the Lord! Halleluja!* then they'd all start. When I was young, church was the big event of the week. You had to start queueing up at five o'clock for the six-thirty evening service if you wanted a seat. Like the movies. And the preaching was fierce. *Fierce!* The preachers would bang their bibles and thump the table and knock their water bottles over, all about hell-fire and repentance. The people loved it, though most of them lived the most blameless lives.'

The Reids came from the Helford River and were a well-known Moonta family. Ken's maternal grandmother was the first white woman to live there and his father, who was born at the Burra mines, had a drapery shop in the town. His Uncle Matt became Captain Hancock's paymaster, accountant and next-in-charge.

'My Uncle Matt was a friend of Oswald Pryor, who did cartoons about the Cousin Jacks and wrote of the old days in *Australia's Little Cornwall.* Uncle Matt often gave Oswald stories about the miners. Oswald worked at the mines himself. It's all true, it was just as he says in the book. But, of course, the big thing was the funerals. Everyone in mourning, shops hung with crepe, undertakers in black frock-coats and top hats with streamers – all from Reid's drapery. The men were wearing frock-coats for funerals up to eight or ten years ago.'

All who could went to the cemetery; those who could not would go inside their houses as a mark of respect as the coffin passed.

'We had two bells at Moonta cemetery,' Ken said cheerfully. 'The first one wasn't suitable. It sounded too merry and people complained. So they melted it down and put in extra silver, which they collected from the locals, to give a more solemn tone.

'In those days you couldn't get a cart through the scrub. They used to take turns at carrying the coffin – it's a long way to Moonta cemetery – and we all walked, two by two, singing like billy-oh. Later on, they had hearses and horses with black plumes. The chief mourners would go in a cab. There was always plenty of good singing out at the cemetery, people got carried away in more ways than one. One woman sang so well at her husband's funeral she got a proposal from one of the mourners. She married him, would you believe it!

'They used to have a chair by the grave, in case anyone was cut up bad and needed a sit-down; then we all went back to the house and had a wonderful feed. People went out of their way to put on a good spread at funerals, sometimes done by professional caterers: chickens, home-cured hams, potted shrimps, pasties. And seedy cake and cheese cakes and saffron buns.'

Moonta's most famous grave is that of Thomas Woolcock, who was murdered by his wife.

'When he died no one was suspicious; but the men started to talk, how every day at lunchtime, down the mine, after Tom ate his pasty, he would sit with his head in his hands and say he felt giddy. So they dug him up and found he was full of poison. She'd been giving him a little bit every day in his pasty. She was hanged, poor thing. She was very young and had had a terrible life. Tom used to drink and beat her. These days she'd have got off. They lived over at Yelta. It's called Poison Flat now.'

Ken's enthusiasm for funerals rather overshadowed weddings, but he mentioned that they often took place at five o'clock in the morning so that the bridal pair could catch the seven o'clock train into town.

'But Christmas was the great time. We had the carols of course. My Uncle Matt was founder of the Wallaroo orchestra. We had our own family orchestra, we all played different instruments. At Christmas everyone sang Cornish carols all round the town, lorry loads of singers; and there were decorations and Swankey.'

Some people say Swankey is not alcoholic, others claim that it is.

'Well, the Rechabites liked to say it was non-alcoholic, but funny things used to happen after drinking it. They gave some to the parson once and he fell off his bike. You never could tell; it was liable to blow up and hit the ceiling. They brought the recipe out from Cornwall. It had yeast and malt and raisins and hops and sugar and God knows what else. You left it for a few days before you corked the bottles and you had to tie the corks to keep them down.

'The poor miners had to have some fun. You couldn't do much on two quid a week, with a wife and family to keep. But people enjoyed themselves. We had bands and singing, and Sunday School picnics and Tea Treats – they called them Tea Treats – what a feed! – and sometimes there were regattas on the bay. A cheap place for entertainment was the mangle-room; you heard all the gossip there. The mangles belonged to the mining companies and miners' widows were allowed to charge a few pence for putting clothes through. It was like the parish pump. When young men were courting a girl they used to carry her basket of laundry to the mangle-room. That was a kind of public declaration.'

When we left Ken, the concertina-player was still droning out his dirge, the old man was still wheezing, the form in the corner bed still motionless. Gillian was upset at leaving that humorous Cornishman in such a macabre setting.

'Ken, of all people! He had always been such fun. The dinner parties we've had at his house! Nothing seemed to get him down. A few years ago he had a car accident and was badly hurt. He crawled out and sat on the roadside all covered with blood. When a motorist stopped and said, "Have an accident?" Ken said, "No thanks. Just had one." '

Wallaroo is almost a ghost town now, though barley and wheat is shipped from the long jetty and phosphate from Nauru and

Ocean Island is unloaded there. By the abandoned smelting works is a high square chimney with W.W.H. (Walter Watson Hughes) picked out in bricks. The sun shines on the far out Spencer Gulf; a long low headland protects the curve of hard white sand. Strangely it seems more Cornish than Kadina or Moonta with its great silent shimmering bay, yet it is a Welsh settlement. Smelters were brought out from South Wales, and Welsh language, Welsh singing and preaching survived here for many years.

Moonta Mines is another ghost town, even more desolate than Kadina Mines though there are more cottages, a big school and a great Methodist church. The cottages are very scattered and at times seem half-buried – they were often dug into the ground – and fences make it hard to see much beyond tin roofs, chimneys, the tops of water tanks. There are no trees, just a high tower against the sky. The old paths are almost invisible and we wound and zigzagged through an ocean of low bushes. The settlement was never properly laid out. As at Wallaroo Mines, the Cousin Jacks just squatted near their work. At one time there were over six thousand people here. They had electric light when Moonta town had only gas lamps.

Mrs Emmy Rodda, a miner's descendant who still lives in a miner's cottage, showed us inside the church. It has a three-sided gallery, once crowded, and pictures and records of the famous Sunday School run by Captain Hancock's son and successor. It had eight hundred members ranging from children under three to extreme old age.

Moonta town itself, which once had twelve thousand inhabitants, is now very quiet. In the broad streets are dignified stone houses and here and there old miners sunning themselves. There are not many left; they like to congregate and talk at a shop known locally as the Houses of Parliament.

There is a museum and one of the miners' cottages has been restored by the National Trust, but Moonta's great attraction is the cemetery. Here they lie in thousands, all the Cousin Jacks and Jennies, arranged in avenues, from St Just, Redruth, Helston, Porthleven, Gwennap; Nancarrows and Nankevilles, Trewathas,

Penhalls, Trembaths, Kittos, Pryors, Tripps, Retallicks, Voyzeys, Polglases, Tembys, Pollards, Trengroves, Trethowens. John Verran, the Cornish miner Premier of South Australia, is there, and someone described as 'An acceptable and useful lay preacher'. There is also a Tossel – the most prevalent name in the village where I once lived – and famous Tom Woolcock. With Mr Ferguson, a friend of the Misses Mitchell, we prowled for hours in the sun, enjoying the clear air, the scent of the conifers, the curious inscriptions on some of the tombstones, but sorely tempted by old Nailsea vases and china jugs left on neglected graves.

These Cousin Jacks would be surprised to see how quiet Moonta has become, how Kadina has changed. Though this town still has its old houses, and the old Wombat Hotel opened in 1862, it is now a prosperous agricultural centre. The poor property of Captain Hughes has been changed by modern fertilizers to valuable farming land, an important district for wheat and barley.

When it was time to leave Gillian took me to the station. As the train came in she handed me a packet saying, 'You'll be starving before you get to Adelaide.'

We kissed and I climbed aboard. We waved, the train hooted and moved out. The hours went by, we passed the Hummocks, the cemetery near Paskerville with the splendid angels. As dusk fell I grew hungry and opened my packet. Inside were two nicely-browned semi-circular pies with beautifully crimped edges. I spread my handkerchief on my knee like a real Cousin Jenny and started to eat my pasties.

6

Strawberry Farm

It seemed years since I left Adelaide. I had travelled hundreds
of miles in dozens of buses, seen millions of dried fruits and
acres of vines along the River Murray, endless sheep flats and
rolling grasslands, large towns and small towns, ghost towns.
Melbourne, after all the kindly people of the countryside, could
not have been more of a shock. The taxi driver from the station
refused to stop outside the hotel and expected me to carry my
bags back to it. A pleasant young woman was sorry I couldn't have
early breakfast before I left the next morning as the dining room
didn't open. When I went to the railway to buy a ticket for the
next day's journey I was told to come back tomorrow. They only
sold tickets for the day they were used. Telephones were out of
order; none had directories.

In the early morning drizzle, unbreakfasted, I bought my
ticket and asked for a porter.

'No porters here, dear.'

'Is it far to the platform?'

'Yes, it's a fair way.'

Against a torrent of workers surging off trains I battled to
a long wet platform and waited, shivering. I asked three fleeting

officials about connections for Stony Point.

'Dunno lady. Could be.' 'Search me,' said the second, and the third was even more enigmatic, 'You never know.'

I jumped in the train and chanced it. 'Sometimes,' a woman passenger said, 'they put up a notice "Change for Stony Point".'

The draughts blew in through the ill-fitting windows. There were glimpses of sodden suburbs and presently little countrified stations. At Stony Point a pleasant young man who had come in the train, carried my bag to a truck for transport to the ferry and walked with me through the teeth of the gale down the long jetty where a beat-up white boat cowered against the wharf and yellow, oil-skinned figures groped about the deck. There, at Stony Point, the young man explained, we were in Westernport, a large bay with a circular passage and French Island set in the middle. Westernport was discovered by Bass in 1798 when he was exploring the coast by whale boat. This harbour was the most western point of his route and west of all then known harbours. Now that it is east of Port Phillip the name can be confusing. The young man's family had a cattle property on Phillip Island. French Island was larger but not so interesting. Bass had taken it for part of the mainland. The island was named by a French scientific expedition, under Captain Baudin, which came in *Le Naturaliste* and *Le Geographe* in 1802.

My instructions were that when I landed at Cowes I was to go to Dave Cook's garage and then he would drive me the seven miles to Strawberry Farm near Rhyll. The young man who introduced himself as Donald Cameron, said his mother was coming to meet him and they would drive me to Dave Cook's. Already the indifference of Melbourne was giving way to country concern for strangers. Dave Cook was just as helpful. Finding I was to stay alone at the farm, he said he would just wait and 'see you safe inside'. The key was not under the mat or behind flowerports, water tank or any orthodox place. Gusts of rain drove in from the sea along the open verandah.

'Come on,' said Dave. 'I'll drive you down to the store. It may be there.'

The post office store was warm and dry and, sure enough, they had the key. 'Will you be all right up there alone?' asked the postmistress. 'Just give me a ring if there's anything you want and someone will come up in the car.'

'You won't be nervous?' Dave Cook asked, as he tried the key in the lock.

'No,' I said untruthfully.

In this weather, the headland was a setting for suspense drama. But once inside, the house had a faint friendly smell of flowers and biscuits and mattresses, a holiday smell. There was a feeling that a foot stepping forward would sink down into the silence as into feathers. I stood absorbing the beneficent welcome, forgetful of wet clothes or the thought of hot tea. The silence was so reassuring.

The rain whispered on; wet hydrangeas brushed the kitchen windows; beyond, the pines in the avenue were dark against brilliant grass. On the table a jug of pink amaryllis held down letters of greeting.

This was once a strawberry farm; the grounds were planted with fruit and teas were served in the garden. Now it is used for holidays, and the house has become part of nature, the sea, the headland. Beyond the garden gate a path wanders through pines and clumps of wild scented amaryllis. The cliff slopes gently, trees and bushes growing out of its face. I looked down on curving margins of red-brown stone and shiny mangroves and out across the lead-coloured strait to French Island. Flotillas of black swans bobbed on the dull, choppy surface. Small groups detached themselves and sailed away. The air was full of sharp little cries. Long ago, in the 1840s, there was an industry here in swan skins. Thousands of these beautiful birds were killed for their down and their eggs stolen for food.

The farm is sheltered and almost concealed by cypress and pines yet there is no sense of being shut in. The garden surrounds the old house as though asking to come indoors. It is a tangle of red and white geraniums, standard roses, pink lilies, hollyhocks, fuschias and blue chicory flowers gone wild. There is an oak on the lawn, a lemon tree by the verandah. Among the garden beds loaded branches are dragged down with enormous quinces, red apples, pomegranates.

I walked to the village through a small pine wood lined with bright leaves and purple flowers. Rhyll is just a post office store and houses scattered on grassy slopes, and by the water, a long jetty and boats at anchor. To the north, beyond Strawberry Farm, are salt marshes and mud flats haunted by curlews, sand-pipers and pelicans. There is a bridge from San Remo on the Victorian mainland to Newhaven on the eastern end of Phillip Island. In summer, visitors flock across for day trips or to stay for holidays. Sometimes they return here to live.

Ken and Marge Lang who run the post office store, were born on the mainland to become devoted Islanders. It is hard to believe Ken came here for his health. On certain days he covers the whole area of the island, every lane and side road, delivering letters, parcels, bread, milk, meat and machinery parts. The day I set out with him the sea was sparkling and steam rising from the ground. I had expected that Phillip Island would be rocky bleakness, but only one coast really faces Bass Strait. Elsewhere is an orderly landscape of pale concave fields, sheep shorn white or wool-grey grazing the hills with coloured cows or stiff-legged black cattle. Much stranger were the chicory kilns crowned with weather vanes above the rows of spinach-like leaves. Chicory has been grown and the sliced root dried here for nearly a hundred years. It is an ancient crop cultivated by the Romans.

The trees in the open country are spaced out, white houses on the hill shelter in cypress and pine but farms and cottages on back roads are deep in eucalypts. The native trees, she-oaks and tea-trees, are everywhere. The tea-trees have been shaped by the wind almost like umbrella pines with thick matted leaves and clean white trunks. The she-oaks are rounded, stylized, like trees in a child's drawing. At midday they stand in tidy circles of shade, inviting the wooden cows.

At the farthest west point of the road Ken Lang stopped at a tea room and advised me to look through the telescope. I put in a coin, applied my eye and gave a cry of delight. About a mile from the coast an islet of grey rocks was seething with action. Hundreds of slippery forms were plunging and diving and twisting, rearing up, raising sleek heads or stretching shining bodies to bask in the sun. The islet, Seal Rocks, is one of the biggest seal colonies in Australia. Every summer thousands come here to breed, first the immense bulls, with manes and tycoon rolls of fat around their necks, then the females. Each male seizes his own territory for the breeding season and when the cows arrive is ready to claim his harem. It may range from six to twenty. The tycoons are so busy frolicking with their concubines and fighting off rivals they have no time to fish for food and end up leaner than when they came. But for some months Seal Rocks is a mass of gleaming fur and flippers. Baby seals lie like shining slugs; plump liquid-eyed cows swim and slop in the water or flounder ashore to suckle their young. Then, when summer is over, they go to sea again until the next breeding season.

Seals are now protected but in earlier days the most industrious efforts were made to wipe them out. Men were put ashore from British or American ships and left for months, free to kill all they could. Sealers were the first known white residents of Phillip Island. You may now go out to Seal Rocks but not to land. Observers from the Victorian Fisheries and Wild Life Department are stationed there in a fortress-like hut.

Close by the tea rooms, the Island seems to fall away suddenly. Off shore from the cliff is a pile of chocolate rocks called the Nobbies, at high tide a sort of Faraglioni. The whole southern coast is rugged, from the Nobbies to Cape Woolamai at the opposite end, a succession of platforms, colonnades, organ-pipe formations, pyramids, cliffs of eroded granite or sea-shifted basalt, tunnels, caves and blowholes where waves roar in. Cape Woolamai, a tied island, rears up beyond an arc of glittering sand, with high granitic walls facing Bass Strait. This side of the island is as unlike the calm bays and drifting swans of the northern coast as the ocean beach of an atoll differs from its tranquil lagoon.

Inland, we stopped in eucalypt forests to watch plump, sedentary backsides wedged in the forks of trees. Koalas which are protected, live and breed on the Island in ideal conditions. The manna gums that they need for food are plentiful and large forests have been declared reserves. Koalas were exterminated in many other areas by fur hunters, by disease and starvation when the land was cleared. Now, fresh forests of manna gums have been planted in different parts of the country and koalas moved from districts in which they had survived.

Here on Phillip Island, they live in freedom and safety, groping their way across the ground, ponderously clambering up and down trees, swaying high like superior sailors in crow's-nests, chewing vaguely, dozing or peering down with mild indifference.

My nearest neighbours are Frank and Helen Janssen. At dusk, flocks of white ibis take off from the fields, disturbing Frank's sheep which begin lurching and stumbling about in their muffled-up way. Helen always happens to be driving to places she knows I want to see and, at the end of each expedition, says that she'd be glad if I would go home with her to eat. She makes beautiful scones with jam and clotted cream, and after dinner, while Helen knits or sews, Frank sits in his armchair under the picture of his father's sailing ship and answers my questions, good humouredly willing to talk, but with the quality of one used to silence.

Helen was born on the mainland but her people have had links with Phillip Island for many years. Her mother can remember how, when she was a child, a tall dark gentleman carried her ashore and sat her on his knee in the crowded coach going back to Melbourne. He gave her biscuits and talked to her all the way. She was too young to know he was Alfred Deakin, the Prime Minister.

Helen was teaching school in Rhyll when she met Frank. His father, Captain Johann Janssen, was a Swede who came here in the 1880s. For many years he sailed in a famous little local ship called the *Swan* and eventually became her owner. When she was sunk in a collision he bought a schooner called *Stephen* and carried timber from the Bass River to Melbourne. Frank grew up with boats and the sea. He became a fisherman, growing chicory in off seasons. Now, though he has a farm, he still fishes and takes boats to sea.

His mother, who is half-Finnish, half-Welsh, came to the Island in 1893 and married Johann the following year, when she was eighteen. They were married by Dr Rodd, the first Presbyterian minister on the Island, and settled at Rhyll. She still lives in the village and though she is over ninety, has plump rosy cheeks, dark Welsh eyes and a very sweet smile. She sits very straight, holds her head well and walks slowly but firmly. The general effect is of such cheerful dignity you forget her careful steps come from increasing blindness.

I wondered one night why Helen was so anxious that I should come to their house before dusk. She had overheard me ask at the store and was going to take me to see the penguins.

The Island's fairy penguins are very small. They go to sea for food and often stay there for several days, if the weather is good, working in groups, rounding up shoals of fish. They always set out and come back under cover of darkness, as protection against gulls or sea eagles, and their evening return to land has become a great tourist attraction.

I was curious though rather prepared for a sort of 'Feeding Time at the Zoo'. At Summerland Beach, where the birds come in, notices said PENGUIN PARADE. NO CARS PARKED BEYOND THIS POINT. CAR PARK ADMISSION 30 CENTS. There was a great deal of cement, high poles with floodlights, a strong fishy smell, but beyond was only a beach with waves rolling in from Bass Strait and a damp wind.

A floodlight suddenly shone grey on the sand and I saw people out in the shadows, sitting on rugs or standing, very docile and quiet. They seemed less like trippers than sympathetic observers feeling privileged to share an extraordinary experience. Until 1955 there was no control over sightseers. Crowds flocked to the beach, trampling on burrows, stealing eggs or chicks, cutting off incoming parent birds from their young waiting to be fed. The penguins might have been wiped out if the State Fisheries and Wild Life Departments had not intervened. The area around the burrows is now a large reserve and the water is out of bounds up to seventy yards off-shore, between dusk and dawn.

Brown kelp was being sucked back and heaved up and flung down by the breakers. The implacable movement brought sinister thoughts of bodies swept away in the dark by a merciless current, dragged down, never found again.

The waiting people were silent. There was a curious feeling as though something supernatural were about to happen; then out in the black waves white dots appeared, floating in, sailing sideways with the currents, ascending the breakers. It was disturbing, awesome, these frail birds coming out of those endless wastes.

Spectators were now directed by loudspeakers to arrange themselves on each side of the lighted area to leave a space for the birds to come up the beach. Small forms gleamed in the darkness. One at a time, in twos or threes, penguins were struggling ashore, sliding upon the broken waves, staggering out of the foam. For all its impressiveness the scene was comic. Unconcerned by the lights, the birds stood, like white Churchills cogitating, conferring, waiting for groups to collect before moving off to the burrows. They wandered about at the water's edge, yelping at stragglers and rounding each other up. Across the lights, moths flashed white and from time to time a bird swooped. At this the penguins pannicked and rushed back into the water with amazing speed.

The birds at this time of the year are almost double their normal weight. Soon they would come ashore to moult, staying in their burrows and living on their excess fat. If they go to sea half-moulted they become waterlogged and drown.

At last a leader made a move. With flippers hanging like the paws of prairie mice, the penguins struggled across the beach, over seaweed and rocks, pausing to rest, stumbling and falling flat on their faces. Too fat, too easily overbalanced, they waddled and plodded on grimly, determined heads pushed forward, gasping and squeaking. At the edge of the beach they all made a great final effort and charged with a rush, calling excitedly, up the grassy hillocks to their burrows and waiting chicks.

The young birds, almost full grown, greeted them noisily and at once began chasing their parents about until the load of half-digested fish was disgorged into the chicks' beaks.

Away in the shadows, beyond the footlights, more birds were coming in, white dots sailing high on dark waves; but a light rain had started to fall. People were going home. As we passed the fenced-off enclosure a little pair of twins, flippers entwined, looked out at us hungrily. I hoped their parents were down there on the beach waiting for their companions, starting and running back, cheeping and calling. Ashore, penguins are absurd and delightful, but on the black sea they are eerie. Those white flashes in the surf are too much like despairing hands being swept away for ever.

Next day there was a pure blue morning with soft clouds on the horizon. Nothing is quite like going straight from bed, barefoot, into a summer garden. One side of the oak is in shadow, the other side gleams. Across the grass in every direction the sea glitters. The tide is out, pale sandbanks exposed. The house is like a ship facing out to sea with the winds blowing through and the sounds of sea birds coming indoors. There is one in the night that cries *Help! Help! Help!*

Helen says that the nocturnal squawks and racketty conversations I hear are plover. I like them chattering away around the farm. There are also lugubrious mopokes, and by day rowdy mynah birds sit on the backs of the cattle and bicker and shriek. The Island has hundreds of land birds, from English larks to kookaburras. Sea birds crowd in endlessly, dipping down lightly into the salt marshes where sea-lavender grows, or to the swamps with bulrushes and yellow marsh-flowers.

My watch has stopped, so now time has stopped. I lie on the cliff top, in a sheltered place, chewing grass. The air is so still I can hear the faint crackle of seaweed down by the rocks. The bay has become a shallow lagoon shut in by a frail golden bar.

Barossa Deutsch

*Grape picking
in the Barossa Valley*

Vintage time

Barossa Valley Church

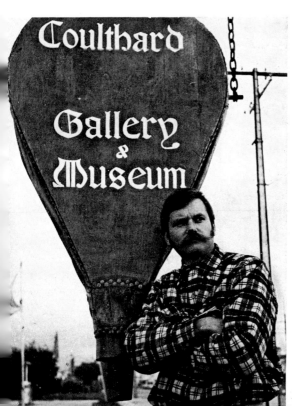

American Settler, Coulthard

Houses of the Barossa Valley

'Good people never stealing'

Valiant Pastor

'Never get anywhere people don't meex'

Old house in Moonta

Moonta mines

Dark Cornish eyes

Cousin Jack

*Just a long jetty and boats at anchor
Rhyll, Phillip Island*

One of the many chicory kilns on Phillip Island

Ossie

Cheerful good humour

Non-nordic look

Mr Walton

Mr Macleay's little paradise
ABOVE—*The gates,* BELOW—*The house*

'My English, My English'.
Estonian chicken farmer's wife

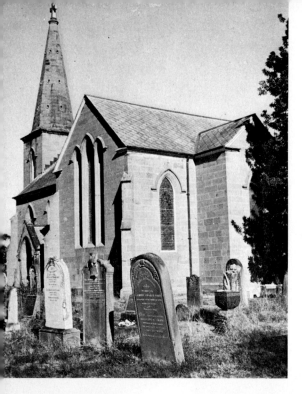

LEFT
Cobbitty Church

BELOW
Group of Estonians

On the milky surface the black swans glide; out on the sandbank spectacled pelicans dab their faces into the water. In the garden, finches, wrens, jackey-winters twitter, very domestic, up to their eyes in flowers and leaves. Butterflies career about, large and coloured, or tiny with white wings. Against the sun, some of the smallest birds might be moths throwing specks of shadow on my book. The seed pods of agapanthus hang down like green spaniel ears.

I am not to take this weather as typical, the Islanders tell me, relating stories of fearful tempests. Old Mr Walton, who lives in Rhyll village, has made it clear that no place has gales like Phillip Island, that over the years the coast has been strewn with wreckage. He tells me about what he calls the *Coramba* storm in the 1930s, when the ship *Coramba* went down with all hands off Seal Rocks. He takes a melancholy, almost warning tone, as though I might be inclined to belittle the Island's wrecks. The most famous I already know from everyone I have met, was the *Speke*, whose relics still rust on the Bass Strait coast.

'A graveyard of ships!' Mr Walton says solemnly. The *Speke* had just come from Peru, and some say the lookout mistook a bushfire for the lights of a town. She ran on the rocks with a terrible hole in her side and was finally broken to pieces.

'A beautiful barque! Ah well, we don't know the Plan behind it all, do we? Perhaps it was meant to be!'

Mr Walton was born at Rhyll and was one of ten – some say twelve – children. His forebears, who lived on the Mornington Peninsula, were connected with sailing ships and he became a boatbuilder. I knew his whole life had been boats, building or sailing, and expected someone more ancient and gnarled. While I walked up the path to his little house by the sea he was waiting for me in the sun, very erect and handsome with no signs of tar or barnacles. He had a pale skin and beautiful smooth white hair, the sort of northern colouring that survives time and exposure.

We began, almost absently, to look at an unfinished boat in his shed and were suddenly deep in conversation about tides and the moon and their influence on fishing, the movements of fish and the waters around Phillip Island, about drownings and tragedies, shipwrecks, storms, even Island smuggling. I could have listened indefinitely but Mr Walton suddenly felt he must be a host and I should have a chair and refreshments.

Inside, the atmosphere changed. Out came the best cups and glass-topped table, the polite chat about cricket and nights at the Club, about high times in Cowes. As he talked I spied a dark, rather wild painting of a lighthouse in a rough sea. But, though admitting he was the artist, he dismissed it carelessly. Now, if you're interested in Art – ' he said, and produced a batch of genteel watercolours and hand-coloured photographs.

Afterwards, driving me back to the farm, very slow and dignified, he showed me the site of Fort Dumaresque, above Rhyll village. It was built in the nineteenth century to keep out the French, who were suspected of having designs on the Island. By the time the little garrison arrived, the French, a harmless scientific expedition, had come and gone. There were only a few Tasmanian sealers living here, peacefully growing wheat and maize.

Ossie was born on the Island. His grandparents, who were from Devon, settled in South Australia but his parents came here after their marriage. As a child his mother had stayed with her uncle, Captain Reid, a Phillip Island identity, a Scottish sea captain who retired to Rhyll over a hundred years ago. The name REID is still carved on a rock at Smith's Bay.

'Mum and Dad didn't have much when they came here,' Ossie said. 'Just a few clothes, a parrot, a violin and an accordion. The dad worked on farms for a while; he managed one for John Cleeland of Woolamai House. Cleeland's horse won the Melbourne Cup in 1875. It was trained on the beach near Newhaven. But the dad didn't see much point in working for other people so he bought some land near Rhyll and built this house. It was only $40 an acre in those days. You'd pay that much a foot now. That was about 1903 and he started with chicory and fruit and vegetables. Then he decided to go in for strawberries –

Strawberry Farm – it's on the old maps of the Island. I took over till we sold up and retired.'

Oswald and Ethel Underdown, the former owners of Strawberry Farm who now live at Newhaven, were down for a visit. They went around the garden like returning exiles, exclaiming and recognizing every tree and shrub.

At a deserted beach, while Ethel stayed in the car, Ossie and I, in bitter wind, clambered over the rough marram grass that holds the dunes together, looking for mutton-bird burrows. A few chicks peered back with startled eyes but most of the birds had gone.

About the middle of April every year the mutton-birds set out from their island home in Bass Strait. Leaving behind their three-months-old chicks, they fly north, across the Pacific, past Japan, to the Bering Sea. Here they moult their wing feathers and stay until they can fly again; then they go on, down the west coast of America to California and home across the Pacific.

For a couple of weeks after their parents leave them the chicks, which are very big and fat, remain fasting in their burrows. When they have lost weight and are light enough to fly they set out to join their parents and, helped by the prevailing winds, find their way by instinct, by the sun and the stars, to the northern wintering grounds.

The round journey takes six months. In the third week of September the birds arrive back at the same island, the same burrow. When they have cleaned it out, they mate, then fly to sea until the eggs are due, late in October. It is said that they mate for life. Each female lays only one egg in a season but both parents take turns in hatching. Then once more, when the chick is three months old, the parents fly off on their endless circular journey and again the young birds follow. But often before they can leave, the burrows are robbed. The fat chicks are very good eating and full of oil which has a commercial value. The Chinese used to extract this beak-oil by holding the birds upside down and squeezing it from their stomachs.

At one time, there was wholesale slaughter. Hundreds of

mainlanders moved to the Islands during the season, not only
for chicks but for the eggs which were used by cake manufacturers.
The burrows are still robbed, illegally; but, though lately the
birds have been dying of a strange disease, there are still many
thousands. When Flinders sailed through Bass Strait he saw a
solid stream of from fifty to eighty yards or more in breadth flying
over for a full hour and a half without interruption.

I dislike the name 'mutton-bird', since they neither look nor
taste like sheep. They are short-tailed shearwaters! They belong
to the petrel family and so are related to the most ancient and
legendary birds of the sea: the great albatross, the tiny Mother
Carey's Chickens, the Bird of Providence. Dampier describes them
thus in the *Voyage of the Roebuck :* ' . . . as they fly (gently then)
they pat the Water alternately with their Feet, as if they walk'd
upon it; tho' still upon the Wing. And from hence the Seamen
give them the name of Petrels, in Allusion to St. Peter's walking
upon the Lake of Gennesareth.'

Across the water from Rhyll village is a low island that seems to
merge with the mainland near Newhaven and the bridge to San
Remo. This is Churchill Island, the first cultivated land in
Victoria.

In 1801, Lieutenant James Grant, with a botanist and surveyor
on board, came in the *Lady Nelson* to explore Westernport.
He was so charmed by the little island off Phillip Island that
he built a log hut and started a garden. He planted seeds given
for experiment by John Churchill of Devon; peaches, apples,
plums, melons, vegetables of different kinds, rice, coffee and wheat.
So he named the island Churchill and wrote of it, 'I scarcely
know a place I should sooner call mine than this little island'.

In the 1860s, the whole island was sold for £210 to a Cornishman
named John Rogers. Since then it has always been privately
owned. It is now a cattle property, belonging to Miss Margaret
Campbell.

To reach Churchill, you enter a wooden gate, near Newhaven,
and drive between grazing cattle to a little white bridge, a private

causeway joining the islands. When the tide is out there are mangroves exposed in the mud. It takes only a couple of minutes to cross, yet looking back, Phillip Island seems already another country. Though Churchill has the same neat landscape, the familiar black and brown cattle, in a smaller compass, the effect is more complete.

A winding road ascends the sand-coloured fields, concave like the roof of a tent, to a gate among cypress and pines. At the top, dogs leapt and barked. Miss Campbell came out to welcome us. She has a strong handsome face, calm, wise and humorous.

Instinctively, without preliminaries, we all went straight into the garden.

We wandered in shaded walks by beds ablaze with colour, feeling rather apart yet united in our tranquillity. From time to time someone would disappear, to be found gazing at a vista or detail; an immense terra-cotta urn on mellow red-brick steps; an ancient tree covered with olives, set round with phlox and yellow daisies, sweet-scented white mandevillea stars scattered over an arch; a sundial; a fantastic science fiction cactus.

Time, love, understanding, helped by volcanic soil, have produced an effect of careless grace, offhand abundance. Planning has been unobtrusive so that all appears to grow by accident, yet in harmony: roses, camellias, zinnias mixed with dahlias and hollyhocks, penstemons among fuchsias, tiny pink chrysanthemums next to marigolds like saffron trays.

There is a garden of native plants packed round with seaweed to keep in moisture, and rows of vegetables in a side bed, like a dignified audience watching the carnival of fruit, corn, passion vines, cannas and flowering shrubs. The air smells of violet leaves, grass and pink lilies, of oleanders and cypresses. Wherever you look, down green avenues, between the trunks of pines, are the mild leonine slopes with black grazing cattle; and all around the milky embrace of the sea.

Old Mrs Janssen took a rest on a chair under the fruit trees. Leaf patterns shifted upon the white table, on the thick lawn, on her calm face. Margaret Campbell bent to inspect new plants, glancing critically at shrubs and leaves. She looks after the garden herself, with only the help of a friend, and runs her cattle property alone. She knows and loves every inch of her island, all the bays where the pelicans congregate, the secluded beaches where strange sea birds gather, the shallows where white ibis come to fish. Her garden is not on the site of Lieutenant Grant's; that was down by the shore. She tells me there is a legend that Bass came here during his time in Westernport. There are letters, now almost weathered away, on the walls of a cave, which might have spelt B.A.S.S.

At the foot of a great Norfolk Island pine is a little cannon which is fired each New Year. It was said to have come from the *Shenandoah*, an American armed raider, and to have been used in the Civil War, but Miss Campbell thinks this is not true.

Behind the main house, among lilacs, is an early settler's cottage with small rooms, low ceilings, thick walls and twelve-paned windows. In the kitchen is a colonial wall oven; in the cellar, insulated with seaweed, trays of apples give out a cidery scent.

The homestead itself has a shaded courtyard paved with worn mellow bricks. Pale green, with narrow white iron lace, the old house might have grown from the earth, so harmoniously does it blend with garden and trees.

We could not bear to go in to tea, though the kettle shrieked in the kitchen and hot scones cooled in the drawing room. Dawdling, delaying, looking back, we ambled inside and found we were all very hungry.

Tea was hilarious. A friend of Miss Campbell's who lives just across the causeway, was stunned at the tale of my journey to Cowes via Stony Point. She cried in her deep, husky voice that: No one but *no one* had ever come that way since Bass sailed into Westernport.

Quite suddenly, the whole house and garden vanished as in a fairy story. Looking back as we drove down the hill I saw only the dark crown of trees, the black cattle on the slopes. The tide had been coming in all the afternoon. Now it streamed under the causeway like a wide river. From the other side Churchill floated out on the sea. At Strawberry Farm, a white moon looked down through the trees. The black swans, asleep with heads under wings, drifted, little dark logs. The tide came in, imperceptibly, flooding the mangroves.

On my last morning, since I have no clock, Helen rang early to wake me. It was raining as she and Frank drove me to Rhyll village, grey and misty as on the day I arrived. I was going in to Cowes with the crew of the Stony Point ferry.

As I got into the car and waved to the Janssens, they were ghostly in the fine mist; then a heavy gust blew in from the sea, and the village, the dark trees around Strawberry Farm were blotted out.

7

My Thoughts are the Northern Flowers

At Thirlmere, near Sydney, there are over two hundred Estonians. Some came in the 1920s. They emigrated during an economic depression at home and settled in this district because Crown land was cheap for anyone who would improve it. They cleared the bush, built houses, established chicken farms, planted orchards and gardens.

When Estonia was overrun by the Soviet Union in 1944, more than 70,000 people escaped from the country. In 1947, many began to come to Australia as Displaced Persons. For years they worked at all kinds of jobs in the cities. Some are still there; some, who had scraped and saved every penny for capital, came to Thirlmere and began chicken farming. They cleared and worked and built, as the first settlers had done. The community grew and prospered; it now has its own hall, two churches and an old people's home.

Most Estonian settlers are peace-loving, honest, industrious. They mind their own business, help each other and cause so little trouble they rarely get into the news. Few Australians know the Thirlmere community exists. I learnt of it from Estonian friends in Sydney, and was on my way to visit the settlement, driving through familiar country, with Arno and Susan Varima and Mr Urm, President of the Estonian Relief Committee.

Passing through Campbelltown I had the strange sensation of seeing Australia through the eyes of a new settler. We who have been here longer are already starting to look back, to want to conserve and preserve before it is too late; but with my Estonian friends there was no bewailing the replacement of historic landmarks with ugly new shops. If you come from an ancient land and have lost everything but your life, the destruction of a few eighteenth century buildings would be hardly worth mentioning. The past, as these people knew it, no longer exists; they can only look forward. I suddenly saw the hideous supermarkets and car sale-yards as reassuring signs that for them a future did exist.

Beyond Picton, Arno turned into flat scrub and approached a small straggly settlement. He said proudly, 'This is Thirlmere!' and waved at a modern building with KUNGLA spelt out on a grey brick tower. 'That is the Co-operative Store. *Kungla* is an Estonian name.'

'It means *Fairyland*,' said Mr Urm. 'The chicken farmers here got together a long time ago to buy food more cheaply. From that grew this Co-operative. In this district are also Finnish and Yugoslav settlers.'

Beyond Kungla the dry scrub resumed; then came green grass and houses among trees. We drove into a beautiful garden with conifers and all kinds of flowering shrubs. In the background were neat buildings for chickens, screened and camouflaged by green willows.

'This is the farm of Arno Enno,' said Arno, driving up to the modern house. 'Here I will leave you and here the Ladies' Committee will entertain you at lunch. Mrs Enno is the President.'

Mrs Enno and her friend Ellen Villig were waiting, both in linen dresses with Estonian embroidery.

'Yes, yes, we do it ourselves,' Ellen said, 'but Luise Victoria is the best. She is champion.'

'I show you,' said Luise Victoria, vanishing and coming back with an immense half-completed embroidery. 'This I do for our Exposition. It is not yet finished, the design. I wait for inspiration.'

Inspiration had not been lacking. The house was full of embroidered cushions, curtains, lampshades and dresses, some worked in double cross-stitch, some in rich bright wools with a look of Orthodox Church vestments. Luise Victoria has great books of traditional designs from which she selects and adapts. Since she helps on the farm with the eggs, as well as cooking and gardening, running the house and looking after her family, I asked when she found time. She said she did it at night, while watching television. Her husband said, 'Mine wife has very much energy and eyes all round the head. She can watch the Tivee, same time make embroidering.'

Other ladies were arriving. Their Committee is very informal, they said, not official like the Country Women's Association. They just meet from time to time during the year to raise funds for good causes, prepare suppers for parties. They also work for handicraft exhibitions and do what they can to preserve Estonian folk arts. Women in other areas weave traditional materials and dress dolls in regional costumes.

The newcomers, Linda Aavik and Sylvia Kongas, both spoke fluent English with no trace of accent. Sylvia, in an orange dress embroidered by Luise Victoria, said, Well, after all, she should, she had been here since she was twelve.

I asked if she had come with her parents.

'My parents were sent to Siberia. I happened to be away from home that night, otherwise – The neighbours told me next morning that *They* came in the night and took them. I never saw them again. You know – the usual story.'

She spoke casually, almost off-handedly, but at the back of her eyes a shutter flickered down.

While the ladies were out in the kitchen, I went around the farm with Linda and Arno Enno. Arno, a fair man with a kindly out-of-doors face, apologized for wearing overalls. He had been working with his chickens.

'Always work. And no holiday. No one to mind the chickens – not until mine boys leave school.'

'Will they come on the farm?'

'Maybe. Maybe one.'

Linda said in her beautiful English, 'Most of our young people go to the city when they leave school, to the University. We are anxious for our children to have the advantages that were taken away from us. This country has so much to offer the young.'

It is hard to believe the wide lawns and trees had been untouched bush when the Ennos first came. They had cleared and worked and watered for years. Arno said, 'And now I grow tired. I grow old. But no holiday for me yet.'

A new Committee member had arrived when we went to lunch, Anni Kaasik, a dark pretty woman with green eyes. She spoke excellent English in an impetuous manner. 'I'll take you this afternoon to see the Old People's Home,' she said. 'And anyone else you want to talk to. You'll find some of the people can't speak much English, so I must interpret. Then we have dinner at my friends, the Kusiks', and there you will sleep.'

I was relieved to see wine on the table instead of vodka or brandy. I had wondered how I would cope with the Old People's Home if lunch was like Estonian hospitality as I knew it. The food was lavish, and, though I dared not say so, rather Russian: beef bouillon with *piroshki;* chicken in sour cream sauce; ice-cream and apple compote; a huge tort with fresh cream and strawberries; coffee and Napoleon brandy. The wine circulated.

'Do you lunch like this every Saturday?'

'No, no. This is for you. We celebrate your visit.'

Except for Linda's husband, who teaches Art in Sydney, most were chicken farmers. They recalled, hilariously, the trials of their early days.

'How could we know?' 'We had never been on the land before, even at home . . . ' 'The mistakes that we made . . . '

'We had no idea how to do the simplest things,' Anni said. 'At our farm we had an old horse but we could not get him to move. Then we found he would only start to music. Maybe he'd

been in a circus. So when he was harnessed we would bring out
the radio and turn it on. Then we had trouble to stop him. One
day my poor husband had to do ploughing. He had never ploughed
in his life. He harnessed the horse to the plough, turned on the
music and suddenly away they went! Full pelt across the field!
Poor Kaasik rushing behind, trying to keep up with the plough.
It was just like a chariot race.'

Martin Villig, Ellen's husband, beamed into his brandy, all
prosperous contentment; yet just before lunch Ellen had told
me tearfully how he had gone back to Estonia, hoping to see his
brother. If you were not on the black list you could visit Tallina,
the capital. You stayed at an approved tourist hotel and your
relations came there to see you. Martin had waited five days.
Messages had been sent but his brother had never appeared.

'I can't be bothered with all that embroidery,' Anni said,
as she drove me away after many farewells.

'But you don't want it to die out, do you? Even if you don't
like doing it. It's good someone keeps it alive.'

'Why?'

'Why? Because people mustn't let their whole background go
just because they've been forced to leave their country.'

'That is peasant art. I prefer to spend time reading; to maintain
the real art and culture of our country. Anyway, *this* is our country
now. Estonia is finished for us.'

'But if you drop all your traditions, even folk arts, what will
take their place? You should be enriching our life here by
contributing what you brought, not dropping it off.'

Anni spoke very passionately. 'We Estonians cannot afford to
live in the past. We want to get on and live well. We have lost
too much too many times to be worried about a few folk dances.
We are Australians. We must integrate.'

'But why can't you integrate without losing your background,
the way they did in the Barossa Valley? You know perfectly well
that the future is built on the past.'

'Our children want to speak English. They want to make their
lives here.'

She was driving rapidly down the country roads, from time to time waving at green clearings in the scrub, lawns, gardens, orchards, modern houses.

'Estonian ... Estonian ... Estonian ... Those are Finns, those are Yugoslavs ... More Finns ... but mainly Estonians. The Finns are closer to us than anyone in language and customs.'

'How many of the new generation will stay here and take over those farms?'

'Hardly any, I think. We have cleared the land and done the pioneering, but still it is ceaseless hard work for most of us: hens, eggs, formalities, paper work for the government. The young ones now all go to the University at Sydney or Wollongong. They will want to be lawyers and doctors and engineers. That's better than battling out here in the bush. For our generation it is too late to think of changing. We have settled, we have done well. But for our children it is different.'

She pulled up at a substantial building, like a house, and said, 'So! This is our Community Hall. Here we have parties and meetings and gymnastic classes. We also let it out to Finns or Australians or people in the district who want to hire it. Cheer up, we are not really throwing away our traditions. We also have here children's classes for Estonian language and folk dancing. And our choir meets every Tuesday night to practise. It's a mixed choir and they sing Estonian songs.'

The hall is hung with the coats of arms of different Estonian provinces and at one end are the portraits of an Estonian president, an Estonian general. Anni said, 'You see, already we are Australianized. It is not usual for us to have portraits hanging in places like this; but Australians have the Queen, so we have our General and our President, whom we lost when we lost independence.'

The Queen is in the Committee room, surrounded by photographs of Estonian cities and buildings.

I asked about the Estonian churches.

'There are two churches. Most Estonians are Lutherans though we have a few Baptists, but we don't go to church every Sunday ...

no no, I tell you, we are not very spiritual people. There is no pastor living here. The Lutheran pastor comes up from Sydney about eight times a year, and of course for weddings or funerals or anniversaries.'

We were back in the car, on the way to the Old People's Home. Anni talked all the time in her quick, rather hoarse voice, humorous, clever, straightforward.

'There's a great deal of pious nonsense talked about us Estonians, how well we get on together, how peace-loving we are. We have to be. We don't make big troubles or stick knives in each other like Greeks or Yugoslavs but you should hear the men on the Vietnam war, for instance, after a few brandies or vodkas. Now, you see . . . here are more chicken farms – Estonian. There are a few orchards and one or two canning factories for sauerkraut and apples but all the rest chickens. This orchard here – acres of apple trees. He has a plant for apple juice. Cars come all the time to buy his fruit.'

This Estonian orchardist has been here since 1937. He speaks like an Australian; but the couple at the next farm, who had emigrated nearly twenty years ago, speak very little English. They live in a small cottage among lawns, shrubs and fruit trees. Orchids and indoor plants flower in a conservatory next to the house. The farmer said shyly, 'I am ashamed of my English. I speak only Estonian, Russian, Finnish, German and Latvian. Not much English.'

His little bright-eyed wife, with a kerchief around her head, made a protesting gesture. 'Please! Please! My bad English!' She cut two immense grapefruit from a loaded tree and offered them, smiling.

I noticed that all the Estonians, except Anni, talk about their Senior Citizens' Home. Even the original address has been changed from Old Road to Estonian Road. It is actually a village, with a central block, separate flats and cottages, and is growing steadily.

Mr Urm, who has been President of the Estonian Relief Committee since 1951, has had much to do with the Home and is building a house there for himself. The Relief Committee was formed in 1945 to help destitute Estonians in Europe, refugees, invalids, children in Displaced Persons camps. When Estonians started migrating to Australia in 1947 the Committee guaranteed them work and shelter. The Estonian House in Sydney was turned into a transit camp and hundreds of jobs and homes were found.

Then, about 1958, appeals began to come from Estonian migrants who were too old to work and had no family to look after them. There were 7,000 Estonians in Australia and many had not been naturalized or been here long enough to receive the old-age pension. The Committee's constitution was changed to allow it to buy property and build a home for old people.

Fifteen acres were acquired at Thirlmere, in the heart of the Estonian farming community. The Commonwealth Social Services Department agreed to give two-thirds of the building cost if the Committee could find the first third. It was raised by a lottery among all Estonians in Australia and the first building was started.

The main block has eight bed-sitting rooms, two bathrooms, a shared sitting-room, kitchen and laundry. It is pleasant, warm and comfortable, beautifully kept, with a resident voluntary matron and a garden where the occupants may work if they like. There is no institutional touch anywhere but its greatest attraction is that everyone is Estonian and it is surrounded by Estonian families. Old people who had lived in fear of being put into homes or hospitals where no one could speak their language, may now end their days among their own people.

The first building was so successful that applications came from all over Australia. Already there are four buildings, including separate units for single or married people. Others are planned. For individual flats the occupant pays part of the building cost and a very small rent for upkeep. When he dies the property is sold again by the Committee. There is a waiting list and priority is given to those who have no family or other resources.

Apart from the first building, financed by the lottery, and those partly paid for by occupants, some of the money for housing has come from legacies. Many Estonians have included the House in their wills.

A number of handsome, cheerful, healthy old people were out and about, chatting, entertaining friends, watching television, cooking in the kitchens. Some were laying out new gardens, others digging energetically in beds full of magnificent flowers. The flats were comfortable and modern, each furnished in the occupant's own taste.

'Come . . . see my bathroom . . . ' 'Come . . . see my kitchen . . . ' 'Come . . . see my books . . . my TV . . . my pictures . . . ' they cried proudly, leading me from unit to unit. They were all so kind, so friendly. Mr Lipping, the secretary, went to no end of trouble to search for newspaper cuttings, to translate articles from Estonian. Someone gave me a huge branch of orchids; someone else gave me a bouquet of hippeastrums. The only flaw was that Luise Victoria's lunch really demanded a siesta. The Senior Citizens were running rings round me. Anni saw my plight; but each time she said, 'Now we *must* go!' another unit, bathroom, kitchen or garden was offered for inspection. The people all around, said the Senior Citizens, are so kind; they invite us to parties, to family gatherings, to functions in the Community Hall; they take us for drives in their cars . . .

'Come!' said Anni. 'This time we go!' Again we shook hands, gave thanks, smiled, waved and called goodbye. Anni pushed me into the car with my orchids and hippeastrums and drove away into the dusk.

'Now we go to Hulda and Max Kuusik's for dinner. Hulda is my great friend. In the old days when we were all starting we lived next to them. We were all very poor and struggling. Our husbands had to work in the city all the week and came home at weekends to work on the farm. In that road was Kaasik – that's us; Kuusik; and Aavik – Linda whom you met at lunch. Our names mean grove or wood of different trees . . . birch, fir and aspen.'

It was late when we emerged from the long bush road on to a wide lawn. There were trees and a feeling of order and elegance, as in a Japanese garden. Diffused light shone from curtained glass walls. Two little black poodles ran excitedly into the headlights. At the front door a man and woman stood waiting to welcome us.

I had a moment's amnesia and thought I was arriving for dinner in Stockholm. Thirlmere, the bush, chicken farms, Ladies' Committees, Senior Citizens, were wiped out. The tall fair man in the dark suit, the slim beautifully groomed woman did not belong to that life.

A Land Rover drove up behind us and Anni's husband got out. He too, in his dark suit and hornrimmed glasses, might have just come from a city professional office or surgery.

Hulda Kuusik led us in through a tiled hall to a great sitting-room. Coarse linen curtains were drawn across walls of glass, facing north and east. From the pale west wall a lofty white ceiling projected, then sloped towards the glass. Heavy brown beams set far apart traced the descending line, emphasizing the vaulted effect. It was simple and bare yet luxurious, a mixture of Lutheran church and artist's studio. Warmth rose from the floor; there were rugs on the polished boards and very plain, elegant furniture. The south side extended into a dining-room and a bar. There were one or two paintings; no indoor jungles, no folk art, no embroidery; only space, simplicity, comfort. The fine Scandinavian silver and glass on the black table, the linen and china had not been brought out to impress; they were part of daily life.

Anni plunged exuberantly from personalities to Estonian history, from mysticism to diet, from Swedish gymnastics to their early days as New Australians. Her husband did not say much but beamed benevolently behind his hornrimmed glasses.

'Why do you call him Kaasik all the time? That's his surname. Hasn't he a Christian name?'

'Because he hates his Christian name. It's Valdemar. In Estonia that's a ghastly name. Effeminate. Like Cyril or Cecil in English.'

Max had been doing his final year Law when the Soviet Army occupied Estonia in 1944. After that there was not much point in continuing his studies; there was only one law. Since he came to Australia he had worked in a car factory, driven a taxi for fifteen years, done grape-picking . . . all kinds of manual labour. Hulda, who had never before worked, had been wardmaid in a mental hospital and process worker in factories. She put her hands over her ears.

'It was the *noise*! When I came home at night I could not stand the noise of the radio. Even now, I cannot bear it when people play music and talk at the same time.'

They had a room at Baulkham Hills, miles from Sydney, and went to work in the city each day. They walked whenever they could, to save money, scraping every penny to buy land. They did not speak English and their other languages were of no use to them. Max learnt English the hard way, in a motor factory; decent men, but they swore every second word and there was no one to help him sort out the permissible from the obscenities.

'And I was so *stupid*!' Hulda raised her hands. Wearing a simple lilac wool dress and a pearl in an intricate modern setting, she looked expensive and fragile as though she had known only a life of luxury. 'I made so many mistakes when I worked in the mental hospital. When I think of them . . . I was stupid and poor. We had no clothes, we never went anywhere. Only work, save, to get money for land! But we could sleep without fear! Without feeling that *They* would come in the night. That is something you cannot understand unless you have experienced it. Fear. Never knowing when . . . '

'Suddenly. For no reason. Just taken away in the night and sent to Siberia. Coming home and finding your neighbours disappeared. It is not hard work that demoralizes,' said Max. 'It is fear.'

'In Estonia,' he explained, 'we had a certain standard of life. We wanted to get it back. Till six years ago, when we built this house, we lived in a garage which I made myself. I was a rotten handyman but I learnt because I had to . . . not because I was brave or more energetic but because I wanted a roof over my head. You must remember that we were not migrants who could change their minds and go home if they didn't like it here. We were Displaced Persons with nowhere to go.'

Hulda said, 'I could not understand it at the factory. When the whistle blew at night everyone left their work, just dropped it. I was always finishing what I was doing before I left; but they told me I was doing wrong. They were angry with me. It was unfair to them, to go working after knock-off time.'

'But in those days,' Max said, 'factory workers were paid only so much, no matter how hard they worked. If you worked overtime you were doing free work for the boss, you were spoiling the others' chances of getting a rise.'

Hulda was still baffled. She had only wanted to finish her work properly. Max thought it was a small matter. Australians were offhand about their work and sometimes unreliable; but at heart they were good. You didn't work among them or drive a Sydney taxi for fifteen years without getting to know them.

'I'm always hearing it said that Australians are lazy, that they're stupid and only interested in beer and the races; but that's because they don't know any better. They don't seem to understand about pleasure in simple things. There is so little real home life in the sense of enjoying each other's *company*. They think a car and a TV take care of all that and when it doesn't they can't understand why. So they go to the pub to forget about it, while their wives stay at home.'

'Yes, yes,' said Anni. 'The streets are dirty, they throw papers about in the parks but they are good. At first it was difficult. In 1948 I had a job as a children's nurse for a Labor member of Parliament. At that time a displaced person was still a curiosity for Australians. They showed me off as though I were a performing dog. They took me everywhere and introduced me to all their friends, but as a curiosity; as *our children's nurse from the Continent.* I did not care for that and sometimes I saw that other people were embarrassed for me. So I left the M.P. and worked in Concord Repatriation Hospital. One day I was called a "bloody foreigner" by an Englishwoman. An Australian girl answered her, "You're a bloody Pommie yourself".'

Hulda said, 'At home in the old days we all had Polish maids. They were refugees and very cheap. When I look back now I feel ashamed. I was never unkind to my maid, I did not ill-treat her or patronize her but she was just the maid. I never tried to think what went on in her mind and her heart, as an exile. Now that I have been through all that myself and been treated as a nothing, I look back and am sorry.'

'Bloody Balts, that's what they called us. But it wasn't only Australians. When I was driving the taxi one day I picked up an Englishwoman just arrived off a ship and drove her from the docks. She kept peering at me till at last I asked if something was wrong. She said, "You're not black, so you can't be an Aboriginal; you speak quite good English but you have a strange accent. What are you?" I said, "I come from Estonia," and she said, "Oh, a Balt!" '

'In the factory,' Hulda said, 'I could not talk to the girls so they did not like me. They called me bloody foreigner; they did not mean harm but I could not join in because I did not know what they talked about. I was so unhappy, I thought all Australians were like that. Then one night we were invited to do our Estonian national dances for a charity organization. For the *first* time I met different Australians. They came over and *talked* to us! They treated us like human beings! We came home so elated, so excited!'

'When we first came here,' said Max, 'we complained to each other in private. We did not say so to Australians but we did not like the dirty streets, the bad transport. It all seemed so rough, so primitive; and we were always homesick. Then last year we went to America and suddenly we realized how much we loved Australia. I forgot all my criticism about lazy ways and dirty streets and bad transport . . . We couldn't wait to get back.'

'Perhaps next year I shall visit Estonia,' said Hulda. 'I am allowed to go to Tallinn; but not Max . . . '

'I can't go back,' Max said. 'My family are on the black list. I long for Estonia. Underneath I am always homesick but I know I can't go so it's no use to grumble.'

Anni said, 'It is no good to go back, even to visit. It's too late. One cannot recapture one's childhood. Better just keep the happy memories and look forward.'

In the room where I slept were music and books and a violin. I woke in the night to hear the little poodles barking, and lay awake, aware of my comfortable bed and the silent bush outside, thinking about Estonia: an ancient country, free for thousands of years, then overrun by Germans, Danes, Swedes and Russians. Since the thirteenth century its people had struggled for independence and in 1918 they achieved it; but only for twenty-two years. In 1940 Soviet troops occupied the country and began their purges. Thousands were tortured, terrorized, deported, murdered. The German army took over in 1941 and stayed until the Soviets drove them out in 1944; then the terror began again.

'In the war you people hated the Germans,' Hulda said. 'But to us they seemed like angels. When they came in 1941 we were so glad to see them we gave them everything . . . brought out our food, our coffee, we hung them with flowers . . . it was so wonderful to be free of the Soviets. They were the *worst* kind of Russians . . . savages . . . The Germans were good to us. And afterwards, when the Russians came back, many people went to Germany. If they could not escape to Sweden they went into German D.P. camps.'

'Ah . . . it was terrible! Every night families would be taken away. One night *They* came to us, by mistake, for the people in the downstairs apartment. I was *terrified*. Those people were taken away and we never saw them again.'

'Our families were considered capitalist. Then one night friends came and told us *They* were on the way, just up the road. So we walked out as we were . . . and left everything. We had a beautiful big Alsatian dog . . . we just had to leave him . . . And eventually we got to Germany . . . '

'In the D.P. camp it was not so bad. We had some fun; we used to sunbake . . . we had enough to eat . . . you get used to most things if you must. It's only the fear, the terror, you never get used to.'

This house is new only in being recently built. Though it and all its contents are modern, they are so quiet, solid and good that there is a sense of maturity. Nothing is raw or unfinished; no gimmicks or startling trends. No self-consciousness or display.

Max goes out early to see to his chickens and comes in about nine for breakfast. His khaki overalls do not make him look like a farmer. Hulda, in check shirt and trousers, without make-up, is squeezing oranges in the kitchen. She still looks young and expensive. Her figure and graceful movements come from Swedish gymnastics. She studied for years at the Idla academy, a system more like ballet than acrobatics. She gives classes here in the Community Hall.

At dinner it was all elegance; at breakfast on the white kitchen table, the stainless steel, thick pottery mugs, little square wooden platters match the black bread, the cheeses and *leberwurst*, salami and Hulda's *kringel*, a sweet loaf we had last night with coffee.

After breakfast they show me the garden, the chicks, the land Hulda helped to clear, the little house Max built, surrounded with creepers and flowers. An older relation lives in it now and helps by grading eggs.

They have many thousands of chickens and every modern labour-saving device. The room with the egg-grading machine is clean as an operating theatre.

'But in a way it has all come too late,' Hulda says. 'We are tired. Now that we have the house and can entertain, or go to town for restaurants and theatres we don't want to go. We have not the energy. It all went in the twenty years of struggling. We just want to stay here. I want only my family, my garden, my dogs. And we have peace. We have freedom.'

There was a very gay prolonged lunch party at the Kaasiks'. They live at Pheasants Nest, near Tahmoor, and Anni's second daughter, Reet, came to fetch me. She is still at school and will go to University next year. Her elder sister, Kai, is already there.

Jean and Joy Roser from Thirlmere were also at lunch. Joy is Australian but looks completely French. All the Rosers and Kaasiks are bilingual. While the adults sat at the table, the families, from small boys to teenagers, flocked in and out, filling their plates, chattering in French, Estonian and English. Anni's cooking is splendid. At the head of the table Valdemar smiled and poured the wine liberally.

Joy was outraged. She had been called a Wog by a tradesman in Thirlmere. Anni asked, 'What does it mean, a Wog?'

'A Worthy Oriental Gentleman. It's a term of disparagement . . . a British sneer at anyone who isn't British, specially if they're dark like me and married to a Frenchman and speak French and look French. But that's not the point. It's the attitude. From a semi-literate tradesman . . . '

'That's why he said it,' Anni cried. '*Because* he's ignorant. This is how you must think of it! Dismiss it!'

'But it infuriates me, not just because I'm as Australian as he is but that he should patronize those who aren't. That all foreigners should be considered inferior.'

'If you had been a Displaced Person you'd have got used to that,' Valdemar said amiably. 'D.P.'s are bloody foreigners whatever country they go to.'

Anni cried ardently, valiantly, 'Why should I feel inferior because a stupid tradesman sneers at me? *I* know what I am. In my own country he would give me respect. Circumstances have changed, but only circumstances. Not me! *I* haven't changed inside. *I* am still the same, just as he is. No humiliations can take away your breeding or background . . . no matter what hardships or indignities you suffer. *They* can't hurt you but *you* can hurt yourself if you allow them to penetrate – if you start to believe them . . . then you become demoralized.'

'In any case,' Valdemar said, 'this doesn't happen much now in Australia. Foreigners are no curiosity here any more. People hardly notice them.'

After lunch Kai took me to meet Anni's mother, Mrs Hageti, who lives across the road. The Hageti's came to Pheasants Nest before the Kaasiks, cleared the land and started their chicken farm. They built the house where Anni and Valdemar now live. It is of local stones, covered with creepers.

Mrs Hageti was a gentle elderly lady sitting in an armchair, reading *Lolita*. She complained that it was rather slow going, perhaps the fault of her English, and wondered if she could get the book in Russian. She grew up speaking Russian, since Estonia at that time was under the Tsar; or in German perhaps . . .

'I read mostly in German now. I can get German books and magazines easily. No, I do not bother with embroidery – someone gave me that cushion – I prefer to read, or to work outside. I like to clear the land. It gives me a sense of achievement!'

She was amused when I asked if she had lived in the country before. She came from the old university city of Tart, where she took her degree. It was a beautiful ancient centre of learning . . . 'But then,' she said in her soft voice, almost casually, 'after the Soviet came . . . it was not so good for us . . . we did not care for their ways . . . so we left.'

She talked in the same mild way of their hardships and difficulties, of terrifying experiences, of being caught in a bushfire at Pheasants Nest with Anni's little daughter.

'We were trapped. We could not go back or forward. The fire was all around us. I put the child into a little cave . . . but fortunately when the fire came it raced across the tree tops, not along the ground, so we were only blackened . . . ' and a little smile as at the amusing memory of some small social mishap.

With Anni, they escaped from Estonia in 1944. They had hoped to reach Sweden but the Baltic was very stormy and no motorboats were going across. They managed to board a German ship. In Germany, Mr Hageti was drafted into the army and Anni had to work in an office.

'Anni came to Australia in 1948 and we came about a year later. Anni and Valdemar met in a German D.P. camp. They married there. Valdemar worked as a sawmill hand, as a grapepicker, a carpenter, a share-farmer. But it is better now. Ah yes, my sister is still in Estonia . . . she writes to me . . . but . . . It is no good to look back.'

That is what they all say. We must look forward, not back. Anni, who refuses to look back in the sense of regretting, is impatient with those who mope or sigh for the past. She even insists on pronouncing her family's Estonian names in English fashion — Reet, Kay, Annie – to her daughter's annoyance, but she speaks for them all when she suddenly bursts out, 'My sweetest memories are from Estonia. I cherish my language, customs, culture . . . In twenty years I have gained something from this Australian way of life but at the same time I have also given something to it.'

When I came back from Mrs Hageti's Anni gave me an English translation of strange and beautiful poems by Bernard Kangro, the Estonian poet now an exile in Sweden. The book was inscribed from the Kaasiks at the poem called 'My Face':

> I have lain here many millions
> Of days like crumbling stone,
> But I am still endlessly conscious
> As if I were sinew and bone.

> The meadow, the pasture, the village,
> The old windy birch by the garth –
> These are I, and my thoughts have been burning
> As a tenuous flame on the hearth.

> My breast has been open to hailstorms,
> My cheeks to the beating rain,
> Full rivers of turbulent water
> Have deluged my lungs with pain.

> The lightning has ravaged my forests,
> Drought crippled my native place,
> And a hundred thousand chariots
> Of war have furrowed my face.

> And I have outlived these and linger;
> My breath and the norther are kin;
> My thoughts are the northern flowers
> That laugh from the arid whin.

On the opposite page Valdemar had written out the last verse in Estonian.

8

Never English Dust

They planted England with a stubborn trust,
But the cleft dust was never English dust.

The part of New South Wales around Cobbitty, not far from
Thirlmere, is often described as 'English'. Among its gentle
hills are late Georgian country houses, grand and stately, with
formal gardens and old trees. Some contain elegant antiques, but
most inherited furniture is unpretentious mahogany brought out
from Home or cedar made on the spot. Hats, Wellingtons,
walking-sticks appear in halls. Dim watercolours by deceased
aunts, Grandpa's ugly armchair, Mother's Edwardian horrors
create a sense of continuity more English than Australian.

Cobbitty village dates from 1812 and its name comes from
'Cobah', the place on the Hill. It was often called 'Cobbedee';
Governor Macquarie, who saw it in 1815, wrote 'Kobady' in his
Journal.

Beyond the village the road descends, past Italian farmers
and fruit-growers, to the river. Here are she-oaks on grassy
banks and a narrow bridge where planks rattle as you cross. Among
green slopes and pastures an earth lane with Devon hedges skirts

the base of a low hill. A grey roof, white chimneys show against dark, noble trees.

The hedge breaks to reveal mellow brick stables, substantial, symmetrical, rather Georgian. Nearby, on a post, is the wooden box where mail and bread are left; then comes an unpretentious white gate, always open, and the name 'Brownlow Hill', in very plain letters.

'Brownlow Hill', which is a district as well as a private property, was named by Macquarie after Lord Brownlow, and lies in the heart of the old Cowpastures. In 1788, the First Fleet's little herd of cattle strayed away from the settlement. Seven years later they were discovered in the Camden district, vastly increased and so wild they could not be rounded up and brought in. The area where they were found became known as the Cowpastures; the route they had wandered across country is still the Old Cowpastures Road.

Governor Hunter, Governor King and Governor Macquarie visited the Cowpastures and all were deeply impressed by its richness and beauty. In 1815, since the herd was still wild and more numerous than ever, Macquarie decided to establish three stations, for the government horned cattle, at Cawdor, The Oaks and Brownlow Hill. The land remained government property until 1826. When the restriction was lifted, the Colonial Secretary, Alexander Macleay of Elizabeth Bay House, applied for a grant at Brownlow Hill. Here, about 1828, he built the present house for his third son, George.

Except for a brief period, the property has belonged only to the Macleays and the Downes, who have lived there since 1858. The original grant of 1,663 acres has been increased to 3,053, now shared by the family. The first two generations of Downeses concentrated on growing wheat, but when rust destroyed local crops, Edgar Downes, of the third generation, began to include dairy farming. This is now the main occupation of his son, John Downes, who also grows crops for feed. The milk from 'Brownlow Hill's' black and white Friesians goes into a great stainless steel cooler and is collected by road tankers. From the dairy farmers' depot in Camden it is sent to the Sydney milk supply.

Entering the drive to 'Brownlow Hill' you move into an earlier century. On one side, Corot trees cast fragile patterns of branches and leaves. An old trunk has curved an arm above the gate in a single span arch; on the other side is a sheet of water, strewn thickly with waterlilies. It was made by damming a creek and the family call it the Pond, but a low wall with creepers and stone urns gives the formal elegance of a landscaped lake.

Ahead, are lawns and tennis court, a gate leading into the fields, but the drive turns and climbs a gentle slope, jalousied with shifting light. Two exquistite Chinese elms have leant towards each other in a natural arch; a plantation of delicate bamboo creates a high green tunnel. At the top, facing the house, is an oval island of very old olives and hoop pines, with staghorns, rock-lilies, agapanthus and aloes.

The building is simple: white columns and walls, flagstoned verandah, grey shutters. The french windows are wide, with little square panes; the roof follows the same gentle curve as a thickly-thatched Japanese temple. Front door and verandah entrance have been raised for more light, sections added as families grew. Colonial purity may have suffered but the house is alive, a harmonious whole.

Joan Downes comes out, in a raspberry-red suit. She has a fair delicate skin, extremely blue eyes and quick movements. Her welcome is easy and warm.

'Well, come on in . . . You know where things are. When you're ready we'll have coffee in the sun.'

The large square hall has a stone-flagged floor and pale Persian rugs; on a built-in stone console table, an arrangement of berries and leaves. There is a lamp like a vast silver candlestick, an ancient family cradle, old polished wood. From the bedroom chest-of-drawers comes the scent of violets tightly packed in a small silver mug.

The top of this hill has been flattened and trees planted low on the slopes, as in a moat, so they do not shut in the house. From the eastern verandah we look down on a lush meadow. White ibis prowl, up to their knees, black and white cows graze. Ethereal feathers of spray rise from an irrigation pipeline, glittering like fountains in the Generalife gardens. The only sounds are their gentle rotating click-click, the flutter of yellow wrens at our feet.

Many fields are divided by hedges. Bare branches of *Celtis Australis* trace winter silhouettes against squares of emerald and brown. In a chocolate field a toy tractor moves slowly; a red truck, too far away to be heard, passes along a hedged road and in the background a ring of amethyst hills shuts off the outside world. But for the warmer winter sun, the gurgle of magpies, it could be England.

Lawns, flagstones, brick paving, wide beds of iris and forget-me-not, fruit trees and violets merge happily. Formal touches remain: a huge stone urn on a pedestal; and beyond the sundial in the rose garden, an aviary with arches, all creepers and broken walls of little red hand-made bricks.

Among the zodiac signs on the sundial is engraved *George Macleay, Brownlow Hill, Camden, N.S.W.1836*. George was a close friend of Charles Sturt, the explorer, and went with him on the expedition down the Murrumbidgee River. They set out from 'Brownlow Hill'. Though he was only twenty, George distinguished himself by his courage and cheerful endurance, particularly by his kindness and sympathy with the Aboriginals.

George, his brother James and cousin William, all lived here at different times. All were quiet, cultivated men, devoted to learning and natural history. Because the Macleays planted the garden, the trees and shrubs are often curious and exotic. The Chinese elms, whose pink mottled bark is peeling off in small patches, have half-red, half-green leaves. Our winter is not cold enough to turn them completely.

Mossy steps lead down to the Wilderness. There is the familiar mushroom smell of damp leaves, mould, vegetable decay. Branches lie about, narrow bars of light glint on ancient bricks, rotting posts, broken urns. Lilly-pilly and loquat trees are swathed with wisteria and monkey vines, olives and bamboos have gone wild; yet though shut in, it is a gentle, unfrightening jungle.

At the old stables it is quiet, a little eerie. Something creaks up in the loft; shadows move across lichened logs; yet close by is the friendly front gate, the hill with the dairy buildings.

The original kitchen and servants' quarters are separate from the main house. Here are stone floors and small-paned windows, a flagged court with pots of red geraniums against white walls; a row of bells for summoning maids. Stone steps lead to the cellars. Down there the porous egg-shaped stone, like a font, was used for filtering water. Jasmine grows all over the little white porch at the back door.

Joan has a multitude of tasks but she makes time for me and our visits about the countryside by getting up earlier, thinking three jumps ahead, and putting things into the oven before we go out.

We drove over to visit Miss Llewella Davies who grew up at Sutton Forest, near Moss Vale, in the old house which later became the vice-regal country retreat. She now lives in Camden, full of cheerful vitality and kindly good humour. When we arrived she was out in the garden wearing a tweed skirt and cardigan.

'I think I shall have to cut it back . . . too close to the house . . . though it's one of the best white camellias I know, apart from those at "Camden Park". Well, yes, so they ought to be, after all Macarthur introduced them . . . Strange they won't grow at "Brownlow Hill" . . . Oh, those little jars are traps for fruit flies. The C.S.I.R.O. people put them there; they come every now and then to empty them. And this' . . . an eager tail swished, paws scraped at her skirt . . . 'he just wandered in, poor fellow, he was a stray. I couldn't turn him away, could I? But let's go in. And Joan! *There's something I want to show you!'*

Books and papers were piled on a mahogany table under the window; a small tea-table was set by the fire. There were delicate spring-flower arrangements.

Llewella showed us an ancient volume. By some imprudent

move, the old Parish Register had been handed to her for the local Historical Society.

'And I'm *sure* I shouldn't have it!' she said, half-shocked, half-joyful. 'Early entries of births and marriages ... surely not for public inspection in *this* country! But they *gave* it to me. They don't seem to value it.'

A musty smell came from the stiff foxed pages. The ink of the entries was brown.

'You see what I mean,' said Llewella. 'Here ... the So-and-sos; and the So-and-sos, still in the town and so grand these days. And all their ancestors' marriages signed with a cross. That means they were illiterate. And these "married by permission of the Governor?" Does not that mean they were convicts? Or ticket-of-leave?'

There was no malice. It was present pretentions, not humble origins that offended.

'After all, we know what people did get sent out for,' she said indignantly. 'Perfectly innocent sometimes; often just for trying to bring about reforms. But why put on all these airs now?'

An occasional page had been torn from the register, perhaps to conceal a secret. One had been replaced, marked with folds, as though posted away in an envelope. There were many deaths of young children and some births entered with no father's name.

'So you see, Joan, why I was disturbed. One mustn't *talk* about these things we have seen though the register *was* handed to me. But what should I do?'

'If you don't keep it, someone else might make wrongful use of it; or worse still, burn it.'

'That's just what I'm afraid of.'

We turned to other books and documents, then to a jolly good countrified tea with four kinds of cake and Florentines made by Llewella ('The recipe blew over the fence from the cooking class at the girls' school next door'). Llewella did so wish they could get a proper building for the Historical Society; she did so wish something could be done urgently about the old bank building, threatened with demolition. How scandalous, the tearing down of the old mill at Campbelltown, how disgusting the destruction of historic buildings by developers with their beastly Home Units and hideous service stations, which could be put *anywhere*! Then Llewella brought out the sherry and recalled wild gentlemen riders, in their cups, hurdling fences in the streets of Camden, and returned to the grave charge laid upon her by housing the Parish Register.

The sun had long set by the time we had been around the big garden, which she tends herself ('And why not? It's good for me'), mowing the lawns, pruning the fruit trees, digging and weeding the beds of flowers, shrubs and vegetables. There is a privet trimmed into a sphere holding a bird-bath ('Yes, I did it myself') and trees loaded with oranges, which she picked and pressed upon us. We returned to 'Brownlow Hill' in darkness. The headlights caught the trees leaning over the drive and threw shadows of lace. From the dining-room came a warm glow, where John had lit the fire.

The long velvet curtains are drawn; firelight shines on polished mahogany, old silver, odd bits of Staffordshire. Over the sideboard, in a bird's-eye maple frame, is the painting of *Nimrod*, a famous horse of John's great-great-grandfather, Jeremiah Downes.

John is tall, quiet, easygoing, but he looks alarmed when, after dinner, Joan and I get down on the floor with the Black Box. He retires behind a newspaper, murmuring, 'Oh God, you'll be up all night if you're going to start on that!'

The Black Box contains the family papers, faded documents, old letters, flowery newspaper cuttings and proceedings of the Historical Society.

Jeremiah Downes came out from Shropshire as a young man of twenty with introductions to Benjamin Boyd, at Twofold Bay. He later went on the land very successfully. He was a great rider and lover of horses and at one time owned some of the best in the Colony. For years he was a judge at Sydney races, but he resigned in protest against dishonest racing and never went to a racecourse again.

In 1850 he went home to England for a couple of years. A fellow passenger coming out in the *General Hewett* described him as a 'thoroughly good humoured, easygoing, peace-loving man' who was universally popular. He gave champagne parties from his own private stores for the First Class and bottles of his good sherry for the Intermediate passengers. On board, he was rather taken with a young Miss Husband, but she married Mr Thomas of 'Saumarez', in the New England district. Years later the Thomases came to 'Wivenhoe', a property near Cobbitty, and their daughter married Jeremiah's son, Frederick.

Jeremiah married a daughter of Rupert Kirk, one of Sydney's first merchants. She was the widow of Nelson Lawson, whose father first crossed the Blue Mountains with Blaxland and Wentworth. The Downeses settled at 'Greystanes', near Parramatta, where Jeremiah lived the life of a local magistrate and country gentleman.

In 1858 he leased 'Brownlow Hill' from Severin Kanute Salting, who had bought it from the Macleays. When the lease expired Jeremiah decided to leave the district. For two successive years his fine wheat crops had been destroyed by floods and he had finally let off most of the land to tenant farmers. (John has the old estate plans with the names of the tenants marked. Some of the paddocks are still known by these names.)

Jeremiah was so loved by his tenants and neighbours that they all joined to give him a huge farewell banquet. It took place in a tent at 'Brownlow Hill' and hundreds came – far more than catered for. Jeremiah was very moved and decided not to leave. He eventually bought 'Brownlow Hill' from Mr Salting.

For generations the Downeses have been magistrates in Camden, members of the Royal Agricultural Society, giving voluntary service to their district, always avoiding publicity. For 112 years they have been known as quiet, unassuming, benevolent country gentlemen, loved for their kindness to tenants and employees, their hospitality, sense of honour and public duty.

In the Black Box are descriptions of 'Brownlow Hill' by nineteenth century visitors. Each writes of the garden, the rich soil, the fine fruits and trees. They also speak of the tranquillity, which is still there. This house has always been owned by people living gentle, peaceful lives.

A few miles across country is 'Camelot'. It stands on the site of 'Kirkham', the house built by John Oxley, the first Surveyor-General. On the far side of Cobbitty village we turned into Kirkham Lane. On a green slope are old whitewashed stables, all that remains of 'Kirkham'. The loft was sometimes used as a church. High, thick hedges stretch on each side of great iron gates. At the end of Kirkham Lane the Hume Highway streamed with traffic. Here, all was silence.

As the drive swept up to the front door of 'Camelot' one saw only the vast chateau, the Loire turrets and Segovia pinnacles of brick, the grey-green roofs and hundreds of windows, some with drawn blinds, some with a blank empty stare.

A little dog ran out, barking excitedly. From the front door came a very tall slender woman with white hair, wearing an elegant black suit: Miss Clarice Faithful-Anderson.

Inside were arches and stained glass and white marble floors. Doors opened into great rooms. On the wide staircase landing stood a bronze bust on a pedestal. Miss Faithful-Anderson said, 'That is my mother.'

'We'll have tea in the little room,' she added, taking us into a sort of salon with an almost out-of-sight ceiling, and paintings, portraits, picture of horses, dogs, carriages, on the high walls. Over the fireplace was a great mantelpiece; tall windows gave a view of the shrubbery.

Hot gem-scones, running with butter, were piled in a silver muffin-dish; there were all sorts of cakes which should have been made by a plump, red-faced cook. But the house was so silent; you could not imagine cheerful cooks clattering about in the kitchen.

Miss Faithful-Anderson's voice was rather slow and very soft.

'The original "Kirkham" was actually where our kitchen-garden is now. This house is on the site of the old mill. It was built by a Mr White who was a great racehorse owner. He had a famous horse called Chester. It is said that this house was built with Chester's prize money.'

She poured tea and offered gem-scones. Her height suited the room; but Joan and I felt dwarfed when we stood up.

'When Chester died they buried him across the road, near the old stables. His grave is still there, I believe. When my parents bought this house from Mr White they found Chester's forelegs preserved in the cellar. Then one of the old gardeners, who had been here a long time, said that he had Chester's ears and tail. We have them still. I'll show you . . . '

I began to feel odd; the huge, silent house, the overcast sky, the thought of Chester's remnants; but Miss Faithful-Anderson was so gentle, talking about Burragorang Valley, the families who lived there before it was flooded for a reservoir, and the farms and houses now under the water. She often rode to the valley as a girl.

'That was one of our carriages,' she said, showing an elegant little drawing. 'My father was a great horseman, both riding and driving. He drove tandem, unicorn and four-in-hand. We still have some of the carriages. I'll show you after tea.'

I gathered that 'unicorn' was some kind of troika.

'Yes. One horse in front and two behind. My father was a wonderful driver.'

Chester's relics were on the wall of another vast high-ceilinged room, among trophies, pictures, photographs of horses and people. There was an impression of things stacked up, of dust-covers. In the great silent drawing-room a large portrait looked down on imposing furniture and *objets d'art*.

'My mother.'

'She was beautiful.'

'*I* thought so. We were everything to each other; like sisters!'

From the windows of an elegant sunroom we looked out on a sunken garden with magnificent black iron gates, patterned with grape vines.

'They really are Queen Anne,' Miss Faithful-Anderson said. 'I found them in England and never thought I could get them sent to Australia; but there was no trouble, so here they are! But the garden has run wild. I'm not here very much.'

It was like an English country house during the war, when all the young people had gone and a few old men struggled to care for the grounds.

More rooms, more balconies, more garden vistas; splendour, silence, loneliness. An empty aviary. Silence again.

Outside, the late afternoon was bitter, the light bleak. A great pine stood dying on the green lawns behind the house. Borer had eaten into its trunk. It would have to come down.

'And this is the carriage house and stables.'

A vast edifice, bigger than a church, with high arched entrance. We pushed open heavy doors and entered. Here were the empty horse boxes, each with its occupant's name still on the wall; a remote, beautifully beamed roof, like a gothic cathedral; carriages lined up, in dusty, dark, black leather, full of shadow – the victoria, the brougham, the dog-cart . . .

Light shone dimly up through slits in the floor. When the stables were swept the rubbish went down, to be cleared away from below. A large round-ended section was closed for repairs.

Beyond were the cottages, kitchen-garden and fields; but all the time my eye was drawn back to the doomed pine tree, the vast empty house with its hundred unseeing windows. The men of the Downes family have always been churchwardens of St Paul's, Cobbitty. Three generations, male and female, are buried in the churchyard.

Thomas Hassall was the first rector here. His father, Rowland Hassall, was a Coventry blacksmith who went to Tahiti in the mission ship *Duff*. Later he came to Australia and about 1812 took up land in this district for himself and his family. His son Thomas, who had married a daughter of the Colonial Chaplain, Samuel Marsden, was gazetted chaplain for the district south of Liverpool, a parish so immense that he spent most of his time on horseback and was known as the Galloping Parson. The Hassall family were very much loved.

There was no rectory, so Thomas lived and worked from 'Denbigh', near Cobbitty. He established churches and schools all over his parish. At Cobbitty he built the little Heber Chapel which is still inscribed 'in the diocese of Calcutta' – and in 1840 the foundation stone of St Paul's was laid. When Bishop Broughton came, two years later, to consecrate the new church, Thomas was away sick and no one could find a flag. Mrs Hassall quickly made one out of a plaid carriage rug. The Hassalls and their servants, including their Maori coachman, now lie in St Paul's church-yard.

The old house 'Pomare', on the site of Hassall's 'Pomarre Grove,' has become a teen-age ranch, painted pink with cart wheels for gates. A few buildings have gone – the stone black-smith's forge on the corner, where the iron gates for the church were made, the slab hut that stood on the edge of the rectory grounds and one or two ancient cottages. Otherwise nothing has changed much in the last fifty years. One cottage, almost hidden behind its hedge, is still inhabited by an old lady who was there when I was a child. There is the post office store, the school, the church, partly designed by John Verge, who built 'Camden Park' and 'Elizabeth Bay House'; Thomas's little Heber Chapel and, across the road, the Gothic Revival rectory with white barge-boards and gables. It was built in 1870 by Thomas's successor, A.W.Pain, who brought his bride there.

I had not been inside the rectory since my childhood. When I came back to Australia after many years, A.F.Pain, the rector, who had been my father's friend, was in the churchyard, the old house was smothered with creepers, the garden gone wild.

Now the jungles have been cleared away, the rectory repaired and restored. From the sunny garden you can see the hills beyond the bright fields; inside, where I remembered Gothick darkness, light streams on pale walls. In the dining-room are cedar and mahogany, blue-and-white china on the mantelpiece; in the drawing-room a bright fire and flowers, antiques and views of the garden. I remember the shutters that pull up from below the window frames and upstairs the long room at the back where an earlier rector's daughter had a school. This is now a cheerful bedroom.

It is pleasant to sit in the rectory drawing-room again. The present rector was formerly a brigadier in the Middle East; he likes to talk about Turkey. Margaret Barham, his wife, and her mother, are Tasmanians; they love old houses. We look at books on Georgian buildings, sipping dry sherry with biscuits. The rector gravely agrees with Joan that Llewella is right about that Parish Register; the church bazaar is discussed, gardening, recipes for grape jam, Llewella's over-the-fence Florentines, the Embroidery Guild and the splendid tapestry Joan has done of the Galloping Parson.

It is rather like living again in an English rectory: the morning fire and the conversation, the little church across the road with its spire and weeping cypresses, its flat tombs and generations of families in the churchyard; but, as in the Barossa Valley, there is always the subtle difference. Outside are gum trees and bright winter sunshine; the air is dry and astringent. The pioneers could reproduce the tangibles – trees, plants, grey stone walls of home, but never the soft air, the muted, pensive, tender light. This is a different country, a wider, harder land.

9

O Pioneers

Sydney is a very strange city. No matter how aggressive or strident its life, how materialistic its people or crowded its shores, the harbour retains its virginity. By day ferries are on the move, warships, liners, coasters, colliers, tankers. Double-decker marine charabancs, like Melton Mowbray pies, lumber over it. A hydrofoil romps by, a flying-boat roars. Yet when the day's work is over the harbour, so churned and criss-crossed, regains its secret self. At Circular Quay, ferries lie in rows like animals tethered in stalls, a subdued glow warms the pale moth-wings of the Opera House on Bennelong Point. Beyond, all is empty; little glimmers far out, the flash of navigation lights, deserted wharves, count for nothing. In the heart of the city, the harbour lies shimmering, withdrawn, completely alone.

SHOCK REPORT. STARTLING DISCLOSURE. TV STAR QUITS.
BODY FOUND – Pictures. SHOCKING SMASH – Pictures.
PACK RAPE – Pictures. TV GIRL'S BREAST CANCER – Pictures.

SHOULD PARENTHOOD WAIT? PREGNANT AT 14 –
SCHOOL GIRL TELLS.
EX-COP TELLS. JOCKEY QUITS. TOP TV STAR
REVEALS.
SPECIAL OFFER. BIGGER. NEW! MONEY! MONEY!

In the morning light the gold sandstone caves around the shore
are primeval. Fifteen minutes from the heart of the city an arm
of the sea wanders inland among olive-green bays and hills
where houses cling to precipitous slopes. In summer, the scene
is Mediterranean with splashes now of colour around swimming
pools; red poinsettia, pink hibiscus fall into pellucid water.
Even in winter there are weeks of endless sun. In the city parks,
deadbeats and pensioners doze in sheltered corners, office workers
stretch on lawns in the lunch hour. Flame and coral trees splash
scarlet against industrial walls and railway sidings. Beams sift
into alleyways. People linger, prolonging conversations. We are
the Sun's courtiers, we dwell in his eye and gaze on his face.

Then comes the west wind. When it blows the place is
uninhabitable, the spirit deeply disturbed by agitated water,
discoloured trees. In summer, it seems to rush straight from
the desert, the whole world is seen through a rusty film of dust and
flying grit; in winter, the dryness is intolerable. Lips and skin
crack, joints stiffen, nerves are frayed. Cold cuts through clothes
and flesh and petrifies the blood. Inadequately fortified, we totter,
blue-faced, through blasts as bitter as Kashmir under snow.

Cyclonic winds blow in from the sea; day after day, gutters
stream; wet leaves are plastered on littered pavements, buses
are steam baths smelling of damp wood. The hills of Middle
Harbour are iron-black against ashen skies. White choppy waves
fleck a battleship bay that darkens to sterner seas between the
Heads. Far out, passing rain-squalls trail endless chiffons of
tears.

Without fine streets or noble buildings, with colour-drained
water and ragged trees, Sydney in winter is dispiriting. This is
the time when people escape, to the inland, the Islands, the north.

By air, sea, car or bus they depart. Transport becomes crowded; tours are booked out.

By bus, you may travel Express, which means driving all night, or by Tour, which includes a chatty guide and sleeping at motels. Tours take themselves rather seriously. As soon as I asked at the Sydney terminal for the Brisbane bus I could see that I had made a mistake. The arctic young woman dressed as an airline hostess averted her eyes and said with offended refinement, 'Passengers joining the Pioneer Brisbane Coach kindly proceed to the Departure Counter for checking in baggage.'

Pioneer buses are run by an airline and all is done to give the impression that you are taking to the air: uniforms, lip-service, luggage labelled, whisked away. Ladies with lightweight 'overnite' bags and fresh-set hair farewell friends in a waiting room. A loud-speaker asks you to kindly board your Coach which is now ready to depart, and in it you find pockets for brochures and sea-sick bags, pull-out ash trays and knobs to turn seats into sofas.

When the Brisbane passengers were all aboard a uniformed man sprang up the steps and addressed us.

'Good morning folks. Allow me to introduce myself. I'm your Coach Captain – Les is the name. On behalf of Ansett-ANA Pioneer Tours I'd like to welcome you aboard your Streamlined Air-conditioned Super-clipper and take this opportunity of extending to you our very heartiest wishes for a happy journey. Now, we seem to have a very nice little crowd on board' (dubious laughter) 'and I think we're going to have a very happy time together. Now, your Coach departs at 8.30 a.m. and proceeds along the Pacific Highway to Newcastle, where you will partake of lunch at the X Hotel. We will be crossing the Hawkesbury River and there will be a comfort stop at X, at 11.0 hours to allow the ladies to powder their noses and partake of a Devonshire Tea, or perhaps those cakes I know ladies like, or anything else you so desire. During the trip I will be pleased and privileged to point out to you any items of interest and do not hesitate to request any little attention or service I may be able to render you. Now we have 629 miles to go to Brisbane but we'll take it easy today. We break the journey overnight at Kempsey where you will partake of dinner and then tomorrow it's ON! 6.45 breakfast!' (Chorus of Ooh and Aah and loud plans about alarm clocks.) 'Now I'm sure we're all going to get along fine. Eh? What do you say? Are we downhearted?'

'No!'

'That's the ticket. Righty-oh then. Sunshine State, here we come!'

The Pioneers leaned back in their adjustable seats, smoothed down their 'crimplenes' and jersey-knits, opened their brochures. Jewels flashed as fingers lit cigarettes and dug into cellophane packets. Conversations broke out between travelling companions. Single passengers kept to themselves. Pioneer Tourists are a special breed, very superior. This was not at all the sort of bus I was accustomed to.

'I'll just have scones and biscuits when we stop.'

'Morning tea's extra. And afternoon tea.'

'Yes, but all the rest's *inclusive*. It says so in this folder.'

Though Sydney sparkled in winter sunshine, tinted windows screened out nature's crude revealing light. Like ambulance patients we peered through smoky topaz at a storm-threatened landscape, listening to jokes for the benefit of Melbourne passengers, about the Opera House, the Harbour Bridge, the River Yarra.

'This is the North Shore Line,' said the driver. 'Exclusive residential area, noted for its Beautiful Homes and Select Colleges.'

Interstate visitors murmured reverently.

When you look about you in a bus like this you wonder who started the legend that we are a young country. It was not the years these passengers had lived but the state of their minds – cautious, conforming, worshipping property and material advancement. It may come from the days when people arrived here with nothing at all but it ends with closed-up faces and beige lounge rooms. No wonder the young rebel; but I am going to be with these Pioneers for two days, I have come on a Tour of my own free will so had better not lose my sense of humour. At least we do not have leaders and plastic flags like Japanese Tours.

By midday we had made our Comfort Stop, eaten our Devonshire Tea, seen miles of monotonous scrub, khaki Hawkesbury River, the scarred blasted world of the new Pacific Highway. Pastel fibro boxes, weatherboard houses with leprous paint, square or oblong motels with multi-coloured doors, shacks, newspapers, bottles, tins, dead grass, TV antennae, FOODORAMA, DRIVE IN, LADIES AND GENTS, SWANSEA ROTARY WEL-COMES YOU, texture bricks, sandblasted windows, buggy wheels, cement storks, koala bears, aboriginals with boomerangs, even monster kewpies lined the road to Newcastle. As some nations despoil beautiful landscapes through poverty, we despoil through prosperity.

At Newcastle we lunched in a plastic hotel – plastic flowers, tablecloths, pepper and salt, plastic light fittings, plastic food. Outside, a coastline of headlands and bays glittered in washed winter sunshine. Old houses looked down from the hill on a brilliant sea, on the smoke of the river, the subtle beauty of ships and docks.

MATT'S MEATS. HOME BEAUTIFICATION CONSUL-TANT. Superb Moreton Bay fig trees and in arid scrub, yellow wattle doing its best against a harsh land. In the bus coiffured heads nodded and lolled. I dozed through miles of drab forest and drought-parched fields and woke with a start to see BILL AND MERV'S HOTEL, with a boomerang up in front.

But now we were crossing the calm Manning River at Taree. The Pioneers stirred, for this is a tea and comfort stop. Wooded islands break the wide stream, grassy banks are lined with poplars and jacarandas. Across the river the afternoon sun was warm on pale-roofed houses, on clumps of bamboo and pine, monkey-puzzles and Moreton Bays in abandoned gardens or burnt-out homestead sites.

'Now folks, we are approaching Kempsey on the historic Macleay River, where you will stay the night. Now, you'll find this a typical friendly Australian town. Your Pioneer Air-conditioned Super-clipper will deposit you at your Guest House where dinner will be served. Now afterwards you may care to take a walk in the town, or drop into the R.S.L. Club, if you so desire, where you will be welcome; but remember folks, Brekky tomorrow at 6.45 sharp! A big day ahead!'

The Pioneers tidied themselves and reached for bags on the rack. In a Turkish, Italian, Greek or Irish bus we would have long known all there was to know of each other by now but though friends have chatted together, the unintroduced have exchanged not a word.

In the garden a caged parrot shrieked outrage at our trooping intrusion. Inside, an elderly proprietess in gleaming black satin bustled about, apportioning rooms. Every surface bore bowls of plastic flowers with electric light centres. Round the walls astonishing pieces of furniture pushed against each other, cedar and mahogany coated with high-gloss treacle, bamboos and black iron tables, *objets d'art* in leadlighted cabinets, immense paper flowers, ladies in crinolines, see-through shelves stacked with china ornaments. In the parlour a great table was set as for a shop-window display, with gilded plates on a lace cloth and, in a corner, large cups, upside down in their saucers, stood on a small bar under a purple-and-gold scalloped baldaquin. The walls were painted with enormous peacocks and storks, the floors spread with beautiful Turkish and Persian rugs. The driver apologized. It was the last time, he assured his stunned Pioneers, the last time the Tours would come here. Next time it would be a proper modern motel.

When I admired the old lady's rugs she abandoned her waiting guests and showed me others in bedrooms filled with ornate high-gloss cedar.

'I got the rugs dirt cheap at local auctions,' she said. 'But these are all genuine antiques. *Solid cedar*. Made by a personal friend of mine, right here in Kempsey, only ten years ago. We have a famous antique factory in Kempsey.'

The Pioneers, changed for dinner and a night at the R.S.L.

Club, have been drawn together by shock. With barriers down, talk at our table became literary.

'Ever heard of Steele Rudd?' asked my neighbour. 'I got two of his books. Dad and Dave, you know, *On Our Selection*. Well, there's a statue of him at Drayton, near Toowoomba, and I was just going to take a shot of it when the wife says, "Look, there's Dad and Dave!" And there's these two bushwhackers coming along, just like in *On Our Selection*. Talk about local colour! So I got them in with the statue, a beautiful shot. Was I pleased! It's one of my most popular slides. I always get requests to show that one.'

'Here's your veggies, love,' said the waitress, plonking down a dish of roast potatoes and pumpkin. 'Tea now or later?'

'Hubby's a great one for slides,' said the wife. 'He must have thousands. He shows them round the Clubs, you know, the R.S.L., the Bowling Club and that.'

'Well, you see, I'm retired. It's the least I can do, the wife and I feel. Help raise a few bob for Legacy. We done well, family grown up and settled, our own home – everything in it, a good car. I can afford it. Been everywhere, done all the Tours, Alice Springs, Darwin, Tassie, even New Zealand. No trouble to take a few slides. Gives some pleasure – it helps the kiddies. Don't want to just live for yourself, do you?'

His eyes were kind in the fat, rather wistful face. The scraggy wife, with too-smart hair and ornate dress, beamed lovingly with all her far-too-young teeth. A warm little current circulated.

After dinner we walked in the town together. The shops were full of plastic – pots, basins, buckets, cups, plates, flowers, clothes-baskets, bunches of chillies. It was seven-thirty and Kempsey had retired, apart from the jolly R.S.L. on the banks of the gentle, dark Macleay River.

The reclining chairs of our Air-conditioned Super-clipper are so efficient that when the lady in front lies back her new perm rests in your lap.

BEAUTIZONE MOTEL. SUMMA BREEZ CABINS.
OVANITE FLATS. MOTEL. MOTEL.

Australians have gone overboard with motels. The landscape
is pocked with dreary oblong structures, with different coloured
doors, sometimes standing alone in forlorn stretches of scrub,
sometimes tacked on to the back of kindly old-fashioned pubs,
which now call themselves 'Hotel-Motel'.

The driver switched on his microphone.

'Now folks, we're in Banana Land. And I'm going to stop now
and so you can see the Biggest Banana in the World. You will
have time to get out and take a shot if you so desire.'

The banana reared up, in cement, like a yellow whale with
WELCOME planted out in the foreground in some kind of shrub.

'Well,' said the fat photographer, climbing in happily. 'That'll
give them something to talk about at the Club.'

The plantations were dry and disappointing, their only colour
the blue plastic bags that protect and ripen the fruit. The North
Coast, which is so much more publicized than the South, cannot
compare with it for unspoilt beauty, and the so-called Coast Road
is too often far from the sea. The yawning boredom was relieved
by delicacy of bare willows, black traceries against old slab huts,
silver sliprails, a winter tree full of great birds' nests like hats;
then the drab beatnik scrub resumed, the drought-stricken fields;
and always, far off, the thick bush waited, like a dark army, to
attack and retrieve.

There had also been drought in the billowing Richmond Valley;
but her beauty, though changed, had survived. Homesteads with
white gates and long drives were deep in trees, pastel cows
gathered for shade under clumps of bamboo. There was a sense
of space and harmony, a feeling of being out on the Downs.

Towards the Queensland border the landscape grew greener,
strangely puckered. The Macpherson Range was all blue and
purple bell-tents and marquees; there were cane fields, pineapples,
orange earth and fat black cattle lying down like shiny leeches;
tropical flowers, mangroves, pelicans, and at last, the crown of our
journey: Surfers Paradise.

Hotels, motels, caravans, caravans, caravans. Gents' Toilets. BLUE HILLS TV. TV antennae. Avis Rent-a-car. Ansett ANA. The SANDPIPER Holiday Flats. PACIFIC BREEZE. OVA-NITE FLATS. DRIFTWOOD. LINGA LONGA (Do they know what *linga* means?) COBBLESTONES. COSTA RICA HOTEL. OCEAN WAVES. TROPIC SANDS. MOANA. TONITE IN THE MARDI GRAS ROOM ... A long, long beach seen between parking meters; boutiques and coffee shops; fat bejewelled women; desperate, sad, last-chance little men; bikinis. A good time for all.

Most of the Pioneers got off here. Late that night we reached Brisbane on the eighth day of a transport strike.

At the large new motel I was whisked to the top of a glass tower and into a vast apartment of suffocating luxury. My feet went down in the carpet as into sinking sand, the double bed would have held the United Nations. The porter pulled a string and curtains swept back from a semi-circular glass wall to reveal the whole of Brisbane. He pressed buttons to demonstrate lights, radio, television, opened and closed bathroom and refrigerator doors.

The view of the city with the scimitar river was beautiful, but, like all the grandeur within, rather wasted when one only wanted to sleep. This was not easy to do. The bed had so many springs or so much foam-rubber that I felt I was floating amidships and sinking down by the head. When I slid open the glass wall to admit a little air, the petrifying drop below gave me vertigo. Convinced I would walk out there in my sleep, I arranged chairs across the opening. This seemed so funny I started to laugh and was then wide awake. When I put on the light the flawless impersonal decor was too depressing to contemplate. With Brisbane beckoning me to take off from the balcony I dozed uneasily.

In the morning I went to the bus depot for the journey to Rockhampton. Nothing could have been less like Pioneer. There were no refined hostesses or receptionists, no ladies in waiting-rooms or even baggage checks, only rather rough amiable men slinging luggage about.

In the confusion, crowds, smells, noise, delays about leaving and finding belongings, was more than a touch of Mother India. People swarmed into the bus. There was no chatty driver. The springs of your seat sagged and there was nowhere to put your legs. You could not lie back with your head in the lap of the passenger behind; but the people were much more matey, the atmosphere far less formal.

'Where did you stay in Brisbane?' asked the grimy little woman beside me; when I told her she gave an angry shout. 'You must be mad! I bet they charged you! Why on earth do you go to a place like that?'

'There was a transport strike; the Brisbane Show was on. It was all I could get.'

'But the cost! That place! I know it! You pay for all that glass! Luxury! If you knew what I've been through! I've just come back from Perth by bus. A wheel fell off on the Nullarbor Plains. We ran out of petrol. Exhausted! Didn't wash my hands and face for five days. You mightn't think so but I'm *filthy*! This dress doesn't show. Brown, I brought three outfits for this trip, all brown. You should always wear brown on the bus, for the dust. How far you going? Rockhampton? I'm getting off there too. I live at Rocky.'

The other passengers, who would be travelling all through the night to Cairns, wore expressions of fortitude and resignation. Across the aisle a large fat man with sad Labrador eyes and long lashes studied a timetable, then said sombrely, 'It says 11.20 p.m. at Rocky. I hope it's true.'

My neighbour laughed scornfully. '11.20! I been travelling on this line for years and never yet known them on time.'

Packets of toffee and potato chips were being passed about and people said *Talk about Laugh!* and *A laugh did you good!* A singalong was organized by a boy with a guitar. The driver made no attempt to educate us, confining himself to simple witticisms: 'Local Ladies Driving School' (a car scrap yard); 'The Dead Centre' (a cemetery).

My neighbour was full of helpful advice. She said I should always book seat Number Nine in these buses because it has a foot-warmer; that she herself always demands a window seat because they have ashtrays; that I should join the Country Women's Association, then I could stay at their hostels instead of those awful motels, all of them robbers.

'You're not going to stay in motels all the time?'

'I'm going to a cattle station in Central Queensland, near Clermont.'

'Clemment! I know Clemment! What's the name of the property?'

'Fleurs.'

'Flooers! I know Flooers! That's a fine property. You'll be staying with the Frasers. *They* must be doing well! That's the Peak Downs country. Very rich land. I grew up in that district. They say Flooers is the best land in the whole of Central Queensland. I suppose you'll go to the gem fields. Be sure you get them to take you to the gemfields.'

Peak Downs, which was discovered by Ludwig Leichhardt, was famous for minerals – gold, copper, and coal. South of Clermont are gemfields where jewels were found in the ground. The towns are called Emerald, Sapphire and Rubyvale and amateurs come there to search. Sapphires are still picked up on properties outside Clermont, usually by accident.

The dreariness of the N.S.W. border had gone. Queensland was growing more colourful, more interesting with every mile. Hibiscus and pine forests, orchards and pineapples, sugar fields; Captain Cook's Glass House Mountains, like gigantic coloured anthills; the Saturday afternoon torpor of Gympie, an old gold-rush town with white wooden buildings and iron lace balconies; faded silver-grey houses on stilts, red-roofed homesteads crouching on hills among trees and purple bougainvillea . . .

A car overtook us, hooting frantically, signalling the bus to stop.

'Lost your privvy, sport!' yelled the man at the wheel. 'On the road about five miles back.'

'Thanks mate,' said the driver; we turned back to pick it up.

Express buses carry their own conveniences.

'We lost ours crossing the Nullarbor,' my neighbour said. 'Never found out till too late. And not a tree for miles.'

Beyond Maryborough people grow drowsy; children had fallen silent, the sun gone behind the high trees. A green dusk was gathering when on the long empty bush road the bus suddenly trembled and stumbled and stopped. We had run out of gas.

Hours passed. The driver, hailing a truck, had gone back to Maryborough for diesolene and presumably dined there, the passengers said resentfully. We did not dine. We sat or got out and walked about while the sun sank, darkness fell, a red moon rose. It grew cold. The bus smelt of feet and potato chips and little girls' wet pants. Behind, a small boy grizzled, fidgetted, kicked the back of my seat, sniffed and crunched. At first, transistors had given out racing results and pop tunes but now people were starting to bicker. A frustrated honeymoon couple entwined on the back seat got out and took to the scrub. Tempers were frayed.

'Forgot to put petrol in! I ask you!'

'Why didn't he put it in in Brisbane?'

'Must of been the strike.'

'Strike! Strike! What's the strike got to do with it?'

'This is the ninth day of the transport strike and no sign of finishing. And who suffers? The public. The poor bloody public.'

'Don't those bloody fools realize they're just tools in the hands of unions run by Reds? The Aussie workman's not a bad bloke but he's a fool. It's part of a world plot. I tell you this strike's not just a flash in the pan ... Red China's behind it.'

For some time before the breakdown a rather loud monologue had been going on at the back with the passionate touch that enlivens conversations in European trains. Now, as I dozed, my neighbour clambered over my feet and lurched away down the aisle to join the audience. She came back full of satisfied information.

'He's an Eye-talian. A sugar grower, on his way home. Just

come back from a visit to Italy. Been here fifteen years and made quite a pile. He flew back to Italy to decide if he'd stay over there or bring his wife and kids back. Couldn't stand it. *Only stayed three days!* Couldn't get back here quick enough. He says, "What's Italy got for me? I'm an Aussie now".'

'What about his family?'

'Left them there! He says, "I got another wife and kids here – an Aussie girl. They can stay there! They can have Italy. I'll send them money but I'm staying here with my Aussie wife and kids!" *Only three days!* Flew straight back! Think what it cost!'

The Italian bigamist was surrounded by admirers. Noise increased, tempers improved and when towards nine o'clock the driver returned with the diesolene people raised a faint cheer.

A Bundaberg, there was the choice of meat pies and Chinese food. Pies were quicker.

'C'mon, the pub's still open!' said my neighbour. 'There's time for a drink. You go and get the pies while I order the drinks.'

Bundaberg is a sugar town, the home of Bundaberg rum, but a tumbler of sweet sherry ('No dry, love. No call for it.') awaited me in the deserted lounge. The chair and table legs were chrome, the walls dark grey, the pies were lukewarm and gristly, the pastry like cardboard, but it was no time for fussiness. My companion finished off my glass and became rather blurred.

'How you getting to Clemment? The Frasers coming to get you in Rocky? You better cummome with me. They'll be gone to bed by now. They won't know if you're at the motel or not. We'll ring the motel in the morning and tell them where you are. Don't you go to any more of those motels. You cummome with me.'

We reeled back to the fuggy bus and I fell asleep at once. At the approaches to Rockhampton I woke as my shoulder was shaken.

'Wake up! Look out the window. We're crossing the Tropic of Capricorn. See that white notice there by the road? Tropic of Capricorn. Won't be long now, Rocky's right on the Tropic. Better than I thought – only half-past one.'

The sweet sherry fumes were wearing off. I shivered. Would this kind friend really take me home and talk to me all night?

The freezing Rockhampton air brought her round. At the bus depot she did not renew her invitation. We hailed separate taxis and parted.

10

Fleurs

While my bus was floundering about south of Bundaberg the Frasers had driven the two hundred miles from Clermont to Rockhampton and gone to bed at the appointed motel, convinced I was lost.

In the morning I woke feeling frayed. I had been bitterly cold in the night but too tired to get up for more blankets. I took a hot shower to restore circulation and ate the bacon and eggs left on my doorstep by a brisk invisible waitress.

Then I heard the Frasers outside – Duncan's drawl, Mary's quick replies. Pawing the ground, pacing to and fro like a large, generous, high-coloured Osbert Sitwell, Duncan beamed, heaved with laughter, took off his hat, rammed it back, thrust his hands into his pockets, pulled them out, waved them, patted his stomach. Delighted relief, benevolent humour radiated, his expansive gestures offered the world.

'Thank God, Thank God! We were just getting ready to drive to Brisbane to look for you. Jesus Christ, we thought you were lost. Can't stand shocks like this. I'm an Old Man!'

His eyes disappeared into creases, his lower lip protruded, his face was suffused with amusement. He has described himself as an old man ever since I first met him thirty-six years ago. Mary, smiling quietly, went on putting back into the station wagon all that Duncan in his excitement was absently taking out.

When the Frasers come into Rockhampton they have many visits to make, usually to former employees grown old or sick. It was a day of warm embraces and handshakes, cups of tea and slabs of cake at kitchen tables. We drove along a beautiful coast where tropical pandanus, hibiscus and bougainvillea grew among casuarina, gumtrees and bottlebrush. There were black rocks against coral white sand, and fishtraps and islands out in the silky blue sea. This was Keppel Bay, where Captain Cook came ashore hoping to clean his ship, but was driven away by mosquitoes and lack of water. He saw enormous masses of butterflies and clay ants' nests in trees and a stranded fish which 'leaped away as nimbly as a frog'.

At Zilzie, where Duncan's son has a holiday house, we called on a widowed neighbour who breeds animals. She lives on a grassy headland, sloping down to a little secluded bay. At the foot of the garden very white sand merges into turquoise shallows and small, ever smaller green islands trail across the deepening water. The colours are rich and clear but not tropical. It is like Anse Vata, in New Caledonia.

The sun soaked into our backs; there were long friendly silences and a disinclination to move. Sunflowers grew wild on the headland. In the widow's garden sapphire-eyed Siamese, yellow-eyed Persians on little chains stared with blank jewelled gaze; white cockatoos rasped in high harsh whispers, horned goats with long silken hair stepped proud and delicate among bougainvillea. The mango trees foamed with orchids.

Rockhampton, which I had not expected to like, is rather charming and stately, on the banks of the Fitzroy River, with wide streets and iron lace balconies. It was settled mainly by Lancashire factory hands, thrown out of work when the Civil War in America cut off England's cotton supplies. It looks extremely respectable now but its past was quite violent. After gold was discovered in the district there were bushrangers, murders and robberies. Rockhampton's most distinguished crime was the Gold Escort murders, when the Gold Commissioner himself, T.J.Griffin, shot and robbed his own Gold Escort troopers.

The rope with which Griffin was hanged was cut up and sold at a shilling a piece. It went like hot cakes. The authorities then buried him in a very deep grave with another body on top, but he was found and dug up and his head chopped off. One of the grave robbers was an eminent Rockhampton citizen who kept the skull as a souvenir.

It was late afternoon when we started the drive to Clermont. Along the Capricorn Highway the sun's rays slanted between high slim trunks and bottle-trees stood like slender urns filled with surrealist branches. Against the sunset a roof showed among trees on a low headland, stretching into an orange lake: 'Gracemere', the home of the Archers, an exploring-pioneer family who founded Rockhampton. The white 'Gracemere Inn' stood on the roadside, hung with vines and surrounded by cottage gardens, and on the rolling downs shabby old wooden homesteads, high on posts, merged into tropical creepers and trees. Far off, the Explorer Mountains were changing colour, sharp-edged, cut from cardboard.

The road went on and on. The slow sunset lingered, lighting the red Natal grass by the edges. A strange bird muttered into the quiet. In the paddocks pale Brahman cattle grazed, with humped backs and crescent horns.

This country has seen explorers, pioneers, gold escorts, bushrangers, coaches, Chinese and Europeans off to the gold diggings, Cornish miners going to Copperfield. Frank Gardiner, a sort of Robin Hood bushranger, was here with his beautiful black horse Darkie and the settler's wife who had chosen to share his life. Gardiner reformed and started afresh with her, as a storekeeper at Apis Creek. Those who knew them have written that they were much liked for their kindness, but years later Gardiner was recognized and betrayed by an old friend, for money.

At Emerald, where we stopped for dinner, there is a fantastic railway station with extravagant arches and columns and iron lace, but the hotel refused us a drink because it was Sunday or too late or we had not travelled far enough. Duncan seethed like a samovar. We all took a swig from the rum bottle in the car and dined rather greasily at the Greeks', then on, in the dark, through a world that existed only in headlights. I was tired; the car was warm, the sound of the engine soothing. I dozed and woke to smell flowers. Along the road, unseen forests of wattle released their sweet honey-scent into the night.

I woke again suddenly. The lights shone on a wire gate. When Duncan got out the crisp night came into the car. With deep happiness Mary said, 'We're home!' There were more gates, seemingly miles apart, smells of earth and cattle and grass; then a distant clamour which intensified as we approached. At the last gate the barking was frenzied; chains and tins rattled as fourteen dogs raced and leapt on their kennel roofs in welcome.

I stood, giddy with fatigue, while the others unloaded the car. There was a feeling of being far out at sea, of something vast and untouched. The night was immense, the air diamond-sharp. Above, in a Lermontov sky, star was talking to star.

In the morning, the light came through french windows that open upon the verandah. It was bitterly cold. Looking out from under the eiderdown I could see several old fine Persian rugs and heavy beautiful silver on the dressing-table. There was a large cushioned basket chair, an antique music cabinet, a reading lamp by my bed. People were moving outside, canine claws pattered and skated on floor boards, crockery rattled and presently the door was edged open and several dogs slid in. A couple laid their heads on the bed and rolled mournful eyes, others sprang about eagerly, as though to get me up; but Mary, coming in with a breakfast tray, said I was to stay where I was until it was warmer.

On the other side of the house Duncan was also breakfasting in bed, sitting up like a Roman emperor, receiving visits from dogs, reading the papers, conducting long telephone conversations around the country and calling instructions to anyone who would listen.

By ten o'clock the sun was shining into the verandah and the air so warm I was taking off fur boots and sweaters. In winter, Central Queensland has bitter nights and early mornings, hot basking days and superb lingering sunsets. The plains are a coloured infinity. It is hard to believe in their terrible droughts, seeing those oceans of pale grass, the huge lakes of brilliant young wheat where neat dark trees stand, as though deep in water. Yellow acres of safflower are splashed across the dark expanses of ploughed black earth. Rich fat cattle dot the landscape, pastel Brahmans, chestnut-red Herefords, Drought-masters, Shorthorns. The horizon is an unbroken circle, except in the east where astonishing peaks mark the sky. From all parts of 'Fleurs' they are visible, changing colour with every hour. You look up suddenly in the cattle yards and see the blue shapes, with down-trickling purple shadows, like erosion lines, rising out of the grass, among trees and clouds, or fading, far off, in reflected sunset. When the air is clear you feel you could touch them.

One could never be lonely with these mountains in sight. They belong to the Peak Range. Leichhardt named them after men in his party, but the locals call them Table Mountain, the Gemini, Fletcher's Awl, Mount McDonald and Wolfang. Wolfang, which gave its name to a great station property and to a nearby creek, is the most dramatic of all.

The Frasers bought 'Fleurs' in 1954 and are Queenslanders by adoption. Both are from grazing families. Duncan's people came from Scotland to pioneer and explore in Western Australia, South Australia and Victoria. His father settled in New South Wales, at Darlington Point, where the family are still graziers, and his mother's people were landowners in the same district. Mary, whose name was McMeeken, is descended from Northern Irish and Scottish stock and her father's family included valiant Presbyterian ministers and settlers. On her mother's side were the Officers, distinguished in Tasmanian history, and the Hebdens, a famous old grazing family. She grew up on a New South Wales sheep station and apart from years at boarding school has lived her whole life in the country.

Mary is happy with birds and animals, shy with people. She was an only child brought up like a boy on a large sheep station, only mixing with other girls at boarding school. When her father died she managed the property for her mother and now runs 'Fleurs' in partnership with Duncan. She is a fine rider, works as hard as a man, takes on any sort of tough job. Her voice is quiet and under her well-bred reserve she is warm and humorous. The land, which she knows and loves, is her life.

Duncan loves the land but he also likes people. Apart from his years as a boarder at Scots, he has always spent time in Sydney. He likes night-clubs, parties, seeing new faces, old friends; yet he shares Mary's dislike for the social pretentions of some station owners and refuses to mix with them.

'Those little fillies in Sydney, they think it's a great achievement to marry a grazier. When a boy goes down to town he goes to have a good time, but when he comes back to the land he has to work, if he wants to run his place properly. But these little fillies expect to keep up the social round all the time . . . they want to be down in town, they won't stay at home and help, they only care about getting their photographs into the social pages, or going abroad or buying new clothes. You wouldn't read about it in picture books, the way they go on. We can't *stand* that sort of thing, and most of them were *nothing* to start with. Let them think we're snobs if they like; we just can't be bothered with them'.

Mary's dogs work hard but live like lords, each in his own domain. They go out with her in turn on the property or stay at home, frustrated, eager, tensed-up, waiting desperately for her voice, restlessly rattling their chains, yelping shrilly when the car is heard. Duncan loves them – 'Disgraceful! Disgraceful to be so fond of dogs. Bestiality! Down you bastard!' – and they give him kindly good-natured affection but Mary is their goddess. She has only to look and they obey. When Duncan roars they seem not to hear.

Duncan says frequently that you wouldn't read about the Aboriginals in picture books. Though he keeps up a ceaseless despairing mutter about their vagueness and bloody carelessness with expensive equipment and even occasionally bursts into roars, they fear him not at all, knowing his heart is soft.

One boy in particular exasperates him. He is young, very black, very dumb, with long legs and a taste in gay shirts. He has a fancy name but we call him the Philosopher because he stands for hours, neither happy nor sad, not even leaning on his spade. He belongs, in a sense, to a Chinese woman in Clermont. Mrs Hee, who is liked and respected, acts as a labour exchange for most of the coloured people, gets them jobs, allows them food, drink and tobacco on tick and even lends them money. She deducts accordingly from their wages which, in self defence, she usually collects from their employers. Quite often, when her debtors – both black and white – get paid they forget what they owe her and do their shopping elsewhere.

The Philosopher never gets out of her debt for he works spasmodically and drinks and smokes regularly. He is also very fond of taking taxis – the taxi is run by Mrs Hee's husband – and has been known to summon the cab out from Clermont when a truck would have driven him in.

'Ah, poor bastards,' says Duncan. 'Let them ride round in the taxi if they like. The poor buggers don't have much fun in their lives.'

There are about three hundred of the Poor Buggers living in a kind of shanty town on the outskirts of Clermont. Some are local, some come from Springsure, south of Clermont, and descend from a most savage tribe who murdered whole families of white settlers. Others have drifted here from all over Queensland and New South Wales and many now from the Missions at Woorabinda and Cherburg. They are locally known as Coloured People or Dark People because, though there are some full bloods and Aboriginal blood predominates, they are really a mixture with white, Chinese and Kanaka strains.

Some work as railway fettlers, as council labourers or garbage collectors. There are not many on mechanized mixed grazing and farming properties like 'Fleurs', though some of the younger ones are now learning to drive tractors, but they work as stockmen on the larger cattle stations, north and west of Clermont, in the more timbered country. Mary says they are not employed on these stations as much as they were; but drovers still use them when mobs of cattle are moved, though most cattle are now carried by transports.

Seeing the houses the Clermont dark people live in, their miserable surroundings, I was staggered to learn that in this district they are paid the same award wage as white men. Those over 21 years get \$37.30 a week, those under 21, slightly less. More experienced men get above the award: \$8.00 to \$10.00 a day, and drovers \$44.74, all plus keep. It will take more than one generation for them to learn the white man's way with money.

When the first petrifying chill has gone from the air I sit in the garden and bask. Because the Frasers love and encourage birds they play all day in the garden or fly into the verandah looking for crumbs. A pale grey and yellow Noisy Miner with downturned mouth and a sharp-curved yellow beak looks at me from his yellow rimmed eye; a little top-knot pigeon comes, very delicate mist-grey with striped wings and tiny peacock crest. There is a sloshing of geese dipping their faces into a bucket of water, in, out, in out – washing or drinking or both. Bees drone by. The cook's silky-haired baby staggers and sways and stares before collapsing boneless at my feet.

Nearby the Philosopher has been working for hours, making a small hole in the ground for a post. At very long intervals there is a dull thud. When I look up to see if he is still there he is standing at gaze, spade in hand. I am not familiar with Aborigines and am intrigued by this suspended action. It does not suggest looking or thinking or even conscious inward withdrawal, as with Orientals; it is simply just not being there. They become empty and absent as Australia herself when she is in the mood.

Though I do not see him dematerialize he is gone when I get up for lunch. The post is in, upside down. Duncan says you wouldn't read about it in picture books.

Out on the plains the brolgas dance, the Native Companions. There is an aboriginal legend that the brolga was a beautiful girl who became a bird and now must dance for ever. The first time Mary came running to call me we found three grey attenuated spirit forms, like Aboriginal drawings, deep in brown sorghum stubble. They were ghostly against the pale dead trees, pieces of bark, but for their long beaks and thread-like necks. They stood silent, part of the pastel landscape, then stretched out their necks and rather slowly took to the air, gradually streaming forward and snooping away to join a conference in the neighbouring field.

Sometimes they stand quite still, then hunch up and peer down into the wheat and go along crouching, very thin, short-sighted professors with pince-nez.

When they dance they are stately and beautiful, bowing and tossing their heads and flapping their great wings to and fro like fantastic fans. They dance with their mates or in groups; then rise in the air with a strange trumpeting honk. There are many of them at 'Fleurs'. It is said they often stay faithful to one mate for life.

Over at the sheepyards in the early afternoon, the woods stand motionless, like trees in English parkland at the height of summer. They are slightly darker, a drabber green but no less leafy and billowing. The grass is still. It all seems to be waiting. Tiny birds like moths swoop and plane overhead, very high in the pale sky. Willy wagtails sit on the fence twitching their tails from side to side, impatiently waiting for maggots from sheep being clipped.

A minute bird flies into a hole in an old dead tree trunk. Mary taps the trunk. There is silence; then as we move off he comes out at a rush, terrified. Perhaps he is building a nest in there.

Faint whistling sighs come from a tied-up dog; there is the clip of shears. A little grey-black bird with orange face, black cap and yellowed wings flies to the fence beside me and cries piteously for several minutes. From time to time the silly sheep cough and stamp.

As far as the Frasers know, 'Fleurs' was once part of Wolfang station and part of another property called Retro. Wolfang was taken up by a Frenchman, de Satge, who came to Peak Downs in the early 1860s and later represented the district in Parliament. Some people believe de Satge named 'Fleurs' for its beautiful wildflowers, others that it was the Hatfield family, who took some of de Satge's land when it was divided up. Most of the Hatfield's land now belongs to 'Fleurs'.

Near the garden gate is a small house of orange-red handmade bricks over stone and *pisé*, built about a hundred years ago by the Hatfields, as a dairy. The homestead, designed for intense summer heat, is large and low, with wide verandahs and high-ceilinged rooms. It is buried deep in athel trees – a kind of tamarisk – and Cook trees, with shiny narrow oleander-like leaves and green fattish poisonous seed-pods. They are said to have been washed up from South America and brought here by earlier settlers. Mary had this information from the Government Botanist at Melbourne Herbarium and feels it should be reliable, but Duncan shakes his head.

'Washed up from South America! You wouldn't read about it in picture books!'

Mary smiles and says, 'Yes, but then you also doubt the origin of coal.'

Duncan has always had individual ways of expressing himself but the picture books phrase is unusual. Most of his metaphors – 'a woman's place is in the stud paddock' – come from the land.

Compared with some cattle stations, which go up to half a million acres in other districts, 'Fleurs' is not big. It is 13,400 acres but the Shire considers it the richest and most valuable land in the Shire of Belyando, for soil, crops and cattle. The property is highly mechanized, for though it is mainly a cattle station it also has thousands of Merino sheep and hundreds of acres of wheat, safflower, sorghum, oats and sugar-drip, some grown for grain, some for feed. Duncan does not believe the high price of beef can last.

'Our families think we've gone downhill terribly since we came to Queensland. If my father knew I was growing *wheat* – I was brought up to believe wheat was for cocky-farmers. Only sheep were fit for gentlemen. Sheep and Scotch whiskey. We drink rum here. Shocking! Vulgar! If my father was alive now he'd turn in his grave to see me growing crops and drinking rum. He was a wonderful man but narrow in some things; as for Mary's people ... She was brought up the most terrible snob. No one was good enough for her family. *Wonderful* people but *terrible* snobs.' He regards his wife as a brand snatched from the burning.

'Fleurs' is seven miles from Clermont – pronounced Clemment – and we go in quite often. Mary does not care for town, though she likes the people, but Duncan enjoys it.

Clermont is the capital of Peak Downs. It is believed to have been named by de Satge after his birthplace, Clermont-Ferrand, and grew from gold. In the early 1860s it was a collection of tents and bark huts around a lagoon, near the junction of two creeks, Sandy and Wolfang, with a store and a pub called 'The Diggers' Retreat'. When gold was found crowds of starving British migrants from Rockhampton, Chinese, adventurers, diggers, prospectors, no-hopers from the south, flocked to the goldfields. At one time there were two thousand people at Clermont and a thousand at Copperfield, a twin town a few miles away, where copper had been discovered. There were brawls, drunkenness, fights over claims. A gold warden of the nineties had described the main street of Clermont on Saturday nights as densely packed with respectably dressed men of all ages and nationalities, with their wives and families, pubs and shops doing roaring trades, two bands playing and eight or ten police on duty to keep the peace.

Then the gold gave out. The miners drifted away. The copper mines closed at Copperfield. Clermont is now a pastoral town handling cattle and grain.

Until 1916 it stood on the flat land near the lagoon. Although there had been several floods, the people, like those who live on volcanoes, made no effort to move away, and in 1916 an appalling flood almost completely destroyed the town. Sandy Creek and Wolfang Creek overflowed and swept down together in a wall of water. Most of the buildings were washed away and sixty people were drowned. The surviving buildings were afterwards moved to higher ground and the town rebuilt.

A day in Clermont with Duncan is like going out with the Squire. Beaming, benevolent, he makes his way down the main street, stopping to greet every man, woman, child and animal on his way. Progress is slow, for a visitor in a country town is always interesting and no feelings must be hurt by missing out introductions. We dodge in and out of shops and offices, hail people in passing cars, greet families on pavements.

'Hullo, dear!' Duncan cries paternally. 'How are you, dear?'

He takes me to talk to old Mr Mills, a former Shire Chairman, young Mr Turner, a present Shire Councillor; Johnny Jones, from Llanstephan, the dark bright Welsh manager of Primaries; to drink coffee with gentle, soft-voiced Greeks from Cythera; to meet a baffled garage proprietor, a busy and self-important butcher. A little old lady clutches my arm and says I must go to Cooper's Creek where she was born; a sad old man with a faint voice holds me, in the teeth of a bitter wind, while my smile grows stiff with cold.

'Ah!' he whispers. 'I could tell you stories for hours ... '

I meet famous riders and drovers, horse-breakers and publicans, Great Lovers and civic leaders, old identities, new settlers. I am perishing, Duncan is thriving.

'Duncan ... I'm freezing ... exhausted ... can't we go home?'

'Just one more, dear, old Mr So-and-so. He'd be terribly hurt if he heard we had a visitor and he wasn't introduced. And old Mrs So-and-so ... She doesn't have much of a life. That's a good girl. I know you're tired but we can't hurt these nice people's feelings.'

Mary takes me to visit Miss Rose Harris, the Rose of Clermont. She lives alone in a little cottage, half-crippled with arthritis but gay as a lark. She is famous, not only as a woman saddler and rider but also as the local heroine. During the great flood, the family saddlery was one of the few buildings not destroyed and, from the upstairs windows, Rose and her father threw out halters and hauled up men who were being swept past. She belittles this episode but likes to talk of her life as a saddler and of the old days of Clermont. In her armchair, or manoeuvring herself around resolutely, making morning tea she says, 'I was known everywhere for the fineness of my work. You see I was *properly taught*. My father was a Somerset man and he believed a job must be done well; but then, I loved horses. I could never bear to think a saddle was going to cause the slightest discomfort to the horse – or the rider for that matter; but the rider could come and complain to me and the horse couldn't.' She was a kind of institution, like a family doctor, to generations of grazing and riding families. When country families are mentioned she says, 'I made his first saddle . . . ' 'I made his father's saddles . . . ' 'My father made his grandfather's saddles . . . ' 'I made *her* first saddle and when she grew up and married I made all her children's first saddles too . . . You see every saddle is different. Each saddle must be the only one you ever made. That's why they came back to me year after year. And I was always happy doing this work because I knew the dear horse would be comfortable as well as the rider. You must always think of the horses.'

The saving of seven men's lives does not compare in importance with the comfort of the horses.

People here think nothing of going vast distances for a cup of tea. Yesterday we went to 'Solferino', a hundred miles there and back. The property is 45,000 acres and when I asked if this was considered large the Frasers said, 'Yes and No. Big for this area but not compared to some in lighter country.'

'Solferino' belongs now to a family called Nicholas, from Victoria. In the past, owners had trouble with water shortage and Duncan is full of admiration for the Nicholases, who it seems, are working the property well. They have been harvesting sorghum with a gigantic header and I must see it in action. Though the work is almost finished the Nicholases have most kindly offered to hold it till I get there.

The road from 'Fleurs' to 'Solferino' is so long and straight that you see it for miles ahead, dipping and rising and dipping, reappearing, always straight, almost deserted by cars, all the way to Charters Towers.

Quarrians – little grey parrots with yellow crests, white noses and pink painted cheeks – flock on the surface, picking grain dropped by trucks; white cockatoos crowd in tree-tops, ruffling their sulphur combs; squatter pigeons and peaceful doves sit trustingly on the roadside, and galahs make mad, ludicrous swoops overhead. We stopped once to allow a huge python to cross the road. He was so drugged with sleep and sun he ignored the prods of Duncan's stick and lay supine while I took his picture.

Mr Nicholas is a big handsome Cornishman. He and his son were waiting for us as though time were of no importance, unruffled, full of good nature. The colossal machine was growling and grumbling among the sorghum and I was taken around in its cabin, high up in the air.

Machinery is not my strong point but I was hypnotized by this monster. It cuts a width of 22 feet and in a good crop can fill 35 bags in 15 minutes. When the huge receiving bin is full, the grain is fed into a waiting truck and driven off to the railhead or bulk shed. All this is done by two men, one in the header, moving a lever and one on the truck. If two trucks are used with this machine, as at 'Fleurs', the work goes on without pause, one truck filling while the other drives to and from the depot. There is an even bigger machine that cuts 24 feet at a time.

The 'Solferino' family are pioneer people. Mrs Nicholas, young-looking, slim and erect, was doing the washing when we reached the house. She left the washing machine to make tea and while we talked around the table, she mentioned casually that she was a water diviner. She discovered her powers as a child, with a forked stick, and has used them ever since. Amused at our slightly awed reaction, she offered to demonstrate.

In the garden she took a piece of fencing wire, bent one end like a handle and held it, horizontal to the ground. Slowly, the wire began to move, swinging farther and farther in the motionless hand till she had to turn her body to follow it. Without hesitation it pointed directly at a nearby artesian bore.

Mrs Nicholas said, 'That only shows what it looks like, since we know water is there; but it is the same when you're searching. Sometimes it leads you on and you just have to follow and then it turns and points to the ground.'

Mary took the wire. Nothing happened; it remained dead and motionless. Then Mrs Nicholas put her hand on Mary's. 'Oh!' Mary jumped. The wire began to move. It flickered uncertainly, then swung slowly, surely towards the bore. Mary looked startled and fascinated. She said Mrs Nicholas's hand on hers was just like an electric current turned on, a warm strange tingling.

I was dying to try but afraid I might unconsciously influence the wire, since I knew where the water was. When my turn came I turned away from the bore facing in another direction. The wire seemed dead in my hand. I waited, disappointed, but as I was about to ask Mrs Nicholas's help there came a strange sensation. My arm and hand tingled faintly and looking down I saw, with a kind of fear, that with no physical effort on my part the wire was starting to sway. It swung slowly towards the right. There was a feeling that nothing, not even I, could stop it; it was like a magnet, the pull of gravity.

I stood, slightly aghast, watching this simple, uncanny movement; then I was being led, only a couple of steps, but compulsively. I followed and stopped. The wire had inclined towards the paddock. I waited but nothing more happened. There was neither artesian bore nor tank nor garden hose to be seen.

When the others came round I had to admit that I had not found water; but Mrs Nicholas said, 'The wire isn't mistaken. There's an underground stream just there. It comes out behind the yards.'

Softly the star-grass floats and descends at your feet or piles up against the gates. The silky barricade seems to melt as you touch it, drifting away like mist.

I have learnt from Tom Hall, who is overseer at 'Fleurs', that the star-grass which I love, is very common, not harmful but not much used as feed. There are all sorts of grasses here: Blue grass, Foxtail, Mitchell grass, forest Mitchell, curly or bull Mitchell, Brigelow grass, button grass, sago grass, green couch summer grass, uracloa or curly grass, a little Flinders grass, white spear and black spear. The spear grasses were one reason why Central Queensland graziers turned to cattle instead of sheep. Sheep were first run in this area but the spears penetrated their skin. They were also attacked by dingoes. The blue grass, which is as common as star-grass, is very good feed and helps keep the cattle in their splendid condition.

When we pass one of the bulls, loafing like a pasha among his harem, Duncan puts on a pained expression and says, 'Disgraceful! Disgraceful! Shocking sight!' The bulls turn their great dopey eyes and gaze, dribbling slightly, too content to bother.

I never expected to so enjoy the sight of cattle. These are magnificent silken beasts; their gleaming coats ripple as they slowly graze or stand majestic, indifferent at our approach. Though proud of them the Frasers are really sheep people at heart.

'The trouble with cattle,' Duncan says, 'is they're so bloody *bovine*! Sheep have more sense.' When I protest, Mary supports him. 'Cattle are far more stupid than sheep,' she says defensively.

Tom Hall and his wife, who live on the property, sometimes come over in the evening to have drinks and talk. Tom is quiet, intelligent, thoughtful. He speaks slowly, as though considering each word. People here, particularly men, are altogether more natural, dignified, less inhibited than in the cities. Like ships' captains in remote seas they talk freely, without self-consciousness or fear of being thought effeminate, about strange things: ghosts, legends, birds, jewels, mystical experiences. No one scoffs or professes to know all the answers, nor is there any touch of Yarns-while-the-billy-boils.

I like the way Mary and Tom talk. Duncan and I get carried

away, exaggerate and embroider to make a good story, expostulate
or collapse in laughter; but the others talk like good writing,
making every word count. Sometimes, hearing them out on the
property, pauses are so long that you think they are finished;
but then comes a remark full of meaning and thought.

Tom can answer all the questions about birds, animals, can
identify all the trees on the property. Some I have learnt to
recognize: collibah, bauhinia with coloured flowers, emu-apple,
which has the bitterest fruit in the world, box, kurrajong and
athel trees. I love the tea-trees and hate the brigelows and
ironbarks but grow confused at the list of unknowns, all the
wattles and different woods – beef - , tallow - , blood - , sandal -
and rose-wood. Mary says that when rosewoods are cut the
timber really smells of roses. Without doubt the strangest of all
are the bottle-trees, and in their own way the most beautiful, with
their swollen filarial trunks and stiff little formalized arms.

There is a huge open-cut coal mine a few miles away, at Blair
Athol, the biggest in the world. You walk to the edge of the vast
black cliffs and look down and across a gigantic crater, the lake
and drowned forests of millions of years ago, at the earth's deepest
secrets brutally exposed to the light. Little trails of smoke wander
up from the cliff face, where coal burns, as though to remind us
that we are here on sufferance. The coal still stretches for miles
under the ground but no one works it apart from a few merry
men in tin hats. The mining town has gone, grass and weeds grow
wild, weird birds roost in dead trees.

On the other side of Clermont is Copperfield, where thousands
of people once lived and worked, at the Peak Downs Copper Mine.
For fifteen years the town boomed; then in 1887 the mine closed.
Now there are only a handful of ruins, a neglected cemetery.

It was evening when we went out to Copperfield, cool, with
scents in the air. From the trees and grass along the red road
came the faint hollow clank of bells, where drovers' horses were
hobbled. There was a bare little store, a couple of houses, then

metal gates leading into the old mine, which is now on private property.

Many Cousin Jacks from Kadina and Moonta came here, but they have left nothing behind – no machine houses, no miners' cottages, only a wilderness of thorny bushes with springing arms. They faintly scratched and brushed against the car as we pushed through the tangle.

It was not spooky like the Yorke Peninsula mines. The sun was behind the hill and all was in shadow – orange stones, orange earth, the remains of a rough orange road – poetic in its abandonment. A broken poppet head sagged silver-grey, among young tender almond-green wattles; the hills where the houses stood are all bright grass; a low foam of trees covers the place where the pubs and shops once flourished.

It is dangerous walking here, the earth may cave in. We picked our way like cats. In a rough clearing, a straight, square-sided chimney rose into the last of the light. The beautiful old bricks glowed orange. Inside the arched entrance you could look up to a tiny square sky, far off at the top, with a frayed crow's nest, like a stork's, in one corner. A long dead kangaroo, dried out like black leather, lay on the ground. There was a clean, slightly chemical, smell.

Among the trees we found a medieval keep with a dungeon full of stones. Its walls flamed red in the descending sun, unexpected as a Welsh ruin, a Roman wall, a Byzantine *kale* in Anatolia; but no jackdaws or ravens croaked on those broken battlements, only the sweet fresh cry of the bucher-bird, the twitter of little birds going to bed.

Down the road, behind a rusty iron gate, rusted railings enclose neglected graves. Great aloes with bent shark-leaves lean like the masts of sailing ships or lie on the ground among their gigantic seed-pods. There are yuccas with cream flowers, but the aloes dominate, they have taken over, pushing aside the fences, collapsing under their own weight. Where the grave is small – *Two years, Three months; Eight years, Nine months* – the living plant completely obscured the name of the dead.

Most of the graves are in vague rows but a few lie farther off, among the trees. These, half-buried in grass, seem even lonelier than the rest. All is pastel, faded, washed-out. I remember an English churchyard and ancient bones by an open grave – frail, thin, pale as tissue. The bones beneath this bleached grass are purified, dissolution's horror long past.

As we return along the road Mary marvels at my enthusiasm for opening gates between fields; but once out of the car it is hard to get in again. One wants to stand and gaze. The horizon is a circle, as out at sea; the sunset lingers as though it cannot bear to leave. As the light burns there comes a purple tinge. The archaic shapes of the Brahman cattle, the deep green crops and smell of dark earth are like Rajasthan on winter evenings. After the sun goes, dove-coloured clouds lie across a pale opal sky.

11

Rachel's Leg

When the Frasers heard I was going to look for 'Exmoor Downs',
the sheep station where Rachel Henning once lived, they decided
to come with me. The fact that it meant driving over two hundred
miles from Clermont into the Bowen district and back did not
concern them. They said they both loved *The Letters of Rachel
Henning*; they wanted to see 'Exmoor Downs'.

Rachel Henning was an English gentlewoman of the last century,
a clergyman's daughter who spent several years on her brother
Biddulph's Queensland property. She had been in Australia before
and disliked it so much she went home; but the second time she
stayed, married and died here in 1914. The letters she wrote to
her sister Henrietta in England, between 1853 and 1882, were
preserved by her family and published in 1951. Though she did
not have the hardships of some women – isolation, sick children,
hostile blacks, hard manual labour – conditions were sometimes
rough for one of her background. Her precise, controlled style
never lapses, even when writing of events or people not usually
encountered in polite Anglican society; and her talk of woods
and meadows, shepherds and flocks, servants, pressed flowers and

evening prayers, gives an incongruous touch of Victorian England
to the untamed scenes she described. She never relaxed her
standards: '*Nobody ever sits in the parlour without a coat* ... '
or gave up her ladylike domestic accomplishments, but she loved
the outdoor life, the challenges and improvisations of her new
country.

Our difficulty was to find out if 'Exmoor Downs' still existed
and who owned it. After a great deal of telephoning round the
country, Johnny Jones, the Clermont manager of Primaries, found
that it not only existed under the same name but that we were
welcome to visit it. Duncan rang the owners.

'A couple of brothers called Comerford. Quite young; very
nice boys. The old Henning house is gone but we can see where
it was.' He gave me one of his gimlet looks. 'Now, keep calm;
don't go up in the air. When I said you were a writer they asked
if you were Rachel Henning.'

We were to drive by the Peak Downs Highway to Mackay on the
coast, sleep there, drive next day to 'Exmoor Downs' and back to
Mackay; then I would go by train to Cairns while the others
returned to 'Fleurs'. All arrangements were to be made by Johnny
Jones's opposite number in Mackay. He would book us into the
motel, inform the Comerfords of our arrival and make my
reservations on the *Sunlander*, the train to the North.

The Peak Downs Highway crosses miles of timber country,
which seemed oppressive after the open grasslands, the peaks, the
empty sky. At close quarters, Wolfang peak was disappointing,
robbed of its colour, a mere barren rock; but there were curious
sights to see: fossilized seashells in cliff faces by dried-out rivers;
a mass of honeyeaters devouring pale yellow blossoms among the
long needles of desert oak; the bottle-trees, beautiful, off-beat
grotesques, Grecian urns, slender amphoras holding stylized
deformed branches with sparse leaves. We lunched by the Isaac
River and at the end of the day climbed through mountains to
a sudden prospect over a valley of sugar, patched with small,
wooded hills and swelling brown fields. Down on the tropical
coast the air was soft and relaxing after the astringent Downs.

Sugar grew by the road, high feathery-grass, close-massed like an army with standards and plumes.

The motel in Mackay seemed as artificial as an iron lung, with its carpets and air-conditioning, well-behaved banana plants and chlorinated swimming-pool; but dinner was good, and crossing the courtyard afterwards we heard a faint cry from over the river.

Mary said, 'Curlews!' We stood in the dark, listening, a cool breeze from the water blowing through our hair.

In the morning, something had gone wrong with arrangements and it looked as though we should not get to 'Exmoor Downs'.

Duncan can give an impression of fearful choleric rage, with suffused face, glaring eye, raised voice. When he lowers his head like one of his own bulls and roars, it would be alarming if you did not know how quickly he can be dissolved into laughter. Heard on the other end of a telephone wire it must have been shattering. Here he was – a busy man – *three* whole days – hundreds of miles across country to bring a *world traveller* to see this *historical* place!

Reparations were quickly made. In the midst of a roar Duncan's frame began to shake, his outraged eyes became two benevolent stars. He growled, then threw up his hands helplessly as though the whole business of anger were too difficult. We set off for 'Exmoor Downs'.

We were to meet one of the young Comerfords at a station called 'Turrawilla'. He would direct us to the old Henning property, where we would find another brother who would show us round. Driving through sugar fields into dry timbered land Duncan said, 'The Comerfords are only young, you know. I expect they're battling a bit, probably a few hundred acres or so. But very nice boys by the sound of them.'

Rachel Henning and her sister Annie came by ship from Sydney to Rockhampton to meet their brother Biddulph and from there they travelled on horseback, in all weathers, through Marlborough to the Port Denison (Bowen) district. I thought ours was a long

trip till I saw on the map the distance they covered. It was a
fantastic journey for two gently reared ladies, but there was no
grumbling; only amusement, good humour and interest in
everything new. They left Rockhampton on 24 August 1862 and reached
'Exmoor Downs' on September 10. Rachel wrote to Henrietta:

It was raining when we left Rockhampton but we were so
tired of the place, and Biddulph was so tired also that we
preferred taking the chance of bad weather ... Biddulph had
our horses waiting on the other side of the river, and by a
superhuman effort of packing we crammed our dresses and
crinolines into a valise which he carried before him, while the
rest of our property went into that little black bag we bought
at Bristol and which I fastened to my saddle ...

In the party were the two girls, Biddulph, his friend and right-hand
man, Mr Hedgeland who later married Annie, and Mr Stewart,
'A quiet, good-natured little man with bad health who was going
up to see if Queensland agreed with him'. They had pack-horses,
spare riding horses and a spring cart, which they picked up at
Marlborough, and formed 'quite a cavalcade'. When there were
sheep stations on the way the girls stayed at them but mostly
they slept in a tent. They rode more than twenty miles a day,
eating lunch as they went, only stopping at night. Rachel enjoyed
it all.

We had some very good damper, fresh beef, cheese and jam
and I was never so hungry in my life, having had nothing since
breakfast and ridden twenty miles. When it got dusk we all
drew round the fire, and I wished I could send you a picture of
the camp ... Annie and I betook ourselves to our tent about
nine o'clock where they had made us up a very comfortable bed
of blankets and rugs, with our carpet bags for a pillow, and you
will wonder to hear that we slept as soundly as possible in
our novel bedroom.

It is hard to tell from the letters which way the Hennings came after they left Marlborough and Tooloomba, but once we had turned off the highway at Nebo, for 'Homevale' and 'Turrawillah', we began to feel we might be following their route. We were travelling at almost the same time of year – early September – and hot and dusty even in our big comfortable jeep; we could imagine how it must have been on horseback, in sweeping riding-habits, for the two Englishwomen.

At first it was pleasant country, with a few large homesteads; then it grew dreary. Compared with Peak Downs, I thought it poor and scruffy, all shaggy ironbarks and outcrops of large round stones. We assumed these were Rachel's 'Small granite boulders from one to six feet high . . . smooth and rounded as if waterworn.' She had found the country so strange and new that she enjoyed the journey, but we did not share her enthusiasm. Duncan kept shaking his head and consoling himself that we had a four-wheel drive. For some miles the road ran on a high ridge, like an embankment, giving occasional views across silvery brigelow into weird ravines and chasms; but for the most part it was monotonous – 'So uniform that the most fruitful imagination could find nothing to say of it,' as D'Entrecasteaux said of the Great Australian Bight. We decided that we would return to Mackay by the shorter road, through Eungella National Park and the sugar fields.

I felt so cut off from the world in this thick smothering bush that it was a shock to suddenly find a notice board nailed to a tree –

ARCADIA SAFARIS

'They bring them in Land Rovers, camping. I suppose people should see their own country,' Duncan said dubiously.

Then it all cleared. We came into an open space with buildings and sheds and a homestead in a garden. An immensely tall young man in a wide hat and a boiler-suit came slowly to meet us. I marvelled at his stately carriage till he told us he was all strapped up with broken ribs.

Dogs barked. A girl with magnificent copper-gold hair came from the house. She was tall but came only to her husband's shoulder. They stood, friendly, smiling, relaxed. 'Isolated? But I *love* it here!' Denise Comerford said. 'I'd never live anywhere else. I grew up in Rocky but I could never go back to a town again.'

The sun was hot but she seemed not to notice it, hatless, not bothering to move into the shade. Danny Comerford, a gentle giant, had large dark eyes and a high colour and spoke in a soft low voice. His manner was modest and simple, talking with Duncan and Mary about his cattle and property. The heat, the absolute quietness, the feeling of being so far away from the world, made me disinclined to move on, but Duncan rounded us up, laughing and stamping and blowing. He had quite shaken off the depression caused by the arid journey. 'Come on! Come on!' Danny had given directions for the rest of the way and his younger brother Errol was waiting out at 'Exmoor Downs' to show us around.

'What a wonderful boy! A wonderful young couple,' Duncan murmured, as we floundered on through the dust. 'Struggling! You remember I said they were struggling?' He shook with laughter. 'Jesus Christ, do you know what these boys have, these young boys? Over two hundred square miles, nearly 200,000 acres. That's all! And 8,000 cattle. That's not bad for a young fellow!'

The thought of the young Comerfords struggling along with their meagre 200,000 acres kept him happy for the rest of the drive. We had to move fast, if we were to get to Exmoor and back to Mackay in time for my train. Close to 'Turrawillah' we passed the track to 'Blenheim', a cattle station which belonged to Biddulph Henning. Danny had suggested the present owner, who is now very old, might have remembered the Hennings, but we dared not lose any more time.

The road was rough and bordered with ironbarks, but blue cranes, white cockatoos and squatter pigeons helped break the monotony. Now and then, we met groups of Danny's cattle, which revived Duncan's amusement at the Comerfords' bitter struggle. Then the road dipped down to a calm, shaded river, winding away among grey stones, with tranquil reflections and still glassy ponds. We felt this must be where the Hennings camped and ate boiled eels for supper and felt sad that it was the last night of their journey.

We crossed the cement causeway and almost at once the landscape changed to softer, more sheltered country, a broad grassy plateau surrounded by low undulating hills. It was rather exciting, identifying this scene we knew only from descriptions written over a hundred years ago. We recognized the wide open plain the Hennings crossed at a gallop when the horses knew they were home, Rachel's beautiful mountains, some rounded 'like the Quantocks', some 'cut down from the summit into a precipitous wall of rock which runs for miles and miles and seems to shut out the world beyond with a natural wall.'

But now at the end of the flat green stretch there are large neat cattle yards, at which the Frasers murmured approvingly, well-kept sheds and a rusty-red two-storey house. A young man and a boy came out to meet us at the garden gate.

Errol Comerford, the young man, is every Australian's idea of the typical Australian: very tall, very handsome, with long legs and brown face, slow speech and easy movements. He wore a check shirt and wide hat and spoke in a very soft voice. He had come to Exmoor especially to show us around, for his elder brother who lives here with his wife, had gone to Rockhampton.

'No trouble,' he said, friendly, leisurely, while we lunched in the big modern kitchen. 'A pleasure.' Duncan was more impressed than ever.

'These three boys inherited the properties when their father died. They run them together. Lucky man, lucky man to have three such wonderful sons! The cattle are in excellent condition. By Christ, these boys know how to do things! Those yards are a model! Wonderful, wonderful boys!'

The house was comfortable and very cool. Red and pink geraniums grew round the doorways, jacaranda and oleander

framed the views; outside in the garden the still hot silence
was broken by far, bitter cries of crows. Nearby, a horse cropped
quietly. It was essentially Australian though no smothering
bush crowded in; there was neither eerie watchfulness nor
aloof indifference; only peace and benevolence and a haunting
quality.

In the foreground, patches of faded rusty earth, a silvery
tinge in the trees, gave a bleached look; but behind, the colours
were deeper, the shapes more dramatic, pinched up into points
like waves of the sea, merging into Rachel's wall of rock.

It seemed perfectly natural to find a kangaroo watching me
attentively, its little dark fore-paws drooping helplessly from the
wrists, like a Victorian lady in mittens.

After lunch Errol took us across the Little Bowen River to
the remains of the old Henning house. The building was already
demolished when the Comerfords came to Exmoor and no one
since has bothered to investigate the site; but it fitted Rachel's
description when she wrote that Biddulph's first house was
moved after she arrived to a better position with 'a rocky creek
at the foot of the ridge in front, and a noble view over a wide
sweep of undulating plains dotted with gumtrees and patches of
scrub like a park, beyond the thick bush and a panorama of
mountains all round, peak behind peak.'

There is plenty of room for a garden round the house, and a
flat of rich soil close by the creek for a kitchen garden. To the
right of the house is a rocky creek with pools of clear water and
pretty trees growing in it ... At the back of the house the
gentle slope rises suddenly into a little steep rocky hill, crowned
with gum-trees and rocks where you can sit down and survey
a most lovely prospect.

The little hill is there and the rocky creek on the right, full of
boulders and torn-out roots, like petrified bagpipes. As well as
the lovely prospect, Errol pointed out that this would have been

a good site for early settlers. The hill behind would protect them from surprise attack by natives and the wide view in front would allow them to see any hostile approaches.

He and his young cousin watched us with amiable interest as we clambered about in the sun. They both had a marvellous stillness, the loose unconscious grace of movement that comes from complete relaxation. Errol listened, amused, to our talk of Biddulph, of Annie and Mr Hedgeland ('more than a friend') and the scandal of Rachel falling in love with Mr Taylor, who was so much younger than she. If he wondered why we had come all this way to look at so little, he showed no sign.

Only a few posts, pieces of metal, the remains of iron roofs and tanks, traces of garden fences. The rooms the young Hennings lined and papered so proudly are gone, the verandah where Rachel tied her tame emu, where they sat with Mr Sellheim, the gentlemanly German who said *apenhalt* before every word. Mary was exploring the rocky creek when, poking amongst a litter of rubbish, I found the remains of a stove. The broken iron frame was half-buried, but by scratching and digging I unearthed a well-shaped, well-preserved leg.

'I've found the kitchen!' I shrieked. 'This must have been Rachel's stove!'

Mary came running and we dug together, uncovering a second leg. The men watched as though we were mad. We dragged the legs out of the rubbish.

'What are you going to do with them?' Duncan demanded.

We looked at each other uncertainly. Errol said, 'Take them. You take them.'

'Do you think we should?' Mary said dubiously. 'It seems rather like vandalism.'

Errol was vastly amused. 'What should I do with them?' he said. 'They'll only rust away there. You take them. You're welcome.'

Mary still looked hesitant.

'Jesus!' Duncan expostulated. 'They're only old bits of scrap-iron. You'd think you'd discovered the Dead Sea Scrolls. But

A Georgian look - Brownlow Hill stables

Camelot

Sydney pensioner

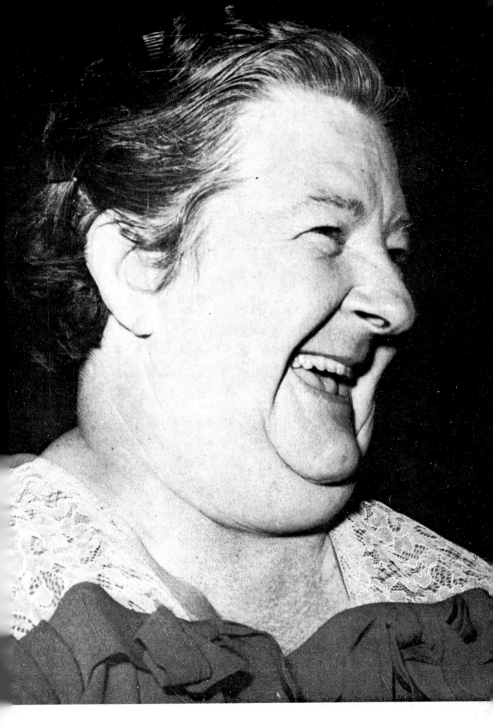

'A laugh does you good'

People . . .

. . . not V.I.P.'s

Queensland horseman

The horsebreaker's wife

Mossman: Like a Samoan church

Rachel Henning's 'Exmoor Downs'

Mossman : Cane cutter

Joyness

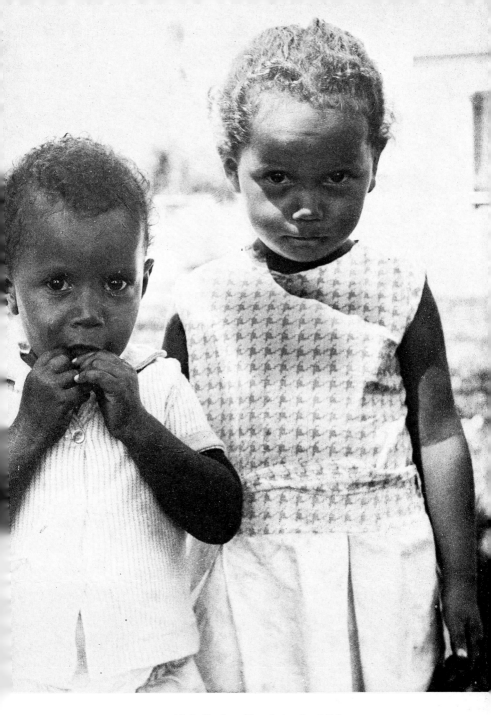

Beautiful little Aboriginal children

Siciliana

Cattle king's wife

Olive grower's wife

The perennial charm of the young child

Abandoned convent

BELOW
Cooktown: The bushes encroach

Always time to talk

take the bloody things if you want them.' He looked at me. 'Are you going to carry yours all round Queensland with you?' We put Rachel's legs into the car. Mary would take mine to 'Fleurs' and bring it on her next trip to Sydney.

I walked up the little hill behind the house to take a picture and sit for a minute looking out at the Lovely Prospect. It was strange to think of the gay young household once living down there; of Rachel dressing a vase of wildflowers every morning; her best white dinner-set, her pretty white-and-gold breakfast china out in this silent bush; of the parlour wallpaper, 'very light green with a small white pattern of wild roses and ivy leaves,' and all the other ladylike details with which she surrounded herself. It never occurred to her that she should not continue to live in her accustomed manner, even in the wilds of Queensland. She loved the wilds, but kept them in their place with gardening, picnics, rides, walks, crinolines and shady hats. She made a pretty garden with English flowers and herbs and vegetable plots and Biddulph planted an orchard. At Christmas, in the hot alien December, they roasted a turkey and grew rather merry on lime juice which the gentlemen warmed with a little brandy.

Of all this charming ridiculous courage there now remains two legs from an old iron stove, a decrepit bauhinia, a stunted bottle-tree, a twisted plum gone wild; but there are also Rachel's letters, which keep it all alive. There is no sadness here and none in her story. She married her young Mr Taylor and lived very happily with him at Myall, in New South Wales, and then in the Illawarra, near Wollongong. Years later, she and Annie, both widowed, kept house once more for Biddulph at 'Passy', Hunter's Hill.

We said goodbye to Errol, to Danny and Denise at 'Turrawillah' and started out on the short route back to Mackay. Frustrated, far too quickly we raced through some of the loveliest scenery in Australia, by a wandering stream in a deep valley, through the green volcanic peaks and white alpine villages of Bungella

Reserve. In fading light we shot down a mountain highway as spectacular, winding and steep as the road from Mussourie to Dehra Dun, in the Himalayan foothills, then through the flat sugar-fields. The lights of Mackay appeared in the darkness, half an hour before my train was to leave for Cairns.

12

To the Tableland

After all the rushing, the snatched sandwiches, the loving farewells, the taxi dash to the station, I found the *Sunlander* was going to be three hours late. At the motel the Frasers would be going to bed, to prepare for their dawn departure. I imagined Duncan's fury on my behalf, and decided to stick it out on the station with the rest of the disconsolate passengers.

The *Sunlander*, which takes three days and two nights from Brisbane to Cairns, is the pride of the Queensland Railways and Tourist Bureau. They speak of it with awe, as of the Trans-Siberian crossed by the Japanese *Hikari*. In reality, though cleaner and with better seats and lavatories, it is not unlike the *Posta* in Turkey. It breaks down or goes on strike and at certain points they take off the restaurant car so that passengers must eat at railway refreshment rooms. This is rather worse than Turkey, where food vendors come to the line with fresh fruit and hot *kebabs*, for there are never enough serving staff, and the food, if you get it, is terrible. You eat it because by that time you are glad to get anything.

I was to spend many fascinating hours in this train, wedged in with nuns, Aborigines, Italian cane-cutters, Girl Guides, campers, schoolchildren on holiday, and once with eighteen beautiful shining black Thursday Islanders, who sang and played guitars night and day. On that journey, the air-conditioning failed and on the second night the engine broke down and we sat for hours waiting for help to come from Townsville. Starving passengers climbed out and walked across the line in the dark to a little store which soon sold out of biscuits and sardines.

When the train at last arrived at Mackay I was half asleep. I had just taken my place when a little man entered, looked at the seat next to me and said angrily, 'Have I got to sit next to *you*?'

I said, 'There's heaps of room.' The carriage was almost empty.

'But this is my reserved seat, next to you.'

'And this is mine, next to yours.'

'But I want more space. I want to stretch out.'

I had also hoped to stretch out. I said, 'All right. I'll move,' and gathered my things together. He said, as to a wanton law-breaker, 'You realize that if you take someone else's place you can be turned out in the middle of the night?'

'I'll take the risk,' I said from across the aisle, putting my legs up on the opposite seat. Almost immediately a red-faced woman bustled in with a snorkel, a rucksack and a wet swimming costume. She brushed my feet aside and sat down.

'But you're really in my place,' she said in a loud English voice. 'You may stay there because I must have my back to the engine.'

She put her rucksack and snorkel on the overhead rack, also the wet swimming costume, which dripped down on me, and began opening paper bags. It was after nine-thirty but she was frighteningly wide awake and energetic, cracking nuts, peeling bananas, munching noisily into apples. As she masticated she asked my views on fluoride in the water and why was the government hushing up the scientific analysis. She could not understand the *apathy* of Australians; they did not seem to care what happened to them or to their country. What about Conservation? Overseas interests *wrecking* the beaches with rutile mines; *raping* the earth, kangaroos slaughtered, wildlife wiped out; the Crown of Thorns starfish eating the Barrier Reef. Was nothing to be done?

I agreed to signing all the petitions and dozed off. I woke to find her standing on the seat trying to open the window.

'They're sealed.' The swimming costume was still dripping down my shoulder. 'The train's air-conditioned.'

'But one can't sleep in this atmosphere!' she said haughtily. 'And in any case I can't stand air-conditioning. We shall just have to open the door.'

'No, you don't!' said the little man who had taken my seat. 'I don't want no draughts.'

'Draughts! Don't you realise we're in the tropics? And we can't all sleep in here without air.' She began struggling again with the window. The snorkel fell down on her head. The little man laughed coarsely and said, 'Bloody Pommie.' Two women behind said loudly and virtuously that *they* weren't complaining and a sympathetic exchange began across the aisle about the rights of others. I pulled my hat over my face and tried to sleep.

Next day, we sped past sugar fields, houses on stilts, bananas, coconuts, rain forests, rivers and flowering trees. The compartment had filled up with families; babies cried, toddlers raced up and down and drummed their heels on the seats. A half-blind Italian was fumbling about, trying to feed himself from a packet of *biscotti*. The dark-eyed woman next to me suddenly thrust her face into mine and said, splutteringly, 'That puir old mon. He's nearly blind. I must gie him a wee drink.'

The Englishwoman, still breakfasting out of paper bags, stopped her chewing and said, 'Are you Scots?'

'No. I'm Bulgarian.'

'Bulgarian? Are you sure?'

'Of course I'm sure. What do you mean, *sure*? What's wrong with being Bulgarian?'

'You don't sound it. You sound like a Scot to me.'

The air was charged with suspicion and disbelief. I shut my eyes and refused to be drawn in.

At Tully, there was lukewarm Irish stew for lunch. I ate it

because I was famished but afterwards dozed in the humid heat. When the train stopped at Innisfail I barely looked out the window. It was not until some time passed that I realized that we were still in the station. The Scottish Bulgarian, the old Italian had vanished; the Englishwoman was striding healthily up and down the platform, filling her lungs. The little man across the aisle suddenly shouted, 'How do you like that! We're not going on! The train's stopping here! It's a strike. A bloody strike!'

I thought it was a joke; but more people were standing up, sitting down, tut-tutting, looking outraged or resigned; then a smiling guard came through the compartment. The Englishwoman followed, emanating hostility.

'Four hour strike!' he announced. 'This train is not going on. It will remain here till 5.30.'

When the Englishwoman demanded, 'Why?' he looked even happier.

'It's a lightning strike. State-wide.'

'But friends are meeting me at Cairns.'

'Well, they'll have a long wait, won't they?' he said nicely.

'It's an outrage. An outrage.'

The guard said she was lucky to be in a station. They might have stopped out in the open. This way she could go in and have a look at Innisfail, no extra charge. There was time for a nice cuppa tea.

Someone said meekly, Ah well, there was nothing they could do, might as well get out and have some tea; others grew loud and angry. It was generally agreed the public-the-poor-bloody-public was what suffered and bloody strikes were wrecking the country. A man said he was self-employed, he couldn't afford to strike, if he went on strike, he'd starve, that's what. He had no union to finance him; a woman asked belligerently what would happen if the housewife went on strike, eh? The man behind said, They called it the Tourist State, he'd been three weeks in Queensland on holiday, had four strikes already.

The conductor was not perturbed; you could see it was not his affair. When I asked if there would be alternative transport to Cairns he glowed with friendliness.

'No dear, nothing. Nothing till 5.30 when we get moving again.'

I looked at my map and saw there was a road from Innisfail to the Atherton Tableland. In the west, high mountains were powder-blue against a pale sky. I got out and waylaid a ticket collector.

'Can I get from here to Atherton by road?'

'We . . . ll.' He pushed back his cap. 'Well, you could; if you had any transport.'

'Is there a bus?'

'No. No bus dear. But there's a mail car.'

'Will he take passengers?'

'He takes passengers sometimes if he's in the mood. He's out there now. You go and ask him nicely, he might take you.'

I raced to the little van parked in the station yard. The man at the wheel raised his head and said rather sadly, Okay, he was going up to the Tableland, Okay he could take me and Yes I could find transport down to Cairns if I wasn't in a hurry and didn't mind staying the night at Ravenshoe.

I said, 'Wait for me!' and ran back to the train for my bag. He seemed surprised at my eagerness, as though no one in their right mind would want to go with him to the Tableland.

'You got friends in Ravenshoe?' he asked.

'No. I suppose there's a hotel.'

'Oh yes. There's a hotel. Two hotels.'

In the clear light of Innisfail, flowering trees and bougainvillea clustered thickly around white buildings, grass grew right into the roads, there were wooded islets out in the river. A cool breeze stirred the coconuts along the lush banks.

'That's the Johnson River,' the driver said.

We went around the town collecting mail, newspapers, bread and meat for the Tableland; then, sighing deeply, he set out towards the West.

I felt the sudden, literal catching of breath that comes with tropical beauty. Colour was in solid blocks; dark trees on emerald hills, young springing crops streaked with yellow, chocolate ploughed earth, orange-red roads. It was vibrant, intense without shrillness. Blue against blue, like the Pyrenees seen from Lourdes. Mount Bartle-Frere basked, a white scarf across her throat.

We seemed to be plunging into the heart of this colour, into fields of sugar, farms with purple bauhinias, shocking-pink bougainvillea, South African tulip trees splashed with orange flowers.

From time to time the driver hurled a rolled newspaper into an open paddock. The hot sun shone into my face and suddenly we were out of the tropics and into cleared land, steep, long-grassed grazing country, high on a ridge, with a prospect of smooth downs spreading out all around.

Then it changed again and became all great trees and gorges and tropical plants, with a cold clear river pouring over black stones. The air smelt fecund and damp; the roadside was starred with blue flowers like forget-me-nots.

The driver said this was the Palmerston National Park. The Highway wound through the fantastic rain forest, emerging at last into verdant highlands, domestic, with trees and cows and white farms. The late afternoon light stroked the red earth, the fawn grass by the road shone like the silky fur of an animal.

'Millamilla,' said the driver. 'You want to get off here?'

Millaa Millaa's white houses and gardens seemed embroidered on emerald velvet. It was restful and beautiful and I was tired and longing for tea, but I shook my head without quite knowing why.

The driver became chatty as we approached Ravenshoe. When I asked about hotels he said I had better go to the best which had a Good Big Lounge. Now that we were up on the Tableland with the sun going down, there was a chill in the air. I asked if the hotel had a fire. Oh yes, it had every comfort, including roaring log fires. Don't worry, I wouldn't be cold.

I was relieved, for already I sensed the mountain touch, could anticipate the glacial stillness of midnight in high altitudes. The sunset was splendid and sharply defined, its colours held in the sky with all the clarity of low temperatures. There was a tang of excitement, of reviving energies after the heat of the plains, a crisp feel in the nostrils with each inhalation. It would be as cold as the Antarctic after dark.

Compared with the rich dairy lands around Millaa Millaa the first sight of Ravenshoe was disappointing. It seemed closed-in and ugly, though the main street is wide. The driver took me to the hotel and offered to wait while I asked if they could take me. If not, he would drive me to the other hotel down the road.

I got out reluctantly. The building rather resembled an Anatolian *oteli*. Inside, the Turkish touch was sustained by grimy dark walls and the dust that covered the furniture.

The girl who came from the bar said cheerfully that I'd be right, there was plenty of room. In fact, this huge hotel housed only two men and myself. We farewelled the mail man, then she led up a vast obscure staircase. In the gloom I discerned a vista of leaden-blue walls with doors painted salmon-pink.

We tramped down midnight corridors, past empty rooms with sagging beds and gaping mattresses, to a true Middle East apartment. All the familiar ingredients were there: the dust, the smells, the lumpy bed, the drawers that stick, the wardrobe door that sags, the absence of windows, the two doors, the one to the passage, one to a long verandah upon which the rooms of my fellow guests opened and which I must traverse to reach the out-of-doors bathroom. There was only a subtle difference in smells. In Turkey it is the all-pervading stench of the urinal; here, it was the more intimate localised reeks of unemptied jerries.

Since this was the best hotel and I had to sleep somewhere there was no point in making a fuss. I asked about blankets.

'Oh yes dear, plenty of blankets. You'll be warm as toast,' said the nice girl. She prodded the traditional burgundy cotton bedcover and bounced away through the salmon-pink door.

The bed was hard and cold, like a couch of stones. I pulled back the cover, revealing two thin grey cotton blankets. There were none concealed in the wardrobe or chest of drawers. I wondered about ventilation, for the smell in the room was strong. Should I open the hall or verandah door? I would be in a draught, for the bed lay between them; but I was going to freeze anyway. I opened the verandah door and gained an uninterrupted view of the man opposite. We were both well-lit by naked light bulbs. There were several enormous clothes-baskets on the verandah, heaped like Welsh coracles.

I went downstairs seeking blankets and tea.

The friendly girl had gone back to the bar, where business was lively. In a grim brown lounge a couple of women in hats and thick coats were drinking beer by an empty grate. There was no sign of roaring logs and the chill air suggested there had not been for some time.

'Tea?' said the girl in the bar. 'We don't serve tea. Sorry dear.'

'Never mind. I'll go to a café.'

'Oh you won't get tea down town dear. Not here. Would you care for a beer?'

Cold beer would not do at all. I could think only of hot tea. I asked if I could make it myself. She looked surprised but said amiably, Well if I wouldn't mind going out to the kitchen she supposed it would be all right.

I groped through shadowy passages to the vast kitchen. An immense fuel stove occupied one wall; there was a large table, a massive refrigerator and a terrible smell of drains. All was covered with grime. A man was wandering about making tea. When he had filled his cup he handed over the pot and told me to get myself milk from the fridge if I wanted it.

I opened the door and saw a lump of blue-black cadaver nestling beside a clot of purple sausage meat. The emanations were startling. Could this be tonight's dinner, or was it pet's food? I decided against milk, though the tea was black as Indian ink.

The man advanced with a plate of thick tomato sandwiches. ' 'ere,' he said sternly, ' 'ave one!'

Silently we sat chewing and sipping. I thought about the kitchen. The stove was magnificent, so was the dresser. If the dark-brown walls were white, the table and floor scrubbed, more windows put in . . .

A friendly woman entered and announced herself as the cook.

'That's right, dear,' she said. 'Eat up your sandwiches and have another cup. Tea won't be ready yet awhile.'

She removed the lid from a large aluminium pot and carefully lifted out three fawn-coloured bodies, boiled to disintegration. They had, in their time, been athletic birds.

'Tomorrow's lunch!' she said with satisfaction, laying them out in a lake of congealing liquid. She bore them off to the refrigerator and returned with the blue-black meat. Then she took a knife and said, 'Now for tonight's tea.'

Outside, the sun had set; pale orange lingered in the sky but Ravenshoe lay in shadow. The air was fresh and I thought of my two little Japanese cotton blankets. At the other hotel there were hot smells of cooking and cheerful grunts from the bar. I wondered why I had come to Ravenshoe.

Cars were parked down the centre of the wide street and by a station wagon a tall, rather elegant woman stood talking to its driver. As I approached she smiled and said as to an old friend, 'Hullo. Where are you off to?'

I answered instinctively in the same way that I was going to the paper shop; then we stared at each other. I knew her, yet had no idea who she was. She seemed to know me for she started to say to her friend, 'Let me introduce . . . ' then stopped again.

'But I know you,' she said. 'I just can't think of your name. How silly!'

I told her my name and saw it meant nothing. She said, 'I'm Nancy too!' Then again, as though we were friends, 'But what are you doing up here?'

I told her about the strike, the mail van, the train I hoped to catch next day to Atherton. Why did she look so familiar? I knew perfectly well we had never met before. She was slim and good looking with a fine fair skin and narrow green eyes, rather fragile and delicate facial bones. I should have remembered if I had met her.

I could see she was baffled too. She asked where I was staying and when I told her, threw up her hands.

'You can't stay there. You'd better come home with me. Be my guest, I'm all alone.'

'But I've told the Hotel . . . '

'They won't mind. They'll be relieved. You'll freeze there. You come home with me. You'll be warm and comfortable and I'd love to have you.'

She waved me into a station wagon and drove to the hotel for my bag.

The house at the end of the town gave a different perspective of Ravenshoe. The sheltered garden where azaleas and camellias grew among citrus and peach, where narcissus and violets flowered beneath apple trees, spilt out beyond the fence into the peaceful trees of the bush.

Nancy led me to a self-contained apartment and told me to rest till dinner. It did not strike either of us as strange that I should be there.

Nancy's husband has a cattle property on the Tableland. When he and their sons are in town they also use the Ravenshoe house.

She was born in Queensland, though her mother's family were early settlers round Sydney and the Hawkesbury district. An ancestor, William Pascoe Crook, was once offered the whole of Woolloomooloo Bay, Sydney for a shilling an acre but declined it because it was not good grazing land. She sighed philosophically.

The name Crook was anglicized from St de la Croix. They escaped to England during the French Revolution. William came out to the Marquesas in the mission ship *Duff* and stayed fourteen years in Tahiti. He was an extraordinary man, born before his time. When he came to Sydney from Tahiti he studied as a doctor, then decided to learn printing. He built the Church with a Chimney at Watson's Bay, where the fire station is now, and had a wharf and a ferry service. He also founded the Congregational Church in Australia. His headstone is in the Collins Street Church in Melbourne. Someone at the University of Queensland, in Brisbane, wrote a thesis on him.

'I'm always meaning to look up the records in the Mitchell Library when I'm in Sydney,' said Nancy. 'As for my father – he was a marine engineer. He left the sea and took a property near Roma, where I was born. He used to bring mother home the most beautiful jewellery but after my brother was born he left us. Just walked out, taking everything but a sewing machine which had been Mum's eighteenth birthday present. Life was pretty hard after that.'

Nancy had a talent and passion for dancing, but there was no money for training. She did her best by reading all she could find on ballet and the theatre and learning at second-hand from girls whose parents could pay for lessons. When she was old enough she went to work in a grocery shop for 13s 4d a week.

'I gave mother ten shillings out of this, so there wasn't much for clothes. I bought my first dress in instalments – a shilling a time! I was studying book-keeping at night but I never gave up the idea of dancing. I went on teaching myself till at last I was good enough to get professional engagements. I was so happy. Then I had a bad accident to my leg and that was the end of my hopes. I had to console myself with teaching.'

When the war came the Tableland was a big military centre. There was no time for moping about lost ambitions and the girl who had wanted only to dance, found herself driving trucks and buses, helping run grocery shops, butchers' shops, hotels and boarding houses, doing dressmaking, buying and managing property.

'There's nothing very interesting about me, I'm afraid,' she said. 'I live a very ordinary life, between town and "Glen Gordon".'

Out on the property she rides, drives trucks, shoots, looks after her husband and sons, manages the books and business affairs, cooks, sews, keeps fowls, paints walls, grows and preserves fruit and vegetables. In town, she manages the flats she has bought, gardens, makes her own clothes, works for the Ambulance. She is president of the local library, vice-president of the Country Party Women's Tableland Section, and is standing for Council. She is very interested in local government, raises money for charity, acts as Samaritan, judge, adviser, scrutineer, campaigner . . .

'The funny thing is that I was born ill. I was such a mess that the doctor asked mother if it was worth trying to save me. He said I'd always be an invalid, never able to lead an active or useful life.'

When I came out next morning Nancy, in lilac linen and a wide leghorn hat, was putting clothes through the washing machine. She threw in my grubby jeans and shirt and led me upstairs to the kitchen. She was full of plans as she made an omelette for breakfast.

I was not to take the train to Atherton, I was to stay on in Ravenshoe. Her husband was coming in from the property in a day or so and if I liked I could go with them to a cattle sale at Mareeba, on the other side of the Tableland. She could drive me to Atherton; I should see something of the Tablelands before I went down to Cairns; if I wanted to go on to Cooktown I could go across country to Mt Mooloy and pick up the bus there; I really ought to see Herberton and Mt Garnet. Also, her friend Ruth Wallis-Smith, the wife of the local Member, had invited us both to lunch in Atherton . . .

I wondered if she had lost count of the eggs she was breaking into the basin.

'Eight. Not enough? I've got plenty . . . '

'For *two people*?'

'For one. I don't eat cooked breakfast!'

'Nancy! I can't eat *eight eggs*!'

She looked faintly concerned.

'They're absolutely fresh, I promise you. From my own hens this morning.'

Ravenshoe is 2,900 feet above the sea. In this warm, sunny country it is hard to believe in the Tableland's bleak winds, its cold mists and rains, but Nancy assures me it is bitter in winter. Visibility is now so clear, the air so sparkling that the view from the hills to the blue mountains brings a sense of liberation, exhilarating as flying.

So far, I have seen cattle country, dairy farms, pig farms; butter factories, bacon factories, timber mills, grain silos. Tobacco, sugar, corn, peanuts, soya beans, are grown; persimmons, figs, grapes, citrus or stone fruit. The scenery is panoramic or intimate, dramatic or domestic. In the gardens are New Guinea crotons, roses, bulbs, azaleas, camellias; along the roads, scarlet flame trees, all kinds of wattles; white, pink, red, purple bauhinia; the orange flowers of grevillea and South African tulip trees. The brilliant blossoms among the dark tulip tree leaves are astonishing, but they are not really suited to the Tableland; they have shallow roots and sometimes blow over in strong winds.

Against the sky are the high-domed shapes of lonely bunya pines, evocative of old houses and early settlers.

Deep green grass covers some of the hills; on others, the silky molasses grass is now turning rust-red. Nancy says that when it matures the red becomes misty, with white feathery tops, like frost.

Parts of the Tableland are so dry that irrigation has been installed. Thousands of acres not yet developed will be served by water from Tinaroo dam, a man-made lake that is also a tourist attraction; yet there are also great rain forests full of cedars and satinwoods, rosewood and pines. Palms, ferns grow among native figs with grotesque roots; mosses, lichens and orchids cling to tree trunks, thick vines dangle in loops like hangmen's ropes.

Strange animals, birds and insects live in these prehistoric jungles; tree kangaroos and great tree frogs, ring-tailed and brush-tailed possums. There are pademelons and spectacled flying-foxes, huge pythons, exotic lizards and butterflies; even the cassowary, with its weird cry and Shinto priest's hat. After dark you can see fireflies.

On the hot days the twilight of these forests is welcome, the moist atmosphere refreshes parched senses, but if you venture too far they grow claustrophobic. The silence is heavy, oppressive; every sound develops significance – branches rubbing together, a leaf twisting slowly downward, a furtive movement behind smooth trunks. The pleasant gloom becomes sinister; innocent orchids turn to poisonous tongues and lichens are lepers' patches. The cool mushroom smell of rotting leaves and wood suddenly speaks of death and decay. There is no sky; the thick trees press down, the vines are waiting pythons. It is time to get out.

There are two highways down to Cairns, the Gillies and the Kennedy, and a good deal of traffic on both. Cairns people come up to escape summer heat; Tablelanders go down for shopping or have holiday houses on the coast. To a visitor, the Tableland seems like the Garden of Eden but most of the residents feel the same way about Cairns. Cairns is Paradise ... warm, beautiful, colourful, exotic; it is full of life and gaiety. 'You wait!' they say, 'Till you get down to Cairns!'

Meanwhile, tourists flock to the Tablelands for the scenery, the gorges and rivers, waterfalls, panoramas, crater lakes and forests. The roads are good, coaches from Cairns make One-Day Trips; there are caravans, parks and hotels.

Yet the Tableland people remain friendly and unspoilt, the little towns are more country centres than tourist resorts. Ravenshoe is busy with timber, Millaa Millaa makes cheese; at Herberton they have mined tin for over fifty years; Melanda is famous for milk and butter. Mareeba grows tobacco and cattle, Atherton has maize. Even Yungaburra is still tranquil and sleepy, though it has a white-painted wooden hotel-motel, and all the cars and buses stop there to photograph the fig tree with roots like a curtain. There is a magnificent bamboo grove; the streets are lined with trees, the houses surrounded with gardens. Below is a prospect of calm dairy country and neat pretty farms.

Since transport is easy from Atherton to Cairns I decided to stay on there, after lunching with Nancy's friend, Ruth. It was sunny and cool as we drove across the hills.

'When you come back,' Nancy said, 'I'll take you out to "Glen Gordon" so you can see the men working the cattle. Meanwhile, you'll enjoy Cairns. I wish I were going down.'

Atherton, the biggest town in the Tablelands, is quite unpretentious, for all its hotels and shop windows full of TVs and washing machines. Prosperity is in the air; cars and station wagons are parked all along the main thoroughfare, trees and gardens planted down the centre. In the quiet back streets, hoses are deep among bouganvillea, bauhinia, hibiscus.

Ruth's flat might be in any big city, anywhere in the world, certainly not in a small country town: very simple and white, with black lacquer and bamboo, a few rich colours. There was Scandinavian china, Italian food, strong coffee and good conversation. Ruth is fragile, gentle, sensitive; warm and friendly.

After lunch Nancy and I parted as casually as we had met. It was very strange; like leaving an old friend you expect to see again soon.

'But of course you'll be back,' she said. 'Any time, whenever you can. Just send a wire and I'll meet you.'

'Do you always ask strangers home to stay on impulse?'

'Well, Queensland people do, much more than in the South. We don't worry much about formalities; but this was rather different. We were old friends. You might have been my sister.'

The Barron Valley Falls Hotel in Atherton is a cut above Ravenshoe's Turkish *oteli*. Downstairs, the decor is Undertaker's Jacobean brown, plywood panelling and stiff gladioli; but the staff were friendly, the meals adequate. In the dining-room plump, red-faced men and ladies with tight perms were being gay over sparkling burgundy. Sherry comes in tumblers. Upstairs are railway-green walls and a room for television. Each time I looked in the occupants were watching a snow-storm, but this may have come from altitude or the interference of mountains.

On the last evening, Ruth took me for a drive to see Tinaroo, the artificial lake. In the tranquil twilight the distant mountains were lilac, the sable ploughed earth seemed to take from the dusk an even deeper, darker texture. In cleared land where men had been burning off, smoke trails lingered and dying flames echoed the last saffron flares in the west.

When we came back it was dark. Far off the rows of little fires smouldered and glowed like an army encamped for the night.

Afterwards, having a farewell drink in the Undertaker's Parlour, Ruth spoke with longing of Cairns ... its tropical beauty, the interesting life you can live there compared with Atherton. She goes down regularly, about once a week.

As I went upstairs I reminded the girl at the desk about my early call. She said Okay, I'd be right, was I going down to Cairns? Half my luck. She wished she were going. There was no place like it. It was a real Tropic Wonderland.

13

Not Quite Tropic Wonderland

Plunging down the Gillies Highway in the early bus we suddenly swept out of mists and rain forests into the tropics again. The sun blazed out upon squares of green sugar and rust-red earth; dark mountains like green woolly Bedouin tents rose straight up from the plain and far off was the sea. Headlands, the colour of jacarandas, receded away down the coast.

This was Cairns, on Trinity Inlet, official Tropic Wonderland of the North, the starting point for tours to the Tableland, to the north, to the Barrier Reef. Every year Australians from southern states flock here by car, train, air or sea, for the winter, as the British in other days went to Egypt.

After all the Tablelanders' talk, the town was anticlimax. Despite its warmth and colour, it is neither exotic nor beautiful. In the morning, bank clerks and pulic servants drive to their offices in regulation white shirts and shorts; there are department stores, chain stores and matrons pushing prams; the sea-front at low tide is a muddy swamp with mangroves. People lead quiet lives and go to bed early. Compared with the strident vulgarity of Surfers Paradise it is a modest and homely town.

This was the height of the season. All hotels, motels and

boarding-houses along the front were full, but there are pleasant old pubs, painted white with wide upstairs verandahs. They are not smart or touristy; locals drink noisily in the bar and dining-rooms run to beetling sideboards and plastic flowers. I got a room in one with a view of the wharves.

The food was Australian Fried Traditional: potato chips, fish in batter, slabs of rubbery toast, strong tea served with tinned soup. Cheese never appeared unless asked for and then it came processed like soap. Fruit juice at breakfast was served, lukewarm from a tin. There was pale greyish bacon with fried eggs and greasy fried bread, but the waitress named Bertha was motherly and the atmosphere far friendlier than in those motels where meals are thrust into one's cell through a hole in the wall.

I became friendly with Bertha, who also seemed to make the beds and sweep the upstairs floors. She was a country girl, very simple and kind, large, slow-moving, with thick ankles and a compassionate smile. She would shuffle in and out of the empty dining-room saying hopefully, 'Ready for tea yet, dear?' waiting patiently for the signal to bring in the large over-full cup. She did not mind if I did not drink it; she knew it took all sorts to make a world.

I seemed to be the only regular. Occasional bearded young men with rucksacks would appear at breakfast, never to be seen again, and purple-faced commercial travellers came and went. This gave me an air of permanence and built up an almost family feeling between Bertha, the publican and myself. Each morning she would ask where I was going that day and how I enjoyed the day before, and when I came back from several days' absence would lean on the back of a chair to hear my adventures.

I never had any trouble getting the same room back when I returned. As I went off the publican would say, 'Ah, you can leave your bag in the ironing-room if you like, it'll be safe there ... no need to pay for the room while you're away. She'll be right.'

Cairns, which was named after a governor of Queensland, began as the port for the Hodgkinson River goldfields. It was still a muddy swamp when Cooktown, Port Douglas and Smithfield were booming, but now it flourishes while they have become ghost-towns or ceased to exist. It survived because of the railway to the interior and is now a sugar town, a port and a tourist centre. I do not know what prevents it being really beautiful. It is like a face with good features but no personality. The town is so wide open that wherever you are you can look up and see the mountains. In some streets are white-flowering trees and the grassy sea-front is planted with poinciana and South African tulip trees. Long green seed-pods droop from bare branches, trunks are thick with orchids like cream lace and ribbon-leaves hanging down.

Houses are mainly wood, a few painted grey like old South Sea traders' houses, and gardens are full of fan-shaped palms, papaws and hibiscus. Frangipani grow bigger than in the south, though not as gnarled or prolific as in the Islands, and there are ever more orchids and vines with taro-leaves clinging to coconut trees. Yet something is wrong, something missing. It is all too predictable, there is too much cement. Our touch, even when well intentioned, is too often municipal, running to public lavatories, red salvia and town clocks.

The Aborigines have a Melanesian look, with brownish skin and solid physique. The women, rather plump and relaxed, sit and chat in grassy parks, surrounded by children, like Islands women.

The white population is partly permanent, partly transient. Sunburnt young men with beards and long hair, on foot, on motor-bikes, in Land Rovers, pass through on their way to the north; the streets are full of white-haired old ladies with hornrims on beaky noses, pale thin-fleshed skin-cancer faces, large hips, sensible shoes and the sort of enormous handbags people carry about on ships. In the evening, with cardigans over floral dresses, they waddle out with duplicate friend or on the arms of depleted husbands. The larger the woman, the frailer the husband. These look rather baffled and lost, with alligator necks emerging nakedly from collars that should have a tie.

There are also flocks of strange little men who come here alone from the south, to spend the winter in second-class hotels and boarding-houses, all alike, with false teeth and mottled faces, open collars and monochrome cardigans. They are not hard up; they go on all the bus tours and expeditions but have no interest in local history, wild life or natural beauties. Most of them emanate a terrible sense of *too late*. Widowers, apron-tied bachelors, they care only for three meals a day and warming their chill lonely bones.

Mostly they like to talk to anyone who will listen, to run over their ailments or the Tours they have done. Their life-stories follow an identical pattern.

'Well, you see there was only me and Mum, after the Dad passed away. The sister, she lived in Melbourne and Mum never wanted to give up the old home . . . I did think of marrying at one time, but it would have meant having Mum to live with us and my Friend said she wanted her own Home. I couldn't very well leave Mum, after the Dad went . . . Well, anyway, now she's passed on and I'm on my own. I can let the Home and come up here for the winter. I get a good rent, it's a good Home, got everything in it. Mum always liked it kept up. I been on all the Tours . . . The Alice, West Australian Wildflowers, Tassie.'

If it isn't Mum, it's the Dad, the Sister, or even the sub-normal Brother. Self-satisfied widowers are quite a relief.

'Yes, well I had a good little wife . . . thought the world of me . . . but after the kiddies grew up and married she kind of went downhill. Had a growth in the bowel. The doctor said *it was a mercy*. Got to look at it that way. A Happy Release. Yes, well I got my mates at the Club . . . keep busy . . . that's the thing. Been on all the Tours. See Australia first, that's my motto.'

In the evening, as the tide goes out, many birds gather in the bay. Cautious pelicans, up to their knees in mud, keep close in shore but waders on long fragile legs range further out into the swamp. Sometimes there are white egrets. Gulls circle and screech and come down on the grassy Front to be fed by little boys in pyjamas. Flights of tiny birds, like spots before the eyes, swoop, sink, soar across the water.

Far out at sea it grows dark. In the east a column of smoke rises from a dip in the mountains. The west is gold. There are shouts from the R.S.L. Club and in the garden of a guest house two men are fighting. Loud TV noises echo from motels, cars roar up and down the road. People are eating dinner; they do not seem to notice that Cairns at this time of the day has become beautiful.

There is a honky-tonk piano in the Lounge just under my room. On certain nights a lady with piston-arms attacks it from seven till ten. At these times it is best to go for a walk or sit on the balcony. In the moonlight you can see the mountain shapes and hear the birds out on the bay.

The talk that comes up from the bar suggests that TAB, the football and how much was drunk last night are the chief concerns of life.

As the cars drive up, doors bang and male forms enter the bar, I wonder how we dare criticize the way Japanese men treat their wives. What are the women doing while these men are in the pub each night until ten o'clock? At home with the kiddies, watching TV if they're lucky, or doing the ironing perhaps, very much like wives in Japan. They may be more outspoken and hostile but in the end they will keep dinner hot, take off the reveller's shoes and put him to bed when he lurches home.

Most of the men come in for a few noisy drinks after work and then go, but others are stayers; you see them reeling away at closing time, sodden, argumentative or being sick in the gutter. Why must they slop around the pubs night after night? At times I blame our Irish blood, the temperament that cannot carry drink yet turns to drink for escape. I feel that these men have come from a groping need to communicate, or from inner loneliness and emptiness. They are not cheery revellers; there is little real gaiety, only a dogged effort to cover up something, to escape questions that cannot be answered.

Cairns has one supreme attraction. Little Green Island, out on the Barrier Reef, is close enough for day trips and in the season crowded boats make the crossing regularly. But for Bertha, I would have missed it. I thought it would be commercialized, like Surfers Paradise. She was shocked to think I was not going.

'But don't you want to see the coral, dear? You'll love the coral. Oh no dear, it's not a bit like Surfers. You go and stay over there for a few days at the hotel.'

The man at the ticket office said I was lucky, school holidays just finished otherwise I wouldn't have a hope at such short notice, but crowds dropping off now. I cannot imagine what it is like when they are on. The boat was packed to the utmost. It could barely crawl out from the wharf and a second one had to be brought up to take the overflow. I wondered why I had listened to Bertha.

But day-trippers are highly organized. Their ticket includes return launch fares, a ride in a glass-bottomed boat, aquarium, submarine observatory, lunch and the showing of underwater colour films. At the long jetty an amplified voice warns arriving passengers that their time is limited; they must hasten at once – as directed to avoid congestion – to the attractions. The majority obey, moving from cinema to museum, from glass-bottomed boat to restaurant, from underwater observatory back to the ferry.

Those who do not join the organized entertainment flock to the beach with lunch baskets to grill in the sun or splash in the crystalline water.

Though eighty thousand visitors come to the island each year, it is unspoilt. From the sea it is still a simple Pacific Island, much as when Captain Cook named it. At closer quarters the jetty, the hotel and TV masts are visible, but the low roof among the coconuts could be the house of a trader; the ugly cabins in the grounds, the cinema and aquarium are hidden in trees.

The sea bears away souvenirs of beach picnickers. It takes more than a few soft drink bottles and cartons to change the essential quality of a coral island. Green Island is not completely South Seas; the mainland across the Passage has contributed more than tourists. Red blossoms from flame and coral trees lie on the shady paths; trees of the rain-forest grow among coconuts, casuarina pisonia, pandanus; butterflies and coloured land birds dance and flit and, on the high branches above where the reef herons wait for the tide to go out, the Torres Strait pigeons crowd like white cockatoos.

Each year these birds come down from New Guinea to breed. By day they go to the mainland for native fruits and berries, returning at night to the island. All day, every day, the air is full of their haunting monotonous call.

This island is richer, more varied than many remote South Seas atolls; but there are no breadfruit trees, no smell of copra smoke, no flower-crowned heads or soft voices singing.

In the aquarium, creatures of inconceivable shapes and shades create a world of colour and drama and humour. Some of the fish faces are so semi-circular it is hard to tell if they are right or wrong way up. A fat pink exhausted starfish flops like a worn-out spaniel over a shell, a thin agile blue one slides irritably about the glass wall, exposing his underside. An almost transparent Tang fish, electric-blue with yellow tail, black markings and Anita Loos haircut peers out pertly; tough little fishes in black-and white, black-and-yellow jersies dart through shoals of greeny-blue Wrasse with pink-and-blue heads, blue-and-pink fins, pink scales and sharp yellow crescent tails.

Tiny orange fish hide among visceral-waving anemones. Portly fish, like aldermen, stand on their heads. A little blue fairy-like creature makes eyes at me from a pink coral, emerging and coyly retreating. Very small turtles with white kid stomachs swim solemnly on the surface of their tanks, to and fro, to and fro, patrolling the glass, like lumbering angels. The big dark fish look glum but the small yellow satin ones look like boiled sweets; the little blue and turquoise Damsels are gay and alert. There are exquisite Butterfly Cod made of Venetian glass, with black-and-white spotted wings and tails and poison-charged spines, large Byzantine turtles, anemones like pink fallopian tubes or purple feather-boas; Trigger fish, Banded Hamburgs, a turquoise fish with blue head and long porpoise snout; striped Angels, Moorish idols, puffed-up clowns and a large green-yellow fish who looks sadly at me with amber-brown eyes.

I never before felt that sea creatures could so directly communicate; but some of these faces are full of expression – depressed, kind, indifferent, bored; or hostile like the Moray Eel, crouched in a corner, brown speckled like the *Dutchman's Pipe*. His face is sulphur-yellow, he has lavender eyes with white studs, two pale nostrils and a wrinkled repulsive dewlap. His gaping mouth opens and closes for breath like somebody dying, ancient, edentulous but for two horrible little fangs. He opens his mouth silently, craftily. Despite his appearance of toothless age, he is evil incarnate.

As the glass-bottomed boat leaves the wharf we all peer down attentively at the blank sand, the odd mutton bones and beer bottles; then the engine is turned off and coral appears, like snow-covered trees in a forest; like mushrooms; like cerebellums, like cooked vermicelli; gold with white stars on the ends of the branches; blue, dull rusty red; citrus yellow.

'It's not very pretty,' a woman complains. 'I thought it would be brighter, like the coloured bits you get at the Souvenir Shoppe.'

When the water is shallow the sun shines through easily upon the coral; moving submarine forms are sharp. Down below all the football teams are out, striped sweaters wriggle and dart. Graceful, beautiful, elegant, luminous green and purple fish cruise through arcades of bare frangipani; tiny electric-blue and yellow forms flit like coloured finches. Now we are hovering in space, looking down into dark crevasses. The sun's shafts cannot penetrate here; they lie in the water like motes of gold hinting at shadowed caves and frightening depths. Far down, objects are covered with concealing fur. *Of his bones are coral made.*

The underwater observatory is crowded but eerie, for we are below the sea. Beach clothes cannot quite dispel the feeling of being imprisoned in a sunken ship. Beyond the portholes are encrusted wharf piles and furred-over chains; fish, suspended, gaze in surprise, or slowly ascend in invisible elevators.

We file round, peering out through the portholes. There is no chance of staying still; if you want to look more closely you must wait another turn, again and again. The turquoise space beyond the windows is polka-dotted with blue and yellow sprites, with black moths in Japanese white-crested ceremonial kimonos. Long thin fish like sticks lie motionless with open mouths; brown and purple forms with huge oriental kohl-rimmed eyes peer owlishly in. From the front, the pupils are black buttons under glass domes. All round is coral like poison toadstools, like the wildest, most gorgeous mushrooms of the Russian forest. Gigantic clams covered with tan and purple embossed velvet lie ajar. Ceaselessly, to and fro wave the graceful anemone arms. In the background, misty trains of large ghosts pass by in stately procession.

The last boat has left for Cairns, the last sunburnt figures have rushed down the jetty and leapt, screaming aboard. The launches churn off across the Passage and quietness falls on the island. Quietness but not silence, for birds are coming home. As the sun moves to the west, flocks circle overhead. On the reef, where the tide has gone out, the herons prowl, dipping their long beaks down into rock pools for crabs and small fish. Across the sea, mists are gathering around the high Fitzroy Island; the dim blue mountains of the coast grow violet. The sky burns. The western beaches glow orange.

On the other side of the island the wind is cool among the dry pandanus. In the deep forest the doves call, the white pigeons crowd high in the flame trees, swaying and crying.

Night falls. Chatters from late settling birds, hotel sounds, die away. No longer a tourist attraction, the little island sleeps. There is no pounding surf, no smell of oil lamps, no fishing lights out on the reef. From time to time the squeaks of flying-foxes disturb the night as they tear at the scarlet blossoms; a sea bird cries. The wind blows in steadily, out of the lonely sea.

Soon, if help does not come in time, there will be no reef,

no coral islands for Torres Straits pigeons to nest upon. If tourists had not stripped the Barrier Reef of the triton shell that protected the coral from the raiding starfish it would not now be in danger of dying.

14

Little Sicily

In the little service car that runs between Cairns and Mossman I was the only passenger. Ron, the driver, who lives at Port Douglas, spends most of his time on this coast. He stopped every now and then to let me enjoy the view.

The Cook Highway from Cairns to Port Douglas and Mossman crosses the Barron River and comes through sugar fields to a wide blue bay, where palm trees and sand attract tourists and caravans. This is Trinity Bay, named by Captain Cook, who discovered it on Trinity Sunday. From here, after groves of scarlet poincianas, the road follows the *Endeavour's* route along the Coral Sea coast.

Looking back, looking forward, a sapphire ocean glitters away to the horizon. Far into the distance, headlands alternate with deep inlets and stretches of yellow sand that might never have been discovered.

'I know it like the back of my hand,' Ron observes, 'and I never get tired of it. It gets more beautiful every day. I come from up Atherton, on the Tableland. It's cold up there in winter, my word! Fogs; but this . . . Would you believe it? Midwinter!'

There are no signs of life beyond sea birds. Here and there, cliffs cascade down to faded rocks; from the road along the heights ribbed sand shows through the shallows and coral patches of the Barrier Reef make dark purple shapes. The sea is so calm its olive-green islands seem set on glass.

'Beautiful! I bought a home at Port, just me and the Dad. Port's a bit of a ghost town now but it's going ahead just the same. Twelve months after I bought my home I could have got twice the price. But I wouldn't sell; not yet awhile. Land's booming. Three good restaurants there now and a motel and caravan park. It's the beach. The best beach in Queensland . . . in Australia . . . four miles of it! Four miles! The tourist buses drive along it. Port's got a big future; but still, it's a good place to live. Take your time, friendly people. Away from the rat-race. You'll like Port. It used to be a big place in the days of the Gold Rush but that's all gone now.'

'They said in Cairns it was full of artists and New Australians.'

'Ah no, not really. People come here, artists and that, because it's pretty and cheap and the climate's good; but for New Australians you got to go to Mossman. Eye-talians. Been there for years . . . thirty – forty years, some of them. Lots of New Australians there.'

'They're hardly New Australians if they've been there for forty years. We're all New Australians if it comes to that, apart from aboriginals.'

'Yes, but you know what I mean. Foreigners. Not that I've got anything against that. You staying in Mossman? Ah well, if you haven't seen a sugar town before . . . Nothing much there except the sugar mill. They take tourists up there in the buses for the day trip, up the Cook Highway to Mossman, then back to Port for lunch. Makes a nice drive; and Port's got good restaurants . . . '

We had left the sea and turned inland to sugar country. The road was lined with sugar, so high that houses and gardens seemed set inside tall fences. Some of the buildings were wooden, square, white, substantial, raised from the ground for ventilation, but here and there a red-brick villa proclaimed extreme prosperity.

'This is an Eye-talian feller,' said Ron as we passed a large ugly house. 'Came here forty years ago without a penny, worked hard, saved, now owns all this . . . ' he waved at the fields around. 'When the daughter got married a few years ago he built her this Home.' – another square red-brick villa – 'That Home,' he said solemnly, 'got everything. Cost all of $20,000. And he paid cash for it all. Every penny! But he's not Lousy. I'll say that for him.'

'How do the locals get on with the Italians? Do they mix much? At Ulladulla, on the south coast of New South Wales, 95 per cent of the fishermen are Italians, but they rather keep to themselves.'

'People get on pretty well together. But there's an Eye-talian community, just the same, Eye-talian food, talk Eye-talian, specially the older ones. Great workers. Now, the feller I work for, he's an Eye-ty. Owns this service car. He's a decent feller, couldn't fault him. And I'll tell you one thing. You can always trust an Eye-talian to pay back money, if it takes him years.'

The sugar fields stretched like a deep gigantic lawn towards the mountains. The heat was enclosing, moist, exhausting but full of excitement. It was another world to the shimmering Mediterranean coast we had left, a lush Samoan scene splashed with scarlet and purple, infused with the gold that underlies tropical landscapes. Only the trees, outlining the river, clustering in forests, showed dark against this intemperate brilliance.

We crossed the river and entered the outskirts of Mossman, with its grassy gardens and flowering shrubs and houses spaced far apart. The wide street that runs through the town and on to Daintree is planted with lawns and shady trees; there are four pubs, and at the far end a single railway line cuts across from the fields to the Mossman Central Sugar Mill. Italian names are painted over shop awnings and doorways. Italian headlines advertise *Il Globo* newspaper.

Ron had accepted my strange wish to stay in Mossman but demurred at my choice of hotel.

'Ah no, I wouldn't go there. Not for you. "The Exchange" is the

best. All the government servants and commercial travellers
stay there.'

'The Exchange', painted baby-pink with baby-blue trimming, is
set on a corner with a wide upstairs verandah overlooking town,
sugar fields and mountains. It seemed homely and pleasant. After
the intense glare, I stood blinking in the cool dark hall. A refined
dehydrated female, drinking with a gentleman friend in the lounge,
turned and stared with suspicious hostility, but the fair girl who
came from the bar had a gentle expression.

'Well, I think it's all right. You can go to room number Eight if
you like.'

'Is the key in the door?'

She smiled, kind and amused.

'We don't have keys here.'

Number Eight was small, clean and hot. French windows
opened on to the great ship's-deck verandah, with a view of the
mill puffing quietly at the end of the town. Across the street were
shops with Italian names; below, the line for the sugar train
and further off the green miles of cane. Mossman is set in sugar;
the fields come literally into the town, round the houses, among
the back gardens. In the west, a line of beautiful mountains
flanking Mount Demi made a blue wall against the sky.

There was a churning sound, a melodious hoot. Down the street
the little diesel train ground and chugged its way, dragging its
load of cane, long poles lying across open platforms and shorter
sections stacked in wire cages. The last trucks were still in the
fields when the engine had reached the mill.

The scene was inland and rural, yet I felt I was in the Islands.
On the other side of the balcony two men in white shorts lay back
in cane chairs, passively watching the mountains. But for its red
tiles, the little stone church of St David might have been in a
Samoan village. Mango leaves foam round the roof, moss stains
the walls, shining crotons and papaws reach up to the windows.
Magnificent trees, which the locals call rain-trees, rise from lush
grass, with staghorns growing thick on their massive trunks, and
from their boughs orchids hanging down like fringes.

Yet, for all its brilliance, the scene lacks the full intensity of the true tropics. The sense of teeming life, of uncontrollable forces is tempered, perhaps by the wide fields of sugar, the openness of the sky; perhaps by Australia's own detached uncaring acceptance.

It was the hottest time of day when I went out; the town was sunk in siesta. Dogs stretched, jaws agape; a few Aborigines sat apathetically in the shade; dark girls with babies and toddlers lay on the grass of the little park. Like the natives at Cairns, they were lighter in colours, more like Islanders than those I had seen in Central Queensland.

The shops were silent, deserted. In a milk bar a sad-eyed Italian woman served me an ice-cream in slow motion. Across the field the blue mountains receded into a haze. Heat shimmered up from pavements.

I took a road out of town, wide, quiet, shady, set round with sugar. A path through the heart of the fields led off to the bank of a river where drowned trees and roots impeded the slow stream. The canes leaned forward, frail coconuts riding out over the beach towards the sea; purplish-brown, shining, marked in symmetrical sections like exotic Regency furniture. Hidden from sight I lay down in the shade and fell asleep.

It was still very hot when I woke. The afternoon was full of soft sounds. A bird called *chock-chock*: doves muttered; the river murmured. Far off, tractors and harvesters purred. At intervals came the hoot, the rumble and grind of the little train curving its way through the sugar.

Above my head the canes swayed and dipped like the masts of ships. There was a gentle rustle and sigh, a faint clattering as when the trade-winds turn the leaves of the coconuts.

This field had not been fired, the canes stood in dead brown trash. Looking into its midst I could see down between the lines of planting, jalousied arcades, aisles and naves flecked with light, trodden and trampled by men, but when I entered I found them hot, claustrophobic. Visibility ceased: the dry trash crackled underfoot. I was lost in a jungle of bamboo, oppressive, stifling.

From the sugar I plunged into long vivid grass but immediately pulled out in panic. Nothing was visible, but malignancy rose from the warm hidden earth. All was calm; but as I stood, shaken, on the path, something curved away from the humid place where I would have walked. I learnt later that there are venomous snakes by the river.

Along the road, the high palisades awaited harvesting. On one side a new crop was coming up, tender green lines across the cocoa-brown earth. These were small fields, curved, semi-circular, S-shaped, intimate, backed here and there with rain-forest or dotted with houses and gardens, strangely refreshing and foreign after the uniformity of the vast ordered acres.

A notice said 'Look out for train'. The line appeared suddenly out of a towering field and crossed the road to a bridge. The river, grown shiny and stagnant, smelt sour and objects covered with floating fur could be glimpsed in the mangrove-green depths. From over the hill, just out of sight, came the sounds of machines and voices. I followed the train line towards the harvesters.

By the time I had climbed the hill the machine was silent. On the line were platforms and cages stacked with cut sugar. In a littered field, four young men, blackened like Aborigines, were drinking from mugs, eating cake and meat pies in the shade of a tractor. Their keen prick-eared dog cocked an eye at me but made no move, too hot and tired to bother. Against a blackened wall of fired cane stood a monstrous machine with a leaf-shaped Picasso attachment and a wire cage behind.

As I approached, the young men exchanged murmurs and then fell silent, gazing sternly at the ground.

I asked if I could come back and take pictures when they resumed work. They stared shyly into their enamel mugs. Presently one said gruffly, 'Please yourself'.

In a take-it-or-leave-it voice, the boss indicated they would be starting work shortly if I liked to hang around. When I said vaguely I might come back some time he tossed away the rest of his tea and mounted the Picasso monster. The others stuffed down their pies and picked up their cane knives. With a shattering roar, Picasso thrust his red leaf-shaped attachment high into the sugar and snipped off the tops while a sinister blade shore through at ground level. Unseen knives chopped the canes into sections; an escalator conveyed them up a red ramp and disgorged them into the waiting cage behind. Two of the young men worked with Picasso, slashing away at the trash round the cane while the third drove the tractor, towing cages to and from the line. The earth shook, dusk flew about; there was a smell of hot oil.

I took some pictures, feeling out of place in this tough man's world. Cheerful Italians, shy Aborigines, cutting by hand were closer my level.

Some of the houses among the sugar look rather ricketty, up on stilts like outdoor sleeping platforms in southern Turkey. Many are wooden, pink with turquoise trimming or poison-green with red; but others are solid red brick or cement, with fancy open-work walls round the car-port. Though reception is bad, because of the mountains, all have television antennae.

From a duck-egg blue house a dog ran out barking. A small Mussolini-faced child appeared and stood aghast, with immense staring eyes. He was clean and well dressed. Tomatoes were set out on drying trays by the wall, onions hung in plaits, there was a lingering smell of *frittata*.

I was moving on when I felt I was being watched. From a shadowy doorway two little black eyes glittered. An old woman, all in black, with small gold earrings was peering out, toothless, yellow-faced, wrinkled.

I smiled and said, 'Good afternoon.'

The black beads gleamed, silent, intent, like an animal from the forest. I wondered if she were a newly imported grandmother or an old settler who had never learnt English. I said, '*Buon giorno, signora.*'

She did not reply. I bowed, smiled and turned away; then a fearful screech sounded behind me.

'Gryce! Gryce! C'm'ere Gryce! S'a'lydy.'

A woman appeared, wiping her hands on her apron. She was dark and faintly moustached and beaded with sweat.

'What's up?' she demanded in broad Australian. 'Screaming out like that.'

The old woman muttered and backed away. Taking the little boy by the hand Grace said in a friendly voice, 'Good-day. You a visitor here? Ah. Been for a walk, eh? Must be hot, a day like this. Like to come in and have a cold drink?'

In the kitchen we sat at the table and drank Coca-Cola. There was a good deal of plastic and vinyl in yellow and red but the smell was of garlic and oil.

'It's me old mother,' Grace said. 'She don't speak much English. Just a few words. Too old to learn. She understands though. Mum and Dad, they're from Sissly but I'm born here. Went to school here. Me husband too. He's same. Born here. Dad, he speaks English. Mum, she never learned much.'

'How long has she been in Australia?'

'Oh, about thirty-five years I suppose. But she never learned much, y'know. Never had to, really, at home with the kids all the time. In those days the women never went out. Always in the Home.'

Everything acquirable was Australian – accents, idioms, furnishings, outlook. She sounded like an Australian housewife, but she was a broadfaced and smooth-haired Sicilian, not the frizzy Arabic type, and her people came from Catania.

'Yes, I know him,' she said when I mentioned the boss of the men on Picasso. 'Quite a nice feller. That's his own sugar he's cutting. You must be tired if you come all that way. You better sit a while and have a rest.'

Our conversation was slow, lazy, and with long pauses.

'Have you been to Italy?'

'No, it's the money see, lot of things to get first for the farm and the Home. I'd like to go for a trip, not to stay though. We're Italian but we're more Australians now. Italy don't mean much to me really.'

The little town comes to life after dark. Suddenly everyone is out, promenading, driving cars, riding motor-bikes. They swirl up and down and round past 'The Exchange', hooting and roaring. From time to time the little train makes its dogged pilgrimage to the mill.

Down at Joe's Service Centre, Italy gathers. This is an unofficial focus of civic and social life. The service car runs from here, so does the taxi. The taxi driver is married to Joe's daughter, who serves in the shop. Among the vegetables, groceries and milk bar supplies, are stacks of *pasta,* jars of olives, tins of oil, Italian salami and cheese. Coffee is served with S-shaped *biscotti.* At the juke box, good-looking Italian boys insert coins and produce loud Italian songs. Older men lean on the counter, drinking milkshakes or sit at the tables reading Italian newspapers. An eight-months-old baby, drawn up to the table in its cot, is cooed and clucked at. A fat mamma with sore feet flops about dishing out food. There is a great deal of noise.

A stranger in the shop is quickly spotted. I had barely started my coffee when a large man with a face like a bandit put down his milkshake and approached. When I smiled he squeezed down opposite, beaming and nodding.

Other craggy faces gathered, staring curiously. The taxi driver's wife and sister-in-law, on their way to and from their milk bar customers, paused to join the conversation. Like Grace, they spoke broad Australian. The brigand spoke a tongue of his own, complicated by a very thick accent.

'Sicilia. Sicilia. Komma Sicilia,' he said loudly. 'Nomme Giuseppe.'

'Siciliano; Siciliano,' echoed the onlookers.

'We're all Sicilians here,' said the girls. 'We all come from Sissly. Mossman's called Little Sissly. Y'know Sissly?'

'Knowa Sicilia? Catania?' Giuseppe shouted, thrusting his granite face into mine, growing excited when I said Yes. He was born near Catania, they all came from Catania. They cried 'Catania! Catania! Si Si Si! Sicilia, Sicilia!'

A young man put a coin in the juke box. A loud mechanical voice sang, 'Oh Italia, Oh Italia, Oh Italia!' with such passion that Giuseppe had to raise his voice higher.

'Sola?' he bawled. 'You sola?'

'Si.'

'Sposa? No sposa? Famiglia? Where you famiglia?'

'In Sydney.

'Aaah! You come my farm, heh?'

'Sugar?' I screamed. 'You grow sugar?'

'Si si, Zucchero. Now alla cut.' He made a swiping gesture. 'Komma I show. Notta far. Hey? *Domani.*'

'Okay. *Va bene. Domani.* Only sugar?'

'Alla sugar. Trya grow vino ... olivi ... ' he shrugged. 'No good. Too hot. Nowa sugar. *Mai ... '* – he made a *cosi-cosi* gesture – 'e croppos. Porco. Milko!' This last was a joke, he giggled. 'Milko, hey. Joosta for famiglia.'

'In Sicilia did you live in Catania or in the country?'

He shrugged again, turning his lips down.

'In Sicilia, a peasant. Very poor. Now make good money. Build a fine house. You come see, hey? *Domani?* I drive.'

'You want some more coffee, love?' screamed the girl at the milk bar.

The juke box sang on, against a background of television voices. The Sicilians seemed unaware of the racket but I was growing limp with heat, noise and the effort of translating Giuseppe's accent. I arranged to meet him next morning at Joe's and after noisy farewells wandered back to the pub. It was quieter there but less gay. A dull murmur, a beery smell floated out into the warm air from the bar. From time to time a drinker emerged and silently drove away. A few Aborigines moped on wooden seats near the doors.

I was so tired I fell asleep as soon as I got into bed, ignoring the cars, promenaders, motor-bikes, even the sugar train. All through the night it comes and goes, for work at the mill continues in shifts. The train is noisy enough when loaded but when the cages are empty the clatter is hair-raising. Towards early morning it seemed to shriek with despair and sometimes stood groaning and churning, just under my window. I did not mind and soon drifted to sleep again.

When I woke the sun was coming up, flooding across the town to the mountains. Mists lay on the peaks and over the sugar fields; mynah birds squeaked, pigeons called. From the balcony I saw the blonde hotel girl coming back from the baker with hot rolls for breakfast. Soon people were going to work, the little train setting out for the fields, Picasso harvesters clanking down the streets like space-age monsters.

At Joe's, Victor, the son-in-law, was hosing his taxi and people were already shopping. The air was full of Italian as sweets, bread, ice-creams and biscuits were bought. Milkshakes were being served to children on their way to school. Australian, Italian, Aboriginal – dark eyes, little dark faces, peered from doorways, gazed into shop windows, smiled from the school bus.

Giuseppe's farm is about five miles from the town. Shouting hoarsely, his brigand's face scowling above the wheel, he propelled his car along the sugar-lined road.

'Two thousand akkres I growa (He meant two thousand tons). Zucchero. Eight men.' He held up eight fingers. 'When plenty men, cut by hand, no men, out machina.' He shrugged. 'Machina no good. Rain komma after machina – ground's all – ' he made a corkscrew gesture with outspread fingers and the car rolled towards the sugar fields.

The fine house, of red brick, was a shrine of TV, chrome, plastic flowers, Estapol, holy pictures and chenille bedspreads. Nothing could have more clearly shown Giuseppe's prosperity or been farther removed from a primitive Sicilian village; but the kitchen was homely with onion plaits and cooking smells. I was glad to sit there when the pigs, cows, sugar and cane-cutting sons had been shown. Mrs Giuseppe, dark and square, served coffee and *biscotti* while her husband declaimed across the table.

'Fifty years I komma in Aoostralya. Old man now. Take a rest. Hey? Eight men work for me.'

He grinned at the thought of the eight men sweating away in the heat, cutting his cane, their brown faces streaked with black.

'Have you been back to Sicily?'

'Si si. Treepa,' said Mrs Giuseppe, making a planing movement with her hand. 'Fly. Airoplano.'

'Would you ever want to go back there to live?'

'No.' Giuseppe shrugged. 'Mama, papa . . . morte.'

'Our home,' said Mrs Giuseppe, looking round pridefully. 'This a good house. Cost money. All paid.'

She sounded very content; but Giuseppe said with a kind of touching dignity, 'In Sicilia, I am *paisan*. Leetra money. Very poor. Grow few olivi . . . leetra vino . . . orangi, limoni . . . ' he spoke the words lovingly, almost nostalgically. 'But land no good. My father very poor. Many bambini. Comma Aoostralya. Worka hard. Buy leetra land. Work hard. Feefty years. Buy more land. Old man now. No more Sicilia.'

His rough old brigand's face was suddenly sad, his huge battered palms turned out in an Italian gesture of resignation; then he shrugged and grinned, showing his grey broken fangs.

'Plenty money now, hey? Eighta men cutta cane. Maybe treep Sicilia airoplane.'

Though less exuberant, the non-Italians are friendly and helpful. There is no bus to where I want to go, say the men in the post office, but the bread woman will give me a lift and pick me up on her way back; the hotel proprietress offers to lend me her car to drive myself, and there is always Ron and the service car.

The hotel is friendly, not at all suggestive of government servants and commercial travellers, apart from being clean and giving generous meals. It has long silent corridors, bathrooms built on to verandahs, a good deal of heat and linoleum but there is the great upstairs verandah with its view of the mountains and the life of the town.

I have picked up odd facts about sugar from locals met at the pub. The mill is co-operative, and the co-op members are both Australian and Italian, whoever owns land to which mill shares are attached. Mills are built where they can best reduce transport costs, and each one is supplied by a certain number of cane farmers. These farmers are paid by the mill for their sugar,

usually three times a year – the first payment on delivery, the other
two during the season. Price is determined by legislation and all
the crushed sugar goes eventually to the Queensland Sugar
Board for selling.

I know now why I see harvesting on one side of the road and
new crops on the other. The cutting season lasts from May to
December and a second crop, called ratoon, comes up after the
first is harvested. I have also learnt why the sugar train draws two
kinds of canes – long poles and shorter sections piled in wire cages.
There are two sorts of harvesters; the whole-stick harvester which
cuts at ground level; the other, the chopper, (or Picasso model)
which cuts the cane into eighteen inch lengths. People say, rather
gravely, that though Picasso does away with much work he has
disadvantages, for bugs can collect and be overlooked in chopped
cane. They differ on whether Picasso is better than a whole-stick
cutter, used with a mechanical loader to take the long canes to
the sugar train, but agree that eventually hand-cutting will
disappear. Already more than half Australia's sugar is harvested
by machine.

There are just under two hundred cane farms in the Mossman
area and eighty-one of these are owned by Italians.

The hand-cutters are all black, by birth or from fired cane.
They wear shorts and old hats, and bend and chop and slash with
cane knives, steaming with sweat. The Aboriginals are very
quiet; they have soft eyes and voices and rather taciturn expressions. The Italians are mixed; most are cheerfully friendly and
curious, others have acquired a touch of Australian caution and
look on me with reserve. My fellow countrymen ask themselves:
Who in their right minds would be out in this bloody heat taking
pictures of anything so uninteresting as this back-breaking bloody
monotonous work?

The town seems to sleep, yet it is busy, the head of Douglas
Shire, with a shire clerk and a big hospital and a good deal of
money being made from sugar and timber. Of 3,338 people in
the whole shire nearly half are in the Mossman area, spread over

town and sugar fields. On modern maps Mossman is printed larger than Port Douglas, which flourished when this town was unknown.

Depending on cargoes and calls, you can sometimes go with Ron to Port Douglas for lunch and come back the same day to Mossman. Ron says I ought to see Port and that you can get a good meal of fish at the Fisherman's Wharf caff. It is run by two foreign boys; they give you as much as you can eat and it's real gormay cooking.

Down at Joe's, two middle-aged Italians were waiting in the service car: Grazia, brown, bright-eyed, with gold earrings, a harsh quick voice and merry smile, and Raffaele, an amiable brigand, like Guiseppe, a cliff-face hacked out of volcanic rock. They both come from Catania and their English is almost incomprehensible.

As soon as I entered the bus they got straight down to business in the Italian manner.

'Youa from Kehns?' Grazia screeched.

'No. I'm going to Port Douglas.'

'Ah. Si si si. Porto. We go Kehns.'

Raffaele leaned over and added a sound I could not interpret. I smiled as though comprehending and said, 'How long are you staying in Cairns?'

'No no no. Notta sty Kehns!' Again the sound I could not interpret. 'Y'know? Conventione.'

'Convention? You are going to a convention?'

'Si si!' they said eagerly. 'Big big conventione. Jovness.'

I said, 'Ah!' Grazia was not deceived.

'You know Jovness?' she said, rather insistently. 'Jovness. Religione. Big big conventione. Five-six day.'

Could it be Jehovah's Witnesses?

'Si si si! True God!' She was starting to shout. 'Y'know? JOVNESS.'

'Yes, yes, I know.'

'Ah si. You believe Jovness?'

I said evasively, 'You both believe?'

Raffaele joined in hoarsely. He beamed. 'We saved! We go big conventions. Alla Jovness.'

'But aren't you Cattolico?'

They shook their heads vehemently and Grazia said, 'Before – Cattolico. Now – *True* God.'

It was just the place for a theological discussion. As the service car bounded through the dust, the mailbags, parcels of meat, bread and groceries began to slip and slide. Grazia's voice had risen. Ron was discreetly minding his own business. Not that he was against Catholics, some of his best friends were Catholics. It takes all sorts to make a world.

I said cravenly, 'How many Jehovah's Witnesses in Mossman?'

'Oh many-many Jovness here.'

'Many-many go to convention,' Raffaele rumbled. 'Gone already. Motta car.'

'Younga people, younga men, sixty-seventy, gone already,' Grazia said. 'Drive themselves. We go train. Nine o'clock tonight arrive conventione. Come back home Sunday.'

I marvelled at the courage of Jehovah's Witnesses pioneering among Sicilian Catholics. I asked, 'What does the Catholic Father say?'

Grazia shrugged off the Catholic Father. She said, 'Deesa betta. Jovness. We saved. No Purgatore now.'

She began to grope into her handbag and presently pulled out a tract. 'Here! You read. You saved like weya saved.'

Ron did not even raise an eyebrow.

I asked how long they had been in Australia.

'Forty-seven year,' said Raffaele. 'First I come. All alone. Work. Save up. Then she come.'

'He come back to Italy to marry me,' Grazia said. 'Bring me out to Aoostrylia.'

'Did you know each other before?'

'Oh yes. Grew up in same vilagio, near Catania. Thirty year married now. Grown-up daughter, married with beautiful grandsons, taller than Raffaele. All work on our sugar farm.'

'Would you like to go back to Sicily?'

'Oh been back two three time. By plano. Been back see famiglia.'
'But to live?'

Raffaele shook his head. 'In Sicilia, very poor. Aoostralya, moocha money.' He sounded slightly homesick, but Grazia said firmly, 'Not live Sicilia. Just visit. Before in Sicilia we young. Now, we old. Betta stay here.'

By the time we reached Porto they knew my whole history. Perhaps with conversion in mind, Grazia urged me to visit her when she returned from the convention. We said a loud goodbye and they drove away, waving and shouting from the windows.

Though it was only half-past eight, Port Douglas was full of moist heat. Ron left me near the harbour, where a grass-bordered street led to the water. There were coconut palms and Coca-Cola advertisements, pale old wooden houses and magnificent South African tulip trees splashed with orange flowers. New Guinea crotons and banana leaves mingled with bougainvillea and poincianas. Frangipani gave off their warm scent, orchids crowded branches of trees. The harbour, darkened with submerged coral, was bordered with mangroves. Across the wide bay, opalescent mountains made a half-circle.

It was silent and soporific. There were no signs of the booming future predicted by Ron, nor of the wild past. The past was gold. When it was found on the Hodgkinson River a new port was needed, so urgently that the government offered a reward for a way across the mountains to the sea. A track was made by Christie Palmerston and the life of Port Douglas began. It quickly became a boom town, full of brothels and shops, and for some years was even bigger and more important than Cairns. When Smithfield, the 'wickedest town in Australia', was washed away in a flood, all its gold and trade went to Port Douglas. Cairns was denuded. Then the gold on the Hodgkinson failed; people drifted away; the railway was built from the inland to Cairns and Port Douglas's grand days were over.

When the Court House was built in 1879 there were twenty-one pubs in the town; now it stands among trees, two-storied, painted white, looking out across a grassy expanse. Shady mangoes, alive with mynah birds, line the overgrown green by the harbour edge. At the end of a stone jetty a pale wooden building on piles hovers above the water.

Though a ghost town, Port Douglas is not haunted. It seems happy, among its orchids and mountains. The harbour is sheltered from the open sea by a high hill, which, they say, was once an island. (One of Port Douglas's names was Island Point.) As I climbed, the view unfolded between flowering trees and over the low roofs of houses, all the bay with its purple shadows, the ring of mountains, for ever changing colour.

Eight miles off this coast, to the north-east, are the Low Islands, sand keys, white coral rock and mangroves, shells, sea birds and silence. Torres Straits pigeons flock there. Only lighthouse families live in the Group but they seem happy in their isolation. One lighthouse keeper stayed there for ten years without even coming to Port Douglas.

A marine shell-gatherer once went to the Low Islands to collect specimens. He was in his element and as he moved about the reef he hummed happily under his breath. Though the people had been friendly at first they grew cooler as the days passed. Finally they told him he would have to leave if he continued to make so much noise.

From the top of the headland, in the direction of Cairns, I looked down on a vast golden arc, curving for miles round a flat cornflower sea, pure, flawless, untouched. Only the little houses, set back in green grass, suggest that this beach has ever been trooden on. This is a different atmosphere from the harbour side's contented torpor, exciting, exhilarating in its beauty and freedom. It is here that Ron's progress – motel, holiday houses and caravan park – has begun.

Ron had warned me that there was not much to do at Port, yet the morning went very fast: a couple of hours on the hill-top watching the ocean, listening to calling pigeons; an hour or so in shell museums and orchid collections; an hour on the grass under the mango trees by the harbour, then it was time for lunch. At the end of its stone quay, the Fisherman's Wharf restaurant was draped with nets and glass floats but there were tables set out in the sun. I ordered coral trout from the German proprietor and went away to the Court House hotel for wine.

'Is this what you want?' asked the man in the bar, dubiously handing out through the hatch a bottle of very good, very cold riesling; and when I nodded, well pleased, 'That's right, dear. Nice to get what you like.'

Alone in the restaurant, though the tables inside were set for a bus tour, I sat in the sun with the water lapping below, watching the mountains, drinking my wine. The young German murmured, filling my glass; a pretty Canadian student brought a basket of French bread. There was soft Italian music, a smell of good coffee and beautiful coral trout.

'Ah, I thought you'd like it,' Ron said tolerantly, as we drove back to Mossman. 'I thought that caff was your style.'

In the evening, tired as I am, I have to go out, caught by its beauty, the sky behind the mountains stained cumquat-pink. Between the lavender peaks is a deep gap, like a pass, and above, in a sky now paling to apricot, the evening star shines out and a white glittering Turkish moon. Smoke from cane-fires drifts across Mount Demi, turning it to a volcano. Soft black flakes float down on me as I walk, following the train line. The chocolate fields have purpled, the ploughed lines that radiate out, threaded with young sprouting sugar, shine luminous, intense, almost phosphorescent. Mynah birds exchange their last-light chitter, pigeons their soft final calls.

To the north, towards Daintree, is a Tahitian scene. In the last of the light the mountains are sombre against an iris-brown sky. A low red-roofed house shows among tropical trees, bananas and coconuts.

Now in the heart of the cane, I can see only the line ahead, between green-brown walls, and the mountains beyond. On each side deep squares have been cut in the sugar, windowless rooms, open to the sky. One could walk here for miles, unseen, unheard.

The warning hoot of the train sounds behind and presently it grinds up, absurd valiant baby-blue engine with yellow wheels, dragging its empty platforms and cages. I have become as fond of this little diesel as of a patient, sturdy horse.

When the young men in the train waved, I waved back and asked if I could come for a ride. They grinned but did not refuse. I climbed into the hot-oil smelling cabin and off we went round the fields.

It was like a toy railway, yet vaguely distrubing, this journey without scenery, with no world beyond the purplish canes and their feathery tops. There was a suggestion of blind corridors, of hunted fugitives; yet how beautiful, for as the dusk deepened two searchlights shone out from behind the engine, pale cold beams that threw moving shadows into the cane, calling up phantoms.

Suddenly, I had had enough. I climbed down and stood listening while the train curved away out of sight. Again came that strange sensation, as though memory stirred. Why did it seem so familiar, to stand hidden, following the course of a train from receding sounds. Far far away it rumbled, tunnelling through the heart of the sugar, unseen, yet with its vibrations encircling, enclosing the whole world.

I turned home in the last burnished light. Blue-white smoke hung like mist above the sugar and lay in soft bands across the mountains. The flamboyants by the church were silhouetted against an orchid sky, the exquisite moon in their branches. The birds were quiet now; there was no sound but a seed-pod rustling down from a tree, the soft distant hiss of the mill.

15

The Cry of the Curlew

Nothing could be less like Mossman than the country between Cairns and Cooktown. There once was a coast road through Daintree, China Camp and Helensvale but it is no longer open to the public. The highway goes inland. You may also fly, or go by boat once a week.

When I went to find out about boats I was given a brochure, with a picture of a bus, which said:

Historic Cooktown. This is the spot where Captain Cook beached the *Endeavour* in 1770 to repair damage caused by a coral reef. Later on, it became the booming port for the roaring goldfields on the Palmer River to the West. Now, however, it is quiet, romantic, steeped in history– a fascinating piece of Australiana. You'll be glad you made this tour and won't stop talking about it to your friends for a long, long time.

I decided to go the humbler way by mail bus and come back by boat. Everyone said the road was frightful and the drive took nine hours.

The bus was a real Guadeloupe affair, informal, broken-down, full of black faces, livestock, boxes, crates and mailbags. They said this was its last trip, that a smarter more comfortable model was about to be installed.

'I thought it would be on today,' a passenger grumbled as cargo was stacked in the back and people stowed their belongings round and under their seats.

'Bill went down to Rocky to collect her but she blew up on the way back,' said the dusky, barefoot driver. 'Should be here by next week.'

He turned on the ignition; the engine whooped.

'Here!' cried a fat woman, nursing a box of chickens. 'You got my fowls' food on board?'

The driver switched off, climbed out and went to the telephone. Presently he returned. 'Okay. She's right.'

We whirled through the streets of Cairns, out into the sugar fields towards the Cook Highway.

Across the aisle an old Aborigine crouched, murmuring to himself, sweating in a thick woollen battledress. He was very thin, very ugly, like a long black frog, with splayed hands and feet and a too-wide toothless mouth in a face of carved linen-folds. He seemed bewildered, hunched in his hot clothes, looking nervously out the window. The man next to me shook his head.

'He's not a local. Don't know where he comes from. Might be an old Kanaka. The abos round here are a good looking lot.'

He himself was a toothless little Mr Punch, with gimlet eyes glittering benevolently under a wide felt hat. He seemed made of leather. His sleevless white cotton vest exposed neck and arms like the skin of a tortoise. He said he was a tin fossicker.

At the Cook Highway junction we turned inland towards the Tableland and climbed through the rain-forests of the Kennedy Highway. The scenery falling away behind was magnificent, but the bus smelt of hot metal and smoke came out. A passenger said ominously, 'She's on the boil, Joe!' Then they all began to make depressing forecasts about our chances of reaching Cooktown, recalling the day they lost a wheel, the night in the wet season when they got stuck and had to stay out all night, the time when the creek was flooded and they couldn't get across. Most of them seemed to be Cooktown locals.

We emerged from the rain forests on the dry side of the Tableland. Where irrigation had been installed there were bright patches of young corn and tobacco, and cows grazing on green grass, but the surrounding country was scruffy, quite unlike the dairy land round the Palmerston Highway. Mareeba, the main town, is clean, with wide streets and, since irrigation, very prosperous with tobacco and cattle.

Some of the passengers got off here, including the fossicker, and the driver said we could have ten minutes for a cup of tea. When I hesitated the woman with the chickens said I'd better take the chance; there wouldn't be another till we got to the Palmer River at lunchtime.

The landscape grew more parched, the road worse, the dust increased. Ventilation was a hole in the front of the bus through which the pulverized road surface poured in. In no time my jeans were white, my mouth full of grit. I swathed my face in a red scarf, pulling it up like a yashmak to meet my sunglasses. Floured like ghosts, the other passengers grinned, their faces cracking.

This vile road was the Mulligan Highway, named after James Venture Mulligan, an Irish prospector and explorer, who discovered gold at the Palmer and Hodgkinson Rivers and silver near Herberton on the Tablelands. It is strange flat land, arid and desolate, with queer immense anthills, like primitive monuments, among dust-covered trees. The dark mountains ahead were the Desailly Range, over which we must pass.

We stopped briefly for mail at Mount Molloy, a silent settlement with a large wooden pub called the Mount Molloy Hotel. James Mulligan who owned it, died there, trying to stop a fight and is buried in the local cemetery. There is an abandoned copper mine near the town, said to have been one of the greatest in the state. The whole atmosphere was of hot desolation, which increased as the hours passed. All was dead, shrunken river, baked-out land, glaring road, frowning hills.

A Lutheran missionary was sitting behind me. With his pale motherly wife and very pale daughter he was coming back, from leave, to the Bloomfield River Mission. They loved it so much they could not wait to get there. They seemed pleasant, harmless people but I noticed the other passengers viewed them with reserve.

The bus wobbled wearily to a little low building made entirely of corrugated iron. The verandah, furnished with old sofas and long chairs, was a hanging jungle of plants in wire baskets; tropical leaves sprouted from oil drums, kerosene tins and sections of motor tyres. It was called 'Wolfram Hotel'.

The missionary said this was Wolfram Camp and there was a wolfram mine nearby. At one time it was big with a town but now only a few men worked here. In the dim hotel bar silent men in cotton vests leaned, sipping beer, served by a resentful woman. The aboriginal passengers repaired to a tin shelter by the road, where they sat sucking at soft-drink bottles.

I could feel the heat, the silence, the queer aridity seeping into my system. There was an inclination to suspend action, speech, even thought. Intense dryness flared into the face, the skin on the throat constricted. Across a yard, paralysed with heat, the wooden privy was hot as a sauna bath. Three months of this and I would be a dehydrated mummy; yet I sensed something strange, a suspicion of fatal attraction. One was drawn, as to the edge of a precipice, towards extinction.

The country grew worse as we climbed the bare mountains beyond Wolfram Camp. There were views back over a plain of dry trees, to distant ranges in heavy heat haze. Dust rose out of the road like sulphur from Volcano Island. It was hateful, oppressive, full of sinister threat but still strangely magnetic.

Across this terrible country, thousands of Chinese and Europeans struggled to the goldfields, through heat, drought, flooded rivers, attacks of cannibals. Hundreds perished. Those not speared and eaten by the blacks died of thirst or starvation, lost in the bush. For years afterwards skeletons were found beside billies containing gold or miners' papers. How merciless those black-trunked ironbarks, the parched river beds and outcrops of white rock high on the mountains!

The bus stopped. There was a tin-and-asbestos cafe and nearby a notice said, 'Palmer River.' The river that produced millions of pounds' worth of gold is here a muddy trickle. A couple of miles away was Byerstown, a goldrush settlement famous for drink, riots, murder and violence of all kinds. It is dead now, as dead as the landscape.

At the asbestos cafe, the proprietor and his wife, streaming with sweat, bustled about with stodgy white sandwiches, tea and soft drinks.

The old Aborigine in the thick clothes had been the first to enter the cafe, but not until all were served did the shopkeeper say impatiently, 'Well Jacky. What you want?'

Bewildered, mumbling, the old man asked for cake.

'Eh? What you want? Speak up.'

'Cake.' The word was humble and hesitant.

'Cake? We got no cake. Come on now, make up your mind. What you want?'

The black frog seemed to shrink. Cake was all he could think of. He stared, perplexed, while the shopkeeper, frowning – busy man – can't hang about all day – said, 'C'mon now. Other people waiting to be served. You better have biscuits. No cake here. You got money?'

There were only a couple of coins in the thin black hand. The old man looked nervously at the biscuits in plastic packets. The cheapest was marked 30 cents.

'Which one you want, hey? Which one you want? This one?'

It was all too quick, the white man was talking too fast. The old blurred eyes could not register, the slow brain was confused.

'This one? Hey?'

Uncomprehending, obedient, the grizzled head nodded. The shopkeeper looked at the coins and said, 'Not enough here. You got more? Well then, you better take these.'

He took back the sweet biscuits and handed a packet of Saos. The old man returned to the bus where he sat alone, eating.

'God!' said the shopkeeper. 'Drive you up the wall. Cake, eh?' You could see he had a great problem; yet he did not look unkind: only harassed and hot.

As we re-entered the bus the old man, grinning childishly, offered his biscuits. Most of the passengers, their stomachs full of ballooning bread, refused with kindly smiles. I accepted, out of curiosity, and found the biscuit stale and flabby. It must have been in the shop for years.

The whole day had been a journey through desolation: abandoned copper mines at Mt Molloy, abandoned wofram mine at Wolfram Camp, abandoned goldfields at the Palmer River; and Cooktown, our destination, was a ghost town. Everything was in the past: all had perished. Only the terrible country survived, indifferent to violence and murder, impervious to futile efforts at conquest, a landscape of death.

The hard blue sky glared down. On a mountain, a great rock stood out, an illusory castle; but the only signs of human life here are the rusted wreckage of cars by the road. The weird anthills had reappeared, grey, a miniature Göreme Valley. The missionary said they are called magnetic or meridian, because their spires point due north and south.

Now a black mountain glittered ahead, a mass of dark rock where nothing grew but lichen. I had just decided that I had had enough, that I am not temperamentally suited for this kind of country and that I might be going mad, when the driver turned off into the old coastal road from Daintree to Cooktown.

Quite suddenly the landscape changed. The bush was mellow and cool; there were glimpses of forked trees, simple and slim as a snake's tongue; of milky pines with grotesque visceral roots, the pale satin nudity of white eucalyptus. We came into a narrow green valley and stopped at a low iron house with bush timber columns. It was almost buried in bougainvillea, hibiscus and mango trees draped with orchid and feathery stalactites.

In a few minutes we had moved from death to life, from arid sterility to tropical lushness, but like everything else on this curious journey the old Lions Den Inn had seen better days. Bus tours bring people to drink in the bar but when they have gone the silence returns, dust settles again on the furniture, the plastic flowers.

I sat with the missionary and his wife on the verandah, waiting for the Land Rover that would come from the Mission to fetch them. People moved indolently, stopping to lean. We talked vaguely, as though tired. They missionaries were dedicated and kind, they seemed to love the Aborigines though their conversation was full of imperatives: 'But they HAVE to . . . They MUST . . . It's as the Lord Jesus said . . . It's God's work.'

Back in the bus, the other passengers expressed the disapproval I had sensed:

'They take the natives away from their villages and teach them all sorts of things and then they're discontented . . . The girls won't go back . . . they get big ideas . . . The missionaries think it's saving their souls but the natives only come in for what they can get.'

Suddenly it was night. The women began to wipe their faces and one put on a crochet cap with huge gold sequins. The fat woman with the chicken said 'Cooktown' very thankfully, and waved into the darkness. I could see nothing. Then the bus stopped and a man approached from a parked car. The sequin cap descended and the car drove off into limbo.

The driver turned and looked at me dubiously.

'Where you going? Hotel or Guest House?'

Brainwashed by heat and discomfort, I could not decide.

'Better go to the Guest House,' the driver said, pushing on into the dark. Dim lights shone, the bus stopped. The driver opened the door expectantly. It was late and he wanted his tea.

On the road I stood, bewildered. I could see no town, nothing but a wooden bungalow with a weak verandah light. Behind the building, against brilliant stars, was the thickened blackness of a high hill. I could not imagine where Cooktown would be.

'Guest House,' the driver said, waving towards the light.

I said, rather panicky, 'Don't go yet. Wait and see if they can take me.'

'They'll take you,' he said heartlessly. 'They'll squeeze you in.'
A woman came from the bungalow and took my bag.
'Just the one? Okay, you'll be right. This is all you got?
Well, come on in.'
The bus rattled off down the hill. I followed the landlady inside.

Beds were everywhere, even in passages, like an overflowing
weekend party. The landlady said they were for when coach
tours stayed the night. She was booked out months ahead, it
was lucky I came when I did. Her name was Betty, what was mine?
Okay Nance, come right on down to tea, it was on now.

I took a quick shower behind a pink door labelled 'Eve' and
went to the dining room. I had just sat down when the landlady
approached kindly with five mature revellers.

'I put this lass at your table. She's just arrived. Now this is
Nancy, Nance meet Shirl, Reg, Merv, Nell, Ern.'

'Howya Nance,' said Shirl, Reg, Merv, Nell and Ern.

'And now I suppose you want glasses!' the landlady said in a
mock What-next voice.

'Too right!' said Reg, who was jolly. 'What you take us for?'

They sat down and unwrapped their bottles: six of beer,
one of Barossa Pearl. Champagne glasses were brought and the
pearl wine's plastic stopper blown off with screams.

'Come on now, girls, pass up your glasses. I know what you girls
are like.'

When the five glasses were filled and another poured for the
waitress, there was a slight pause. Reg said, 'Have some wine,
Nance?' He was doing the right thing, though there was barely
enough to go round. I asked if I could have beer. 'Sure, sure! One
beer for the lady. Coming up!'

I was tired and perhaps this made me feel there was something
frightening about them, they were so hard. They belonged to the
Sydney of takeovers, fast bucks and sales talk. Those who did not
conform to their ways or values would be swept aside.

I did not belong; furthermore I had not Dressed. The other
ladies had taken trouble, they glittered all over. Brilliants sparkled

from the frames of their spectacles, cultured pearls gleamed round their necks, diamonds blazed from eternity rings, false teeth flashed and sequinned bosoms shone like wet fish. Each head was expensively coiffured.

They ate with enormous refinement, holding their knives and forks by the tips of the handles, putting very small pieces of food in their mouths and chewing absently as though up to something shameful. The men were less finicky, shovelling in as though it were their last chance. They held their implements as children were once taught to hold pens, or like playing a cello, the fork vertical, pining the prey, while the knife sawed across horizontally. Shiny and red-faced, their casual shirts bulged at waist and neck. Coronary occlusions stood behind each chair like invisible waiters.

To please the girls, they had tolerated all that fiddle with wine glasses, sipping uneasily, rolling the prickly sweet brew round their tongues. Wine! But now it was finished and they could get stuck into the real grog. The girls were good sorts. The laughter became louder, the jokes more unrestrained. Sledge-hammer innuendoes crashed round the young waitress in a mini-sundress.

'This dessert's real good,' said Shirl, though of course she despised such carnality. 'I think I'll have a return.'

'Me too!' said Ern boyishly. 'Hey beautiful! Got some more dessert for your sweetheart?'

'Maybe!' said Sweetheart tantalizingly. 'Might be off though. You never know.'

'Ah!' said Ern. 'You wouldn't do that to me, would you?' His little eyes rolled into the back of his head.

Outside, it was quiet. The sounds of the revellers died away. The stars were immense, the air warm, peaceful, indifferent. I walked to the top of the road down which the bus had disappeared. Where was Cooktown? I could see nothing but bush. A lonely street lamp, hoisted up very high, sent down a soft yellow beam. Beyond, the darkness was thick and complete. Far away, at the foot of the hill, a weak verandah light shone.

There was a sullen smouldering smell. Parts of the domed hill behind the house wore a subdued orange halo . . . a bush-fire, a rising moon . . . it was of no importance in this strange utter silence.

Everything waited; everything listened. So intense was the silence that there was an illusion of echoes, far far away beyond human hearing. Numbed with fatigue, I had ceased to exist as a physical entity. I was listening, not to but with the night.

In the hall, the landlady bounced up, red and shining with friendliness. She was decked out in bejewelled spectacles and a tight emerald-green mini dress.

'We're having a bit of a sing-song. Come on and join us.'

When I said I must go to bed she reminded me there would be plenty of time for sleep when we were dead, but bustled away to the party.

My little room was hot and smelt of lionoleum. In bed, I still felt the uneasy lurch of the bus. Downstairs, draught-horses were pounding piano and drums. 'Ta ta ti-*ta*, ta-ta-ta-ta-ti-*ta*. Ta ta ti-*ta*, Ta-ta-ta-ta-ti-tiiii' – from the film of *Dr Zhivago*, drawing it out like elastic, over and over, cloying like glue in your hair. 'C'mon now . . . BORN free . . . ta titi BORN free . . . ' I fell asleep.

When I woke the singing was over. Enormous silence had moved in, surrounding us like a huge soft cave. The faint snores behind the wooden wall only intensified its absolute quality. I lay, sticky with sweat, waiting. I heard again the weird voiceless echoes.

The smell of smouldering drifted as I leaned from the window. The orange halo glowed on the hill. The sky was clear yet there was the feeling that mists were closing in on the lonely house, pressing it down softly, inexorably, till no trace remained. Gently, implacably the silence would wipe us out, leaving only the darkness that moved upon the face of the waters.

Then from the hill came a sound, faint, piercing, anguished. *I cannot accept this loneliness*, the curlew cried. *I cannot accept this desolation!* The frail voice wept on, but the silence brooded, indifferent, all-encompassing.

16

Voices in Silence

In the morning I woke completely refreshed, like a child, with
no sense of time or responsibility. Before six, I was walking
up the orange road on Grassy Hill, behind the boarding house.
Though the sun had risen, on this shadowed side night had not
completely retired. Lighting was still diffused, left-over mosquitoes
whined. The knowledge that this early hour could not last intensified its enjoyment. Red flowering grasses along the edge were
damp with dew, the air was full of heat, with promise of more to
come.

The sinister fires no longer burned on the hillside; only a faint
scent of charred wood hung in the air. Nothing moved; no house,
no human being was visible.

Activity was an effort. My clothes were sticky, my forehead
beaded, my legs, feet, thongs, smeared with a red paste of dust
and dew. If I sat down to rest tiny green ants swarmed over me.
I plodded on. It was horrible, uncomfortable, then suddenly
wonderful. As I came round the curve of the hill I saw the Estuary,
still in its nocturnal sleep, and the Endeavour River, winding
away among green mangrove swamps to the mountains.

A horizontal shaft of light struck the white beaches across the water and they flared like snowfields at midday. The tide was moving in slowly. Soon the sandbanks that lay like pale stranded porpoises would be covered.

Last night the silence was vaporous; now it was solid, like the heat-weighted air. Yet it was no less strange. Pigeons had begun to call, familiar but never before sounding like this. Silence had muted the edge of their voices. It surged up between each note, deeper and stronger than ever.

At breakfast, Ern said, 'This is Cooktown, that was!' Shirl marvelled at me, 'You're not going to *stay* here?' They all agreed that Captain Cook had made a blue in discovering the place and drove away in a tank-like car. They had come here by accident. Never again!

The landlady said no tours would be through for a while and I should go down town and buy some shell-jewellery at the far end of Charlotte Street. I was surprised to hear Cooktown really existed.

Charlotte Street lay at the foot of the hill where I had looked down last night. It was long and silent. Notices at the kerbs announced 'Angle Parking' but no cars were visible. The disembodied verandah where I had seen the light was now the post office and across the road, at the Sovereign Hotel, pink and orange bougainvillea was draped like shawls over trees. The motel, an oblong with a few coloured doors in the hotel garden, was empty.

I felt I had stumbled upon an abandoned city. Spaced out among overgrown allotments were grand and elegant buildings, in decay, patched with tin or corrugated iron stuck on anyhow. Iron lace rusted, verandahs sagged, window awnings drooped down like eyelids. Some of the empty spaces are charred from burning off. It gives the impression that fire has ravaged the town. A creamy Italianate facade still bore the name 'Con O'Leary' but trees and bushes were crowding in.

Nearby, like a splendid bride at a funeral, stands the Bank of New South Wales, rescued, restored, palatial, with white columns and tiled floors and lofty ceilings designed for chandeliers. Beyond the post office is a little Albert Memorial with drinking water, dedicated to Mrs Watson, a woman who died of thirst.

I walked down Charlotte Street, spellbound. I had never seen anything quite so strange. Ancient cities of Europe, abandoned, like Pompeii, or rebuilt over and over, like Syracuse, offer far more, yet are less surprising. Cooktown's impact lay in its complete unexpectedness, its relics of splendour in this primeval setting.

In Furneaux Street, on the hillside, the abandoned convent of St Mary is half-hidden in a wilderness of weeds, frangipani and mango trees. Hot, rusty, haunted, with dormer windows broken and iron lace fallen away, it peers out with blind eyes, like a mad woman from between shutters. The stone arch of the front door is inscribed 'Trespassers Prosecuted'.

A group of beautiful Aboriginal children approached, healthy, clean, well-dressed. They carried shopping bags and were smiling, friendly and curious. Several small cats sprang out of bushes, slim and agile as lizards. There were no other signs of life.

I walked on and came at last to the cemetery. There had been a fire, the brassy morning light revealed black earth, blackened trunks and grass. Round about were great grey boulders and sparse trees growing as though blown by violent winds. The silence was broken only by the rustle of lizards or snakes, the cheep of invisible birds.

I wandered among the dead Kellys and Daleys, O'Neills and O'Learys. Nothing could be more unlike the green land they came from. There were a few lonely Scandinavians and Germans, an enclosure of nuns and endless small graves. Well apart from the rest is a Chinese shrine, inscribed: *March 1887. To respect as if they are present. Erected with respect by the Chinese community of Cooktown.*

Back in the town, people were moving about. The pubs were open. Paint had been used here and there with good intentions but rather disastrous effect. It is all very well for the Commercial Hotel to be a dull blue; it is old and wooden and has a ramshackle charm, but the Leisureland Motel, Cooktown Boutique and

Tropicana Bar were glaring green and purple where there was no need for man-made colour.

Bougainvillea splashed purple and red about, hibiscus, orchids, frangipani, grow wild; and Cooktown does not need waking up. It is awake in the true sense, a deep tranquil awareness. The outer world has dropped away, the breath is held, but not in suspense.

It is haunted, like the Gilbert Islands, the Lizard in Cornwall, not with visible ghosts but a presence. It listens, rapt, to its own silence. This is not the watchful waiting of the Australian bush; more an absence, an else-whereness against which our thin clatter has the power of snickering gnats.

Into the listening silence the pigeons call, two notes, purling and echoing, on-and-on, faint from the hill, on-and-on . . . *oodle-oo*; *oodle-oo*. All day the sad sleepy incantation goes on, like a mantrum; mesmeric, monotonous. A strange bird cries *tohok*! a hammer against the silence. Then the sounds die, the listening returns, the faraway unheard echoes.

It is hard to believe in this town's commercial past. One can see the *Endeavour* sailing in, like a beautiful bird, hear the creak and rattle of sheets running through blocks, the hammers of carpenters repairing the hole in the ship. Such sounds, even occasional shots, would only emphasize the silence. Cook did not stay long, he did nothing to change the landscape; but the gold rush lasted for years; it created a city and brought people from all over the world.

The town literally grew overnight. When James Mulligan found gold on the Palmer River people flocked there in thousands. Two government cutters were sent out to find a site for a gold port. They came into the Endeavour Estuary in October 1873 and the very next morning before they could make their report, a ship arrived from the south with officials, police, engineers, miners, horses, machinery and supplies. The miners rushed ashore, tents were put up, cargo unloaded and by evening the life of the town was in full swing.

From that time on, ships crowded into the Estuary. In their

eagerness to get to the goldfields passengers swarmed ashore without waiting to berth at the wharf. Cooktown's white population was 35,000. Imported foods, drink, clothes, textiles came from every part of the world. The streets were lit with kerosene lamps and Chinese lanterns. Grand houses looked down from the hills. There were fine banks and government buildings, ninety-seven pubs and almost twice as many brothels.

Hundreds of coolies arrived from China. The Chinese merchants of Cooktown got much of the gold that was found and more than half the town property was in their hands. There were 20,000 Chinese at the diggings and two and a half thousand in Cooktown; Chinese market gardens, Chinese sampans in the harbour, a large Chinatown, a magnificent Joss House.

By 1899 it was all over. The alluvial gold had given out on the Palmer, the miners had moved to other fields. Now, apart from a handful of buildings and graves, there is nothing to show they were here. The silence, which had retreated, moved in again, as the sea wipes out the wake of a ship.

In the little museum in Charlotte Street, the curator is always ready to talk about the exhibits. He bewails the fact that no one cares about Cooktown, that it will decay, that the government and the National Trust do nothing to preserve it.

Parts of the Chinese Joss House are here, wall and door carvings in scarlet and gold, polychrome figures, a bell, a great pig-skin drum, the temple gong. It was one of the oldest Joss Houses in Australia, its magnificent carvings and figures were sent from China, but when the Chinese left it was pillaged and sold up.

The cooking pots for the funeral feasts are here. Funerals were lavish, but since Chinese like to be buried among their ancestors, the bodies were often dug up and the bones shipped home in big jars; sometimes, it is said, packed round with smuggled gold-dust.

Here you may read in the copy of Mrs Watson's diary which was found with her body. Her husband was in charge of a *bêche-de-mer* station, on the Lizard Islands, miles off the coast. During his absence blacks attacked the house and killed one of the two Chinese servants. Mrs Watson fired at them, then with her little son Ferrier and the other Chinese, Ah Sam, she put out to sea in half an iron tank used for cooking *bêche-de-mer*. They drifted for days, seeing and signalling ships, unregarded and finally reached a deserted island where they all perished of thirst.

From 27 September to 12 October, Mrs Watson kept a diary. The last entry says: 'No rain. Morning, fine weather. Ah Sam preparing to die. Have not seen him since. Ferrier more cheerful. Self not feeling at all well. Have not seen any boat of any description. No water. Nearly dead with thirst.'

There are a few hundred people living in Cooktown, some old inhabitants, some retired from other parts and a few younger families. They all say they would never live anywhere else. They love the climate, the peace, the freedom. The soil will grow anything, there is wonderful fishing, living is cheap. There is always time to talk to people; everybody is friendly; no hurry or stress. An English couple who came a few years ago have taken an old house and made a wonderful graden. They hate going away, even to Cairns.

Though no one says so, it is more than good climate and fishing that holds people here. You either, like Reg and Shirl, hate and dismiss the place, or you surrender, become caught up in the silence and never want to leave. It is like the Gilbertese atolls. There is the same hot drowsiness, the midday shimmer, the cool afternoon breeze, the coral blue sea, and the feeling of being very close to another dimension.

At the far end of Charlotte Street, towards the Estuary entrance, are Cooktown's monuments: a little cannon, sent by the government to protect the town against Russian invasion; a memorial to Edward Kennedy, the explorer, who was killed by blacks while finding a way to the north in 1848; a column marking the spot where the *Endeavour* was beached and Captain Cook came ashore on 17 June 1770. The column stands in a neat little garden of

crotons and hibiscus and is not unlike a sewer-vent. It was erected
a hundred years ago but as yet has no figure on top. Nearby a
small heap of coal, all grown over with grass, was found during
the last century. The *Endeavour's* log mentions landing coal.

In the 1880s, the Cooktown people went out to search for the
cannon Cook unloaded when he ran on the reef. Though nothing
was found then, the cannon have since been brought to the surface.

Near the monument you may sit in the shade of a mango tree
and feel a small breeze from the water. Boats, marooned in mud
by the departed tide, are pulled up where wharves once stood.
Clumps of mangrove expose their roots like teeth in receding gums.

Two hundred years ago there was a little village where I am
sitting, tents for supplies and for those sick with scurvy, a smith's
forge and carpenters' benches. There was plenty of food: pigeons
and kangaroos, turtles and shellfish, fish from the reef and the
Estuary, green leaves for vegetables.

The natives who came to investigate found it hard to believe
the white men were flesh and blood till they felt some of the sailors
all over. When Cook gave one an old shirt to cover his nakedness
the man wound it round his head like a turban. At first they were
harmless; then a disagreement rose, over a turtle. They set fire to
the grass round the camp and damaged the smith's forge. When
Endeavour finally left the whole district was burning.

Most of the cards and explanatory texts in the museum are written
in the same hand, upright, guileless, done with a sharp nib and
plenty of initial capitals. They are the work of Mr Stan Boyd,
who built the collection and looked after it until his health failed.

He is over eighty, has a strong battered face with a bony crooked
nose and grey eyes. He sits straight and holds his head high, tilted
back slightly so that he seems to look down on one in rather a regal
manner.

I met him one day on the post office verandah and we have
become friends. I visit him in the little house which he shares
with another pensioner, in Furneaux Street, opposite the abandoned convent. The front verandah had gone, blown away in a

cyclone, and the old men have no money or strength to replace it; but Mr Boyd has planted a clump of lilies at one side which he tends and proudly displays.

Wearing a cotton vest and trousers he receives you with dignity. He sits rather formally at his table, writing slowly with his sharp nib, making his capitals. He is writing his reminiscences.

His grandfather, William Boyd, came out from England and worked for Ben Boyd at Twofold Bay. He does not know if they were related. William's son, John, the father of my Mr Boyd, was a drover. He brought cattle overland hundreds of miles and pioneered in the remotest parts of Cape York Peninsula.

'I am sorry I can't offer you a cool drink,' says Mr Boyd, 'but I have no refrigerator. I live on the pension.'

He speaks without apology or complaint. It is very hot. We lapse into a friendly silence.

'There are two very good kinds of bees in that part of the Peninsula,' Mr Boyd says. 'A small black bee in hundreds, always has a large hive and a bite just enough to make you brush them off. They make dark soft honey called *Yejuchee*. Then there is a much larger brown bee, not many in a hive and they produce golden-coloured honey called *Onedeelar*. The natives carry the honey in vessels made from messmate bark.'

As he talks on I think of Reg and Ern, with all their dreadful prosperity. Mr Boyd has only essential dignity, independent of everything, even the physical shell. At times he has trouble with breathing, his heart is bad; his eyes are slightly clouded as with cataracts, but a great spirit looks out through the ruins, seemingly undismayed.

'I had only twenty months' schooling, away from home . . . We lived in the Peninsula . . . My father worked for Watsons, you know them, the family at "Coen and "Rokeby" and "Merluna Downs".'

In those days the mail was carried on horseback across hundreds of miles with rivers in flood and cyclones and plagues of marsh flies, sandflies, mosquitoes. Now it is delivered by air. Mr Boyd talks of hobbled horses drowned in the night, stores under twelve feet of water, bogs, heat, vermin; of his parents' life in areas where no white man had been before, of hostile blacks and murders, of long isolation and hardship. His mother was often the only white woman for hundreds of miles. When one of the Watson brothers was killed by blacks she read the burial service.

He remembers so clearly, describes in such detail that everything comes alive. You hear the men riding in tired and hungry, you smell the batch of bread that his mother had made, the mince pies and little cakes; you see the man swimming the river with a rope in his mouth, the grass springing up overnight after rain, the blacks padding off with the mailbags, walking four miles an hour.

'Are you writing all this down?'

'Yes, I'm trying to set it down before it's too late.'

In the long pause the strange bird outside cries *Tohop*.

'When we came to Cooktown to live, the place was going downhill. The days of the goldrush were over. The buildings and houses were there but people had started to leave.'

Those who stayed were returning to *bêche-de-mer* fishing and sandalwood-getting, for which men had come before there was a town. Cairns was booming. Cooktown residents moved there in search of work. Some of the houses were pulled down or stripped of their cedar and taken to Cairns; others were left to decay, to be wrecked by vandals, burnt in bush fires, or blown down by cyclones.

'Not that we have many here. They talk rubbish in the south about our cyclones. It's just an excuse to let Cooktown fall to pieces without making an effort. No one cares . . . the government, the National Trust . . . no one does anything and we have no money. They bring tourists through here in buses but that doesn't do much good. They just stay the night and move on.

'A few years ago they thought sugar was going to bring us prosperity. They were planting here. Land prices went up from next to nothing to ridiculous figures; then the sugar market fell. The land prices stayed up, though they're still very low by southern standards. But before that you could get a mansion for a few pounds.'

I asked what he thought about suggestions for developing Cook-town as a tourist attraction.

'You'll have big modern hotels with swimming-pools, up on Grassy Hill. They'll revive the gold rush days; restaurants decorated with shovels and gold-washing cradles, waitresses in poke bonnets, publicans in miners' hats. Cobb and Co. coaches will run tours to the Palmer. The buildings will be dolled up with reproduction iron lace and old identities, like yourself, hired to tell yarns in bars.'

He was disgusted.

'It should be preserved as a National Monument. If I had the money, that's what I'd do. The old houses should be properly restored, saved from falling to pieces. This town is Australian history and no one cares. Putting on fancy dress and re-enacting Cook's landing doesn't get anywhere. We need money for preservation. I tried to do what I could at the museum till I had a heart attack and had to give up. It was only a drop in the bucket, but at least it was a start. I can't understand how people can be so indifferent, in a rich country like this. They just don't seem to value their history.'

Just before dawn the curlew gives his last anguished cry; then briefly the waking birds sing together. The sun rises. Out in the kitchen are soft voices and padding feet where native girls from the Mission are murmuring and singing. There are sounds of fowls, the smell of woodsmoke.

From Grassy Hill I watch the morning sun shine on Mount Cook. A low cloud lies on its top, like lazy white volcano smoke. The estuary is silky, unruffled, withdrawn. A faint bar of mist lies across the red roads and pale roofs of the town.

If you want to swim you can drive to the sea or walk through a hot sheltered valley. Pandanus grows here among scorched gum-trees; curlews hover nervously on long delicate legs, black-and-yellow butterflies reel about. On the slopes are strange outcrops of grey rock, a miniature Montserrat, and anthills resembling ruined castles, Japanese Jizos, Lilliput mountains. There are

lizards like tiny prehistoric monsters with yellow goat-eyes.
They watch you with supreme attention, round head cocked on
slender neck, body raised on stiff little legs, rigid as wood, fearless
and very intelligent.

At midday the town lies stupified. The streets are deserted.
Not even a dog ventures out. Pavements are hot-plates, surfaces
dazzle, outlines shimmer; but the heat is dry, healthy. Later,
the sea breeze will rise and cool the air.

Occasional Land Rovers pass driven by young men with beards.
Sometimes visitors drink in the bars or at the open-air tables at
the 'Sovereign'. In the old days a police officer rode his horse
half-way upstairs in this building, chasing the publican who had
ordered it out of the bar where ladies were drinking.

A few young Americans have wandered through, a few Nordics,
They shout drinks to an old Aborigine who looks professional
in a small way. He chats on obligingly but seems embarrassed
when a liberated American girl keeps holding his hand.

Out at the wharf, near the Estuary entrance, a man fishes
lazily; a barge unloads silica sand from the north to be taken to
Japanese ships. People lean about, watching. Across the Estuary
the mountains are green and fluted with grey, as though indented
with lava. The dark low bushes and fine white sand, the sparkling
water might be in the atolls but for two tin W.C.s, fair and square
in the foreground.

No matter how hot in the town, there is always a breeze up
on Grassy Hill. At the very top is a small white lighthouse with
a red hat. From here you can see the Pacific, the headlands and
Estuary, the river, the town, the mountain named after Cook by
Lieutenant King. He came to Cooktown seeking traces of the
Endeavour.

To the right, steep green slopes, small bays with black rocks.
Below is a drowned continent of headlands and long peninsulas.
The more you gaze, the clearer grows this dim submerged world.
Strange snail-tracks form on the forget-me-not surface yet no
ship or boat is in sight. Far off, sand-banks and coral keys of the
Barrier Reef are ivory, under turquoise glass.

The blue is infinite, constantly changing. Gulls cry, the sea rustles down on the rocks like a waterfall. The southeast trade blows steadily and leaves make the little sound of crackling fire.

Away in the north is an opal promontary. In the river-mouth seaweed traces dark scallops under the water. The white triangular navigation signs might be petrified sails.

I spend whole days on this hill, watching the sea and the tides, the drowned continents. It is like being in a little ship, with the constant soft wind blowing in, blowing in. A small plane flies over, taking mail to Mr Boyd's far Peninsula. Down in the town nothing moves, no vehicle, animal, human being. The streets are empty, the houses silent. No sound of bells rise up, no clocks, roosters, cars or voices. The iron roofs shine white, the trees stand unmoving in their own shadows.

The tide has gone out; the sandy banks on the Reef have emerged to the sun. The river is now a muddy winding passage. The mangroves are soft, thick, like a closepacked garden hedge. Lieutenant Hicks wrote in his log that the natives called the river *Charco*, a term of admiration; but though the Estuary itself is clear and beautiful the winding stream has a sinister air. It is so silent and still. There are alligators in the mangrove creeks.

Joseph Banks went across to those sandhills and mangroves and found hundreds of pigeons and crows. I wonder if they are the same kind of pigeons calling now. Later, he took a party up the river. They found many *Indian* houses and some very strange creatures: a mouse-coloured animal, extremely swift, about the size of a greyhound, that leapt or bounded on two legs; a wolf, exactly resembling those of America; straw-coloured animals shaped like a dog and the size of a hare; goats, wolves, pole-cats, spotted creatures. One seaman saw the devil, which he said was 'large . . . as a one-gallon keg, and very like it; he had horns and wings, yet he crept so slowly through the grass, that if I had not been *afeared*, I might have touched him.'

Along the roads are flattened, dried-out toads, like scraps of black leather. They must have been run over, though few cars are seen.

In the evenings they spring from the bushes and flop rather startingly round your feet. Sometimes little slim sprightly cats appear and come walking. They leap and skip in and out of the shadows, putting their paws around your ankles, rubbing and purring. Like everything here at this hour, they are strange.

I had not really expected to like northern Australia; I came here out of curiosity. When I flew from Cairns to Weipa, on the Gulf of Carpentaria, it did not appeal at all; but now I can see why those who know the north belong to a closed circle. You must experience it to understand. It is too immense and intangible for interpretation. But once you have known it, it never leaves you. In the heart of the city you remember the silence, in cold foreign countries you feel the hot stillness.

At sunset every ancient instinct revives at the sight of the sky. The whole of the west is on fire, the Estuary a bowl of reflected flame, the river a scarlet snake. Against the burning, a bare black twisted tree makes a silhouette; high up, a thin young moon and two stars shine like ice.

The orange light glows on Grassy Hill, startlingly, drawing out each individual leaf on trees, burnishing the red grass, catching the red earth. Nothing stirs or breathes. All is suspended.

The fire in the sky goes on long after the sun has set. The mountains become filled with mist, they are long shallow headlands in a smoky sea. A little breeze rises; birds twitter; crickets sing countinually.

It grows darker. Bats and flying-foxes swoop, small insects scuttle and seethe. Two demented birds suddenly shriek. Toads come out on the road and leap and plop. Night falls. Down the hill the pale lamp burns on the post office verandah, the frail fan of light. On the black hill the fires are smouldering; the smell of smoke, distant cries of dingoes, come through the thick darkness. The Milky Way is a long pale scarf.

Now, the faraway sounds begin, the unheard echoes. Always one seems to be picking up messages from one does not know where, too long ago, too remote for deciphering; far more ancient than anywhere else in the world.

All night the stars are very close and immense; in the silence one seems to hear them sing in their courses.

Then comes the curlew; some Aborigines believe he is a man who is losing his sight; that he cries *I'm going blind! I can't see!* but the feeling evoked is beyond deprivation and grief. It is the very essence of loneliness; the core and soul of this country.

In the south, now, it is spring. In Sydney, the morning sun will be lighting the harbour, a cellophane surface splashed with glitter; the plane trees outside our apartment in Macleay Street will be in young leaf; in our mountain garden, lilac and wisteria, jasmine and fruit trees are flowering. The blackbird sings all day in the orchard.

There is no need to say good-bye here; no sadness, as in lands to which you may never return. This is home. In your own country, leaving is easy.